D087442

ENERGY POLICY
—— IN AN ——
ERA OF LIMITS

ENERGY POLICY
— IN AN —
ERA OF LIMITS

Thomas C. Lowinger

PRAEGER

PRAEGER SPECIAL STUDIES • PRAEGER SCIENTIFIC

Library of Congress Cataloging in Publication Data

Lowinger, Thomas C.
    Energy policy in an era of limits.

    Bibliography: p.
    Includes index.
    1. Energy policy—United States.   I. Title.
HD9502.U52L695   1983   333.79'0973   83–6315
ISBN 0-03-060423-0

WIDENER UNIVERSITY
WOLFGRAM LIBRARY
CHESTER, PA.
DISCARDED
WIDENER UNIVERSITY

HD
9502
.U52
L695
1983

Published in 1983 by Praeger Publishers
CBS Educational and Professional Publishing
a Division of CBS Inc.
521 Fifth Avenue, New York, NY 10175 USA

© Praeger Publishers

All rights reserved

3456789 052 987654321

Printed in the United States of America
on acid-free paper

CONTENTS

TABLES

ix

FIGURES

ENERGY POLICY
—— IN AN ——
ERA OF LIMITS

ENERGY POLICY
—— IN AN ——
ERA OF LIMITS

Introduction and Overview
— 1 —

In the summer of 1979 I found myself, along with millions of other frustrated Americans waiting in long gas lines in a suburb of Washington, D.C., while contemplating with apprehension the roots of this crisis and our ability to deal with it. What a difference three years can make! In the winter of 1982-83 the world market is flooded with oil, with crude oil prices under intense downward pressure, and the Organization of Petroleum Exporting Countries (OPEC) seemingly in a state of disarray and internal discord, with several OPEC countries lowering their oil prices below the cartel's official prices.

Saudi Arabia, Kuwait, and the United Arab Emirates have kept their price structure intact, and consequently have seen their share of OPEC production plummet. In 1981 these three countries produced an average of 12.4 million barrels a day (MMb/d) of oil, which amounted to about 55 percent of OPEC's total oil output. In August 1982 they were producing only 7.8 MMb/d, and their share of the total fell to 44 percent. It is clear that for the time being OPEC has lost its grip on the world price of petroleum, and some industry analysts see oil prices falling from their present $31-32 per barrel range, to $25 per barrel or even lower.[1]

This turn of events is due to a combination of declining demand for oil in industrial countries and increased production of oil in non-OPEC countries. Oil demand by Organization For Economic Cooperation and Development (OECD) countries declined 8 percent in 1980 and another 7 percent

1

in 1981 due to a combination of both cyclical and structural factors. Conservation and fuel-switching investments made both before and after the second oil price shock will continue to have a major impact on oil and energy demand throughout the 1980s. In the United States, consumption of petroleum products has declined by about 15 percent from 1978 to 1981, with further decline taking place in the first three quarters of 1982.

Because the decline in consumption was coupled with increased domestic production of petroleum, net oil imports of industrial countries fell by about 25 percent from 1978 to 1981, and the share of imported oil in total consumption of primary energy declined from more than one third to less than one fourth. In the United States, with its large domestic output of petroleum and other primary energy sources, the above ratio declined from about 22 percent to about 15 percent during the same period. Further reduction is expected in 1982.

Although the decline in total energy used in industrial countries was less marked than the drop in oil consumption, it has nevertheless been significant over the last three years. This decline reflected to some extent the depressed state of economic activity in OECD countries, particularly in their industrial sector, but the major reason behind this development has been structural--the improvement in the overall efficiency of energy use. Between 1973 and 1981, the amount of energy required to produce a unit of gross domestic product fell by 17 percent in the United States, and by 16 percent in the OECD area as a whole. The long-term impact of the 1973-74 oil price shock and conservation policies adopted in its wake had just begun to produce significant changes in the way energy is used in advanced countries when the second sharp oil price increase occurred. The permanent reduction in energy consumption following the oil price increases of 1973-74 involved a slow process, one that requires replacing much of our energy-using capital stock. Adelman reasons that by 1981 only one half of the overall effect of the first price shock has been felt, while the second sharp oil price increase has barely begun to make an impact on energy use patterns.[2] The current deep world recession may have accelerated this process in that it forced several basic industries to eliminate aging, energy-inefficient, and technologically obsolete plant capacity.[3]

The conservation-inducing effects of the first oil crisis, together with demand reduction attendant on the second oil price shock, have combined to produce the recent decline in energy consumption. Available evidence indicates that the major factor behind the large improvements in energy efficiency and the fall in oil consumption has been the effect of the sharp increases in the real price of energy in general and of petroleum products in particular.[4]

Energy policies put in place by industrial countries have been instrumental in furthering energy conservation and promoting the substitution of alternative energy sources for oil. In response to the rise in the real price of energy and certain tax and other incentives provided by governments, investment in more energy efficient-capital equipment has increased significantly, while at the same time there also has been a noticeable shift in the structure of industry toward less energy-intensive lines of production.

Perhaps the most important factor has been the recognition by policymakers of the central role prices must play in providing incentives for energy conservation, and for the substitution of non-oil energy sources for oil. The overall direction of policy has been to permit the higher world price of oil to be reflected fully in product prices faced by consumers. Initial decontrol, followed by the complete elimination, of oil price controls in the United States in early 1981 was probably the most notable step taken in that direction in recent years. Although it now appears that real energy prices have peaked in response to the 1979-80 round of price increases, some added stimulus to energy conservation came about as a result of the price decontrol measure taken by the Reagan administration. Continued high real prices of energy meant that further energy savings are likely to materialize as a result of continued substitution of labor and capital for energy, the continued decline of the output of heavy industry, strong efficiency gains in the household sector, and the introduction of new more energy-efficient technologies.

New technologies now being introduced in industry, transportation, and in residential structures are much more energy-efficient than the typical technology now in use. Combined with structural changes in both the production and consumption sides of the economy, this means that energy demand could be stabilized while the economy continues to grow.

A balanced and forward-looking energy policy must also ensure that unnecessary and self-defeating obstacles to enhanced domestic production of energy are eliminated. The lessons of the 1970s suggest that free-market policies should be relied on to bring about an overall equilibrium between energy supply and demand. The gasoline shortages of 1974 and 1979 and the natural gas shortages of the early 1970s show convincingly why a free-market policy in energy is an absolute must. Trying to keep energy prices below their market levels not only creates artificial scarcities but it also results in unnecessary waste due to resource misallocation.

The United States has adopted several measures that taken together moved the country closer to a free-market energy policy. Oil price controls were abolished, and deregulation of natural gas (NG) is proceeding, although fitfully and capriciously, under legislation now in effect. The Natural Gas Policy Act of 1978 established more than 17 different categories of NG for pricing purposes. Under the provisions of the act, roughly half of domestically produced gas will be released from price controls by 1985.

As a part of its effort to encourage the exploration and production of domestic energy sources, the Reagan administration has announced a new five-year offshore oil and gas leasing program. The new plan is designed to increase the pace and quality of offerings and achieve early leasings of potentially promising areas. Furthermore, the Economic Recovery Act of 1981 provides additional incentives for domestic oil production.

In response to rising energy prices, the total number of oil and gas wells drilled approximately tripled between 1973 and 1981. Exploratory activity, as measured by the number of wells completed, total footage of wells drilled, and the number of rotary rigs in operation--all attained a new high at the end of 1981.

In spite of the sharp increase in such activities, it is generally recognized that domestic oil production will continue to decline as large, productive, and readily accessible oil deposits are becoming increasingly scarce. New oil has been discovered in smaller and deeper reservoirs, some of which are also situated in more hostile environments. In the United States, Alaska remains the last major frontier area for oil development in the United States, with good prospects for giant field discoveries. In all, even assuming that Alaskan output remains stable in the 1980s, U.S. conventional oil supplies are likely to decline by 1.5-2 million barrels per day by the late 1980s.

U.S. natural gas policy during the 1970s has been characterized by a maze of unwieldy regulations that restrained prices, decreased system flexibility, and delayed investments in NG projects. Those factors among others have constrained exploration activity leading to a decline in NG reserves and to reduced production for interstate markets.

In both 1979 and 1980, there was a small increase in domestic gas production, a direct consequence of a much higher level of drilling activity the industry has experienced even under gradual price decontrol. Although the number of gas wells drilled in 1981 was up by some 14 percent over 1980, this compares unfavorably with the 40 percent increase in oil wells drilled, during the same period.

Despite the Reagan administration's repeated pronouncements that appear to favor the speeding up of gas deregulation, it appears unlikely that natural gas decontrol legislation will be acted on by Congress before the 1984 presidential elections. Yet, complete deregulation of NG prices is essential for a climate in which gas exploration and production can attain its greatest potential. Current policy is dominated by uncertainty, preventing producers, consumers, and distributors of NG from making optimal decisions.

Nuclear power is another area where for a variety of reasons, full production potential is far from being realized. The size of the nuclear contribution will directly affect the overall supply of energy and thus the prospects for economic growth in the 1990s and beyond. The depressed state of the nuclear industry is unlikely to change without a substantial change in public perceptions, and in the regulatory regime governing the licensing and construction of nuclear power plants.

The major areas of public concern that must be addressed are the safety of nuclear plants, the disposal of high-level radioactive waste, and the nonproliferation issue. The nuclear energy policy being promulgated by the Reagan administration is designed to remove some of the obstacles and uncertainties that stand in the way of faster development of nuclear power in the United States. The government has outlined several new initiatives that could lead to a speed-up of licensing procedures for nuclear plants and to a resolution of the outstanding problems of nuclear waste disposal.

Yet it is very important that in attempting to restore the nuclear power industry to health the government act in a way that will tend to alleviate public concerns with respect to safety, cost escalation, and regulatory control.

This book was written with two primary objectives in mind.

First, it contains a detailed albeit selective evaluation of the formulation and implementation of United States energy policy in the post oil-embargo period.

Second, it seeks to gain a better understanding of the reasons and factors behind our all too obvious inability to forge an effective and consistent set of energy policies in the past decade.

Repeatedly in recent years market forces have been thwarted and prevented from bringing about a state of equilibrium between energy supply and demand. It is the thesis of this book that an effective energy policy should reinforce the signals provided by free energy markets rather than to attempt to blunt their impact.

Chapters 2 and 3 examine the effects of government intervention in the petroleum and natural gas markets and the cost imposed on the economy by such policies. The experience of the last decade has taught us that the only way to avoid energy shortages is to rely on free market pricing and allocation. Tampering with NG and oil markets not only leads to a misallocation of resources but also places a heavy administrative and compliance burden on affected industries.

Chapter 4 discusses the critical state of the nuclear industry today and the uncertain outlook for its future. In spite of technical and economic factors that tend to favor nuclear power--it is invariably less costly than oil and in many cases it may be even cheaper than coal--the industry suffers from a lack of public acceptance, which acts as a major drag on its near-term development. The failure to realize the full potential of nuclear power could jeopardize efforts to reduce our oil dependence and to ensure an adequate provision of electricity, so as to provide a better balanced energy system.

Chapter 5 provides an overview of energy conservation policies in the United States. It underscores the point that many measures to improve energy efficiency in the United States are economically viable, given present energy prices. Government, though, must adopt policies that would support and reinforce the conservation gains that have been made throughout the 1970s.

The last chapter draws a number of lessons and guidelines for the formation of a more effective energy policy in the 1980s--the key issue being whether free market forces will be allowed to work to the fullest extent possible and thus help the country avoid some of the worst energy problems we have encountered in the past.

The price mechanism should be the basis for a consistent and effective energy policy, one that enables the United States to adjust to any adverse changes in energy prices or fuel supplies.

NOTES

1.   Youssef M. Ibrahim, "Geneva Discord: How OPEC's Oil Pact Collapsed at 11th Hour over Price Discounts," *Wall Street Journal,* January 27, 1983, pp. 1 and 16.

2.   M. A. Adelman, "OPEC as a Cartel" in James M. Griffin and David J. Teece, *OPEC Behavior and World Oil Prices* (London: George Allen and Unwin, 1982), p. 51.

3.   For example, Bethlehem Steel, the second largest steel manufacturer in the United States, has closed or sold nearly one fifth of its obsolete steel-making capacity. In addition to closing inefficient facilities, the company has attempted to modernize its operating plants. "Bethlehem Steel Reports Net Loss of $1.5 billion," *Wall Street Journal,* January 27, 1983, p. 3.

4.   After falling in the 1960-73 period, real energy prices increased sharply in the 1973-80 interval. For the seven largest OECD countries, the real price of imported oil increased by 25 percent per year in 1973-80. In industry the real price of oil and of non-oil fuels rose 15 percent and 10.4 percent per annum, respectively, while in the residential-commercial sector, oil and non-oil prices increased 14.5 percent and 4.5 percent a year, respectively. International Energy Agency, *World Energy Outlook* (Paris: OECD, 1982), p. 80.

The Petroleum Market

— 2 —

Costs and Effects of Government Policies

PETROLEUM AVAILABILITY IN THE UNITED STATES:
OUR DEPLETING HYDROCARBON RESOURCE BASE

It is now a generally accepted proposition that U.S. petroleum production from conventional sources is expected to
decline over the 1980-2000 time span. President Reagan's
recent energy policy statement boldly asserts that due to
his administration's economic initiatives, ". . . There is
good reason for optimism about the future effect of this
policy on the discovery and production of domestic oil
reserves."[1]
Conventional oil production in the United States amounted to 8.6 MMb/d in 1980 and 1981, a 10 percent decline
from the peak level of 9.6 MMb/d attained in 1970.[2] The
production level for the first ten months of 1982 was
slightly above the 1981 level.
Recent Department of Energy projections show a steady
decline in the domestic production of crude oil over the
next 20 years, with the 1990 forecast output put at 7
MMb/d (with a range of 6.3-8.2 MMb/d). The Congressional Office of Technology Assessment is considerably more
pessimistic with regard to future U.S. petroleum production. Their midrange forecast for 1990 is 5.2 MMb/d (with
a likely range of 4.2 to 6.2 MMb/d).[3]
The path of future production of petroleum depends in
large part on the amount of economically recoverable crude

9

oil available in suitable geological formations. The Department of Energy estimates put the amount of recoverable crude oil that remains in the ground at about 70 billion barrels; other estimates range from a low of 45 to a high of 140 billion barrels.[4] Gross additions to reserves averaged about 1.5 billion barrels per year from 1975 to 1979, with a high of 2.2 billion barrels attained in 1979 (for net reserve additions see Table 2.1).

The Department of Energy expects additions to reserves to remain roughly stable over the decade of the 1980s, due to the offsetting influences of rapidly increasing drilling, on the one hand, and a declining success ratio (also known as the return-to-drilling ratio), on the other.

In the final analysis, it is the size of our potential hydrocarbon resource base that will determine future additions to reserves and consequently the amount of crude oil that will be produced in the United States in the coming decades. However, of almost equal importance with the resource base are the incentives accorded to producers through higher prices and higher expected returns to drilling. As petroleum prices rise, the higher expected returns encourage a more intensive search for petroleum deposits in both known and new but potentially promising areas.

It is evident that both large and small oil producers have responded to higher current and expected prices of petroleum--in terms of a vastly expanded exploratory well-drilling effort. (See Table 2-2.) The number of exploratory wells drilled in 1981, the first year of complete decontrol of crude oil prices, rose by 38 percent above its 1980 level, and this is on the heels of a 33 percent increase in 1980.

The average number of drilling rigs in operation in 1981 was 36 percent above their 1980 level.[5] Total drilling footage also rose significantly dramatically by about 27 percent in 1981 following a similar increase in 1980. In addition, vigorous geophysical activity is being carried out, with the number of active seismic crews near an all-time record. Thus, all available evidence points to an enormous expansion in the intensity of exploratory activity in the United States.

Of course, it cannot be guaranteed that such an unprecedented burst of exploratory activity will bring forth the hoped for results in terms of major discoveries of new fields. Yet using the 1980 results, one can be at least cautiously optimistic. In 1980, the United States added six oil fields to its list of giant discoveries. Two of these are in the Overthrust Belt of the Rockies, three are in the

TABLE 2-1. Production and Proven Reserves of Crude Oil in United States, 1950-81

Year	Annual Production[a] Quadrillion (10^15) Btu[b]	Million barrels	Proved Reserves at Year End (billion barrels)	Net Change in Reserves During Year	Ratio of Reserves to Production (years)
1950	11.45	1,974	25.3	-.-[c]	12.84
1951	13.04	2,248	27.5	2.2	12.28
1952	13.28	2,290	28.0	0.5	12.23
1953	13.67	2,357	28.9	0.9	12.30
1954	13.43	2,315	29.6	0.7	12.81
1955	14.41	2,484	30.0	0.4	12.10
1956	15.18	2,617	30.4	0.4	11.60
1957	15.18	2,617	30.3	-0.1	11.61
1958	14.20	2,449	30.5	0.2	12.50
1959	14.93	2,575	31.7	1.2	12.33
1960	14.93	2,575	31.6	-0.1	12.30
1961	15.21	2,622	31.8	0.2	12.14
1962	15.52	2,676	31.4	-0.4	11.76
1963	15.97	2,753	31.0	-0.4	11.27
1964	16.16	2,787	31.0	0.0	11.15
1965	16.52	2,849	31.4	0.4	11.06
1966	17.56	3,028	31.5	0.1	10.43
1967	18.65	3,216	31.4	-0.1	9.78
1968	19.31	3,329	30.7	-0.7	9.25
1969	19.56	3,322	29.6	-1.1	8.78
1970	20.40	3,517	39.0	9.4	11.11
1971	20.03	3,454	38.1	-0.9	11.04
1972	20.04	3,455	36.3	-1.8	10.52
1973	19.49	3,361	35.3	-1.0	10.50
1974	18.57	3,203	34.2	-1.1	10.69
1975	17.73	3,057	32.7	-1.5	10.72
1976	17.26	2,976	30.9	-1.8	10.40
1977	17.45	3,009	29.5	-1.4	9.83
1978	18.43	3,178	27.8	-1.7	8.77
1979	18.10	3,121	27.1	-0.7	8.69
1980	18.25	3,139	29.8	-0.7	8.41
1981	18.15	3,128	29.8	0.0	9.50

[a]Crude oil and lease condensate.

[b]British thermal units.

[c]Not available.

Source: Annual production and reserve data 1950 through 1981 are from U. S. Department of Energy, 1980 Annual Report to Congress, vol. II, April 1981, pp. 5, 41; and U.S. Department of Energy, 1981 Annual Reports to Congress, vol. II, May 1982, p. 45.

TABLE 2-2. Exploratory Oil and Gas Wells Drilled in United States, 1950-80

Year	Wells Drilled (thousands)				Footage Drilled (million feet)				Average Depth (feet)				Successful Wells (percent)
	Oil	Gas	Dry Holes	Total	Oil	Gas	Dry Holes	Total	Oil	Gas	Dry Holes	Total	
1950	1.58	0.43	8.29	10.31	6.9	2.4	31.0	40.2	4,335	5,466	3,733	3,898	19.5
1951	1.76	0.45	9.54	11.76	8.1	2.5	31.0	49.3	4,609	5,497	4,059	4,197	18.9
1952	1.78	0.56	10.09	12.42	8.5	3.4	43.7	55.6	4,781	6,071	4,334	4,476	18.8
1953	1.98	0.70	10.63	13.31	9.4	4.0	47.3	60.7	4,761	5,654	4,447	4,557	20.1
1954	1.98	0.73	10.39	13.10	9.4	4.4	45.8	59.6	4,740	6,050	4,408	4,550	20.7
1955	2.24	0.87	11.83	14.94	10.8	5.2	53.2	69.2	4,819	5,964	4,498	4,632	20.8
1956	2.27	0.82	13.12	16.21	11.1	5.2	58.0	74.3	4,901	6,301	4,425	4,587	19.1
1957	1.94	0.86	11.90	14.71	9.8	6.0	53.4	69.2	5,036	6,898	4,488	4,702	19.1
1958	1.74	0.82	10.63	13.20	8.7	5.5	47.3	61.5	4,993	6,657	4,449	4,658	19.4
1959	1.70	0.91	10.58	13.91	8.5	6.0	48.7	63.3	5,021	6,613	4,602	4,795	19.8
1960	1.32	0.87	9.52	11.70	6.8	5.5	43.5	55.8	5,170	6,298	4,575	4,770	18.7
1961	1.16	0.81	9.02	10.99	5.9	5.2	43.3	54.4	5,099	6,457	4,799	4,953	17.9
1962	1.21	0.77	8.82	10.80	6.2	5.2	42.2	53.6	5,124	6,728	4,790	4,966	18.4
1963	1.31	0.66	8.69	10.66	6.4	4.2	42.8	53.5	4,878	6,370	4,933	5,016	18.5
1964	1.22	0.56	8.95	10.73	6.7	4.2	44.6	55.5	5,509	7,541	4,980	5,174	16.6

Year													
1965	0.95	0.52	8.00	9.47	5.4	3.8	40.1	49.2	5,672	7,295	5,007	5,198	15.4
1966	1.20	0.70	8.42	10.31	6.8	5.8	43.1	55.7	5,700	8,321	5,117	5,402	18.4
1967	0.99	0.53	7.36	8.88	5.7	4.0	38.2	42.8	5,758	7,478	5,188	5,388	17.1
1968	0.95	0.49	7.44	8.88	5.6	3.7	41.6	51.0	5,914	7,697	5,589	5,939	16.2
1969	1.08	0.62	8.00	9.70	6.6	5.0	45.9	57.5	6,054	8,092	5,739	5,924	17.5
1970	0.79	0.48	6.42	7.69	5.1	3.7	36.5	45.3	6,399	7,369	5,687	5,882	16.5
1971	0.65	0.44	5.83	6.92	3.7	3.3	33.3	40.4	5,702	7,616	5,716	5,835	15.7
1972	0.68	0.60	6.25	7.54	4.0	4.6	36.4	45.0	5,850	7,641	5,828	5,975	17.0
1973	0.62	0.90	5.95	7.47	3.9	6.2	34.8	44.8	6,226	6,856	5,844	5,997	20.3
1974	0.81	1.20	6.61	8.62	4.9	7.7	37.7	50.3	5,961	6,421	5,709	5,832	23.3
1975	0.91	1.17	7.07	9.21	5.7	8.0	40.1	53.8	5,863	6,831	5,678	5,844	23.3
1976	1.05	1.40	6.78	9.23	6.1	9.2	37.5	52.8	5,864	6,550	5,525	5,719	26.5
1977	1.21	1.48	7.78	9.96	9.1	9.7	40.9	57.7	5,834	6,550	5,626	5,788	27.0
1978	1.12	1.60	7.95	10.68	6.8	10.8	45.6	63.2	6,039	6,747	5,740	5,923	25.6
1979	1.24	1.78	9.46	10.48	7.5	11.8	43.2	62.5	6,023	6,599	5,794	5,958	28.8
1980	1.60	1.97	8.34	11.92	9.3	13.7	46.9	69.9	5,787	6,974	5,625	5,870	30.0
*1981	2.22	2.38	10.62	15.23	13.3	16.0	60.5	89.8	5,989	6,694	5,697	5,896	30.3

*Preliminary.
Source: U.S. Department of Energy, Energy Information Administration, 1980 Annual Report to Congress, vol. II, April 1981, p. 35, and U.S. Department of Energy, EIA, 1981 Annual Report to Congress, vol. II, May 1982, p. 37.

13

Williston (North Dakota) Basin, and one in Alaska's North Slope.[6]

Another reason for the upbeat view of our future petroleum prospects lies in the more widespread application of enhanced oil recovery (EOR) techniques. This term refers to the use of steam drive techniques designed to ease the flow of highly viscous oil; other EOR methods involve in-situ combustion and miscible gas injections. By raising well pressure, these methods allow for a substantial increase in potential recovery from a given oil reservoir. In the United States, conventional production methods are able to capture only some 30 to 35 percent of the crude oil in place. This percentage can be increased significantly through the use of EOR techniques. EOR techniques at this time add only about 0.25 MMb/d to the domestic production of oil. However, it is conservatively estimated that by 1990 additional production due to EOR will range from 0.4 to 1.0 MMb/d, and some analysts have even forecast additional production as high as 3 MMb/d by that date.[7] The Department of Energy's projection of potential recovery of petroleum due to the use of these advanced techniques (some of them still at an early stage of com-mercialization) ranges from 10 to 30 billion barrels.[8]

Further on in this chapter we will analyze in somewhat greater detail the effect of government policies past and present on the petroleum market. Yet even at this juncture I must emphasize that federal price controls in effect during the 1970s that effectively kept the average price of U.S.-produced crude oil below the world price have caused serious inefficiencies in the allocation of our nation's resources to the production of crude oil. When the alternative to domestically produced oil is crude oil supplied from foreign sources (petroleum that is available essentially without restrictions at the world price), efficiency requires that domestic production be undertaken to the point where the incremental cost of the last barrel of crude produced in the United States is just equal to the landed price of imported oil.[9]

The system of price controls in place prior to February 1981, reduced domestic production below its economically efficient level, with the difference being made up by additional imports. Federal price controls caused a re-duction in the production of crude oil from existing oil fields, but perhaps more significantly, they discouraged the expansion of *potential* supplies of crude through investment in EOR techniques and in the exploration and development of new oil-bearing structures.

A recent study provides a rough quantitative estimate

of the domestic oil production foregone as a result of federal price controls.[10]   Even under an assumed *low* response of production to higher price, the study concludes that in the absence of price controls, production of crude oil *would* have been 10 percent higher in 1976 and 29 percent higher in 1979 than the level of production actually attained under controls.[11]

Given the possibility of somewhat greater supply responsiveness to higher oil prices, the potential loss of production due to controls could have amounted to 13 percent in 1976 and about 47 percent in 1979. Even if one does not accept these numbers at face value, it is clear that a substantial volume of domestic production was sacrificed as a result of government-imposed controls, with the undesirable outcome of increased dependence on imported petroleum.

THE WINDFALL PROFITS TAX

In undertaking to decontrol petroleum prices, it was the intent of both the Carter and Reagan administrations to encourage the production of domestic crude oil in order to cut back on imports. In conjunction with the price decontrol action, President Carter also requested that Congress enact a windfall profits tax of 50 percent on the additional revenue that would be garnered by oil producers as a result of decontrol, or due to future price hikes by OPEC.[12]

President Carter was convinced that without a tax on the earnings of the oil companies, his decontrol action would be unacceptable to the liberal wing of his own Democratic party.[13]   It was projected at the time that the tax would raise as much as $227.3 billion over the ensuing ten years.

More important than the revenue-raising aspects of this tax is its impact on U.S. production of crude oil. As a matter of fact, this tax is not designed to produce tax revenue as a proportion of oil company profits. More precisely, it is a federal excise tax, computed on the difference between the decontrolled price of crude oil (the world price) and three arbitrarily determined "base prices." Producers are classified as either "major" or "independent," with the latter category taxed at a somewhat lower rate than the former.[14]   Further discrimination is applied in terms of a lower tax rate being levied on newly discovered oil, and oil that is produced through the use of EOR techniques.

As noted previously, it is most appropriate to analyze the effects of such a tax in terms of the standard economic theory of excise taxes. If one accepts the notion that the crude oil-producing industry is workably competitive, then it is correct to view it as subject to a long-run supply curve that is positively sloped.

Given the existence in the United States of some 9,000 independent crude oil producers that are responsible for about 25 percent of the industry's domestic output, the assumption of the existence of workable competition in this segment of the industry can be readily accepted.

FIGURE 2-1.   U.S. Crude Oil Market: Effects of Windfall Profit Tax

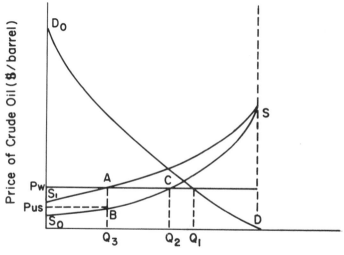

Volume of Crude Oil (barrels)

Figure 2-1 shows the effect of the windfall profits tax on U.S. crude oil production, based on the assumption-- relaxed later on in this chapter--that the United States cannot influence the world price of crude oil through changes in its own demand or supply of crude oil.

The effect of the tax is to shift the domestic supply curve of crude oil from $S_0 S$ to $S_1 S$. At the given world price of crude oil (P_w), the disincentive effect of the tax is clear, it reduces U.S. production from Q_2 barrels to Q_3 barrels of oil, because the *net* of the tax price of crude received by sellers in P_{us} instead of the world price - P_w. Given our assumptions, the price paid by consumers is unchanged and thus their welfare is also unaffected. Furthermore, there will be an increase in imports of crude oil by the amount of Q_2Q_3 barrels. The excise tax results in net social loss, because of the misallocation of resources approximated by the area of the triangle.[15] Clearly such a tax creates perverse economic incentives in the U.S. crude oil markets. It reduces domestic production of crude oil, it leads to an increased level of imports, and most important, it wastes our nation's scarce resources.

It has been pointed out recently that the windfall profits tax also leads to a peculiar convergence of interest between the United States Treasury and OPEC.[16] In fiscal year 1982, the U.S. Treasury expected revenues of about $27.6 billion from this tax, based on the expectation of steady oil prices over the next twelve months. In fact, though, the world price of oil dropped during that year.[17] As a rough rule of thumb the Treasury could lose $1.4 billion in tax revenues for every dollar fall in the world price of oil--thus to date the decline in the United States government's tax receipts from this source alone may be close to $3 billion.

Notwithstanding the revenue impact of the tax, its most serious effect is in terms of its disincentive impact on U.S. production of crude oil. A study done at the Federal Reserve Bank of San Francisco estimates, based on a con- servative set of assumptions (primarily regarding the low supply response of oil production to higher prices), that the production of crude oil--assuming complete decontrol of oil prices and *no* excise tax--could have reached 3,628 million barrels in 1985 and 3,248 million barrels in 1990.[18] Given the existence of the windfall profits tax, production is likely to be only 3,255 million barrels in 1985 and 2,936 million barrels in 1990, a 10 percent decline relative to the *no tax* case. This study points out the major problem with the excise tax; it curbs domestic production. A genuine tax on oil producers' net earnings would not contain the perverse incentive present in the current excise tax scheme--on the other hand, such a tax would not generate significant amounts of revenue for the U.S. Treasury.

OIL IMPORTS: ARE WE "TOO" DEPENDENT
ON FOREIGN SOURCES?

The import dependence issue has exerted an important influence on U.S. energy policy making for at least two and a half decades, and in fact it was used as the primary rationale for the imposition of oil import quotas by President

Eisenhower.[19] I will not provide a historical narrative of this issue since it has been treated at great length by other authors.[20]

In terms of current policy, the question we will be addressing is aptly summarized in the following quote: "Because imports are expensive and uncertain and create economic and political vulnerabilities and because the trend is toward greater imports despite the elevated prices of recent years, a central question of U.S. energy policy is *whether oil imports should be singled out as a target of direct government action.*"[21] (Emphasis added.)

The share of imports in the total United States domestic petroleum consumption has risen inexorably throughout the 1960s and 1970s. From about 20 percent of total domestic demand in the second half of the 1960s to 30 percent in the first half of the 1970s, and finally reaching the highest level to date--in excess of 40 percent--in the second half of the 1970s.[22]

There is good reason to believe that the upward climb in the U.S. import petroleum share has been arrested--in fact recent data for the first nine months of 1982 show that share hovering at around one fourth, back to its level of the early 1970s. Yet, the more fundamental question that needs to be addressed is the following: Should the United States as a matter of *public policy* target a particular (presumably lower than current) level of foreign petroleum dependence?

Quite clearly, it is not the *level of dependence* on imported oil that worries our public officials and prognosticators, but rather the fact that the bulk of this oil comes from areas--such as the Middle East--that are unstable and vulnerable to internal upheavals (as in Iran), to superpower rivalry (in North Africa and Afghanistan), and to violent regional conflicts (case in point, the Iran-Iraq war).

In that sense, the fact that about 30 percent of our 1980 crude oil imports originate in the Middle East, with another 38 percent coming from Africa--from countries such as Libya and Angola--is indeed the stuff that nightmares are made of.[23] In 1980 the United States imported about 941 million barrels or 60 percent of all imports, from sources that must be considered actually or potentially insecure and subject to future disruption.[24]

These observations point to another problem. Given that in 1980 about 2.5 MMb/d of oil came from insecure sources, it is practically impossible to try to reduce imports selectively--namely, just from those sources. Thus it appears that if one is going to reduce the degree of U.S. dependence on foreign sources of oil (including from those considered "secure"), it must be done through an overall reduction of the level of imports. The first question therefore concerns the desirability of reducing imports of petroleum *below their market determined levels.* The strongest case for such intervention can be made by invoking the "market failure" argument. To wit, imported oil is inherently "insecure" or unreliable and therefore the full social (marginal) cost of such oil is higher than its market price. One obvious solution would be to impose a tariff on imported oil, thereby internalizing these "external" costs.

In a well-publicized study carried out by researchers associated with the Energy Project at the Harvard Business School, the authors wrote, *"even world market prices would still be much too low to reflect the real risks caused by oil imports.* These include such things as higher oil prices, slower economic growth, and international political tension."[25]

While higher oil prices bring about several adverse economic effects, such as lower growth rate and increased balance of payments deficits, none of them can be considered an adequate justification for government intervention. The primary reason for government intervention to limit oil imports must be based on broadly conceived national security considerations. The argument here being that the activities of private economic agents--in terms of production, consumption, and trade--have undesirable and unintended effects on the wellbeing of other individuals and the nation as a whole. Such a negative "externality" would provide justification for the imposition of a tax on this activity (in this case a duty on the imports of petroleum would be called for).

An "optimal" import tax would add to the private marginal cost, represented by the world price of oil, a levy that is just sufficient to offset the harm suffered, on the margin, by society as a whole. By adding such a "security premium" to the world price of oil, which is the private incremental cost of this commodity to the buyer, one could bring home to the private sector the full social cost of using imported oil. Of course, in practice, we may not know what constitutes a "safe" level of imported oil and therefore the exact height of the tariff necessary to achieve the socially optimal volume of imports.

An alternative solution to the national security problem is the creation of an adequate national stockpile of both crude oil and petroleum products. A strong case can be made that such oil storage capacity should be internationally coordinated, possibly within the framework of the International Energy Agency (IEA).[26]

In the absence of an internationally coordinated effort in this regard, the Reagan administration is quite correct in proceeding with its own efforts to fill the nation's strategic petroleum reserve (SPR). The SPR's planned capacity of 750 million by 1989 is to be filled as "rapidly as possible, consistent with world oil market conditions."

The Reagan administration's energy plan at least intimates that *private* as well as the government's own oil stockpiles will be used to mitigate the harmful effects of sudden and substantial oil supply interruption from abroad.[27] The stockpiling program is vastly superior to previous policies that would have imposed a cumbersome system of direct allocations and controls of petroleum products, such as a gasoline rationing program, in case of an emergency.

The government's stockpiling program plus the yet unspecified measures to encourage private entities to build up their own emergency stockpiles should be adequate to the task of ensuring our national security. The only specific proposal along those lines is the one that suggests that the government "Remove factors that have discouraged private firms from building up their own emergency oil stockpiles." In addition, I have proposed elsewhere that a modest, and preferably variable, duty on imported petroleum be levied if the market determined level of oil imports is considered "too high" from the standpoint of national security.[28] Furthermore, the tariff revenue collected by the federal government could be used to finance an accelerated program of national stockpiling.[29]

As M. A. Adelman has observed, an ad-valorem tariff on imported oil imposed by all IEA member countries would have the additional virtue of transferring revenue from OPEC to the oil-importing countries. To the extent that such a tax would limit the increases in OPEC's oil prices, it would benefit all oil-importing countries including those that do not belong to the IEA (principally the less developed countries).[30]

A more comprehensive analysis of the economic effects of an oil import levy indicates that the justification for its imposition is based on two lines of argument. First, because of the existence of imperfections in world petroleum markets, the United States and other oil importers incur certain additional costs (over and above the world price of oil) due to their excessive reliance on oil imports. This results from the fact that the international supply of oil is not determined by free market forces but is in fact con-

trolled by a group of exporters that have used their monopoly power to extract large rents from oil importers.
Second, given that the flow of oil to the United States can
be suddenly disrupted, the government has a duty to try
to minimize the macroeconomic effects of the resulting oil
price shocks. Bohi and Montgomery, based on a more
detailed analysis of the security aspects of oil imports,
conclude that "a combined policy of a tariff and a strategic
petroleum reserve effectively addresses the separate issues
inherent in the oil import premium. The two are *comple-
mentary* because the tariff reduces the long-run demand for
oil imports, making the economy more efficient in the use of
energy, while the stockpile reduces the short-run demand
for oil imports, enabling the economy to use its capital
stock more efficiently."[31]

The Carter administration, though, chose to try to
reduce imports through indirect means. President Carter's
National Energy Plan of 1977, included numerous proposals
consisting of pricing policies, and involving the creation of
regulatory mechanisms and a variety of administrative
measures. The Carter plan called for a set of *indirect* oil
import-reducing measures that included conservation of
liquid fuels, encouragement of the production of crude oil
and synthetic fuels, and measures that encourage substitution away from liquid fuels. Income tax credits for home
insulation, fleet mileage standard for automobiles, and
prohibition on the use of petroleum in new electric power
plants were just a few of the policies that would have some
effect--however unpredictable and indirect--on the consumption and importation of petroleum.[32]

These measures in toto did not add up to a program
that could effect the level of imports of petroleum in a
substantial and predictable way; these roundabout schemes
of import substitution have been justly criticized as costly,
ineffective, and wasteful of our economy's resources. This
point was made bluntly and directly by then Congressman
David Stockman (now the director of the Office of Management and Budget), "If we were actually foolish enough to
extract unlimited fiscal resources from the economy in order
to finance a great energy pork barrel containing all the
contending alternative brands and schemes, we would get
nothing less than a foolish result. . . ."[33]

A ZERO-SUM ENERGY POLICY: THE CASE
OF THE PETROLEUM MARKET

It has become fashionable in some quarters to argue that
the primary obstacle to the implementation of a market-

oriented energy policy in the United States is the zero-sum nature of such a policy.[34]   A zero-sum game is defined as any game where the losses and winnings exactly offset each other.

A market-oriented energy policy is one where the major decisions as to amounts of energy consumed, its costs, and its availability (supply) are made primarily through impersonal market forces and processes.

Despite lip service being paid to the effectiveness of the market mechanism in allocating energy resources to their most valuable uses, rarely has the market been allowed to play this role in the past; this is especially true with regard to the petroleum and natural gas markets. While there is no evidence that government regulation, taxes (subsidies), or public ownership of production facilities have been more effective than reasonably free and competitive markets in dealing with energy problems--this has been the direction in which energy policy has been increasingly taking us in the past.

Furthermore, as a result of energy developments in the 1970s, there has been a dramatic increase in the weight of government regulation in the energy sector as a whole, and in the petroleum market in particular. Measures that called for voluntary or mandatory standards of energy conservation and subsidies dedicated to the introduction of alternative energy supply technologies have been introduced.

The most prominent case of such an ill-advised energy policy can be seen in the government regulation of prices charged for oil and natural gas. During the 1970s, price controls held the domestic price of oil and natural gas well below the world price level. To illustrate, in 1980, the average price paid by refiners for domestically produced oil was $24.2 per barrel while the average cost of imported petroleum was $33.9 per barrel.[35]

Regulation of petroleum prices initially came about through the interaction of state and federal regulations. In the 1930s in order to conserve crude oil, the major oil-producing states passed market demand prorationing laws. State regulatory agencies were established to limit the rate of crude oil production. The aim of this policy was to restrict total output and bring about higher crude oil prices. It also meant that crude oil producers, owners of oil-bearing land, and taxpayers of oil-producing states enjoyed substantial rents that they naturally were reluctant to give up. This cozy arrangement continued unimpaired until the mid-1950s when cheaper Persian Gulf crude oil became available in ever increasing quantities, and thereby undermined the previously successful efforts to fix a high price for U.S.-produced crude.

Initially, voluntary oil import quotas were implemented in an attempt to stem imports, but finally bowing to oil industry pressure, President Eisenhower established a mandatory oil import program in 1959. Because the supply of imports was restricted, the demand for domestic crude was raised, and this extra demand could be satisfied only through more costly domestic production. President Nixon's Oil Import Task Force noted that as a result of oil import controls, the domestic price of crude oil was roughly $1 to $1.50 per barrel above the price of imported crude of equal quality.[36]

Beginning in 1971, control over oil prices was gradually transferred from the states to the federal government, bringing petroleum pricing under President Nixon's wage and price control policies.

The 1973 oil embargo brought in its wake a more complex set of oil price regulations. Production from domestic oil fields up to their 1972 production rates was classified as "old" oil. Old oil was allowed to sell for $1.35 per barrel above its May 15, 1973 price.[37] Output over and above the 1972 level and from fields not yet in production at that time was deemed "new" oil. Therein, for each barrel of "new" oil a producer was allowed to release a barrel of "old" oil from price controls.

In January 1976 new rules were promulgated under the Energy Policy and Conservation Act of 1975. This legislation established a three-tier pricing system. Output not in excess of the 1975 level of oil production was defined as lower-tier crude. Production over and above the lower tier level and from fields not producing prior to 1976 was designated upper tier. Stripper oil, federally owned crude, and imported oil were all free from price controls. In addition, an entitlement program was put into effect in November of 1974 to equalize the average cost of crude oil among refiners.

Under this program the Department of Energy provided monthly issues of "entitlements" for low-priced crude to each refiner. The number of entitlements awarded any refiner was equal to the number of barrels of inexpensive (controlled) crude that the refiner would have used had he operated at the national average ratio of controlled to uncontrolled crude. If a refinery used controlled oil in excess of this ration, it had to purchase entitlements. On the other hand, if a refiner purchased less controlled oil than he was entitled to, he could see any remaining entitlements to others. The price of an entitlement roughly equaled the difference between controlled and imported crude. Under the entitlement program refiners perceived the marginal cost of crude oil as being less than the world market price. In effect, the entitlement program allowed refiners to produce petroleum products whose value to consumers was less than its incremental cost. Price controls in conjunction with the entitlement program artificially stimulated the consumption of petroleum products and unduly expanded the use of imported oil.

Estimates place the net cost to the nation of the subsidized consumption of refined products at about half a billion dollars based on 1979 data. To the extent that the world price of petroleum does not reflect the *full* cost to the nation of imported crude oil, the total cost of government petroleum regulation may have been even greater. [38]

Considerable waste of the nation's scarce resources resulted from the discouragement of domestic crude oil production--the additional supply that would have been forthcoming if the incremental cost of a domestically produced barrel of oil was equal to the world price.

Over the longer haul, the domestic effect of price controls is most telling in its impact on the rate of exploration and development of new oil fields, and results subsequently in excessive reliance on supplies of petroleum from abroad.

Based on a conservative estimate the annual cost of domestic underproduction of petroleum resulting from federal price controls is put at about $2 billion. It is possible that investors may have taken an even dimmer view of future returns from oil exploration under price controls, thus conceivably doubling, to $4 billion, the welfare loss due to long-term supply-side inefficiencies.

While the inefficiencies resulting from the overconsumption and underproduction of oil, stemming from the regulation of petroleum prices, had the most serious consequences for the nation's welfare, the full reckoning of costs does not end there. The enforcement of petroleum price regulations by government and the compliance of the business sector with such requirements calls for the commitment of real resources on the part of both the public and the private sectors. A conservative estimate of the annual cost of administering the price controls puts it at $700 million. In sum, a reasonable estimate of the total annual cost to the economy of price controls resulting from the static misallocation of the nation's productive resources is in the range of $3.2 to $5.2 billion. (See Table 2-3.)

While there is widespread agreement with regard to the net economic costs of these energy programs, controversy flares and rhetorical sparks fly when distributional aspects

TABLE 2-3. Annual Welfare Costs (Net) of Federal Price Regulation of Petroleum

Type of Costs	Costs (billions of dollars)
Demand side costs	0.5
Supply side costs (range)	2.0 to 4.0
Administrative and other costs	0.7
Net social costs	3.2 to 5.2

Source: K. Arrow and J. Kalt, Petroleum Price Regulation: Should We Decontrol? (Washington, D.C.: American Enterprise Institute for Public Policy Research, 1979), pp. 14-22.

of these policies come up for discussion. It is generally recognized that price controls have resulted in a transfer of wealth from domestic producers of crude oil to domestic users of crude petroleum. Those benefiting from federal regulations consist of intermediate users of crude (refiners) and possibly also final users of refined petroleum products such as gasoline, heating oil, and kerosene.

Another way of looking at the distributional consequences of deregulation is to realize that they amount to a wealth transfer from the users of petroleum products in general to individuals that hold property rights to crude oil. It stands to reason that the transfer of income from refiners to crude oil producers need not concern us when questions of equity or fairness are aired.

It should also be borne in mind that decontrol may have had a proportionately greater impact on poorer consumers than on those that are better off.

In any event, a careful summary of distributional losses (see Table 2-4) indicates that the most likely impact of decontrol would be a net after-tax loss of less than $3 billion, or about $13 billion for every resident of the United States. However, it is possible that this view of the *distributional* effects of decontrol although generally accepted is seriously flawed.

The following analysis is based on the working assumption that the United States is a *price-taker* in the world petroleum product market, such as the motor gasoline or heating oil markets. This implies that the United States faces a perfectly elastic foreign supply curve of refined products at the *world price*.

TABLE 2-4. Distributional Losses of Consumer Wealth Due to Oil Price Decontrol

		Assumed Pass Through	
	55%	40%	25%
	Total Loss (billions of dollars)		
A. Gross transfer	8.0	6.0	4.0
B. Net transfer	7.4	5.3	3.7
C. After tax	3.8	2.8	1.9
	Per capita loss (billions of dollars)		
A.	36.4	27.2	18.2
B.	33.6	24.0	16.8
C.	17.3	12.7	8.6

Source: Recomputed from K. Arrow and J. Kalt, Petroleum Price Regulation: Should We Decontrol? (Washington, D.C.: American Enterprise Institute for Public Policy Research, 1979), pp. 31-34.

Figure 2-2 describes the situation in such a market, with price controls on *crude* oil (but not on petroleum products) in effect.

Price controls on crude oil combined with the entitlements program, have effectively subsidized the refiners' production costs of petroleum products by lowering the cost of their most important input--crude oil. The domestic supply schedule of petroleum products, S_0S_0, takes into account the existence of such a subsidy; under these circumstances, the amount of petroleum products consumed is Q_4, the amount produced domestically is Q_3, and the United States ends up importing (Q_4-Q_3) barrels of petroleum products.

With the complete decontrol of crude oil prices, the cost to the refiners of their most important input--crude oil--

inevitably rises to the world level as the subsidy is eliminated, and consequently the refiner's marginal cost
increases, and the industry's supply curve shifts to S_1S_1.
The decontrol action per se would have no effect on product prices, which are set in the world market at the level
P_w--but it will reduce domestic production to Q_1 and
subsequently lead to a higher level of imports--(Q_4-Q_1).
The analysis to this point is incomplete because it does not
take into account the possibility that the United States can
have an impact on the world price of crude oil. With the
decontrol of crude oil prices, U.S. demand for imported
crude oil falls because of the greater domestic output and
somewhat diminished demand for petroleum by refiners.

FIGURE 2-2. U.S. Petroleum Product Market

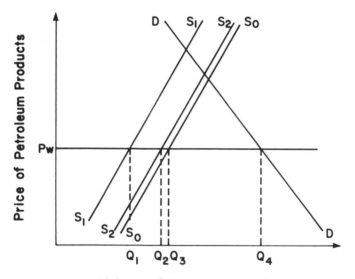

Volume of Petroleum Products

In Figure 2-3, we depict such an outcome as a shift in
the world excess demand for crude oil from ED_0 to the
lower level of ED_1. Given that the world excess supply
curve of crude oil is unchanged, a decontrol action by the
United States leads directly to a lower world price of crude
oil--a fall from P_c^0 to P_c^1.[39]
Next, one has to take account of the impact of the
falling world price of crude oil in our examination of the
U.S. product market in Figure 2-2. The effect of this

development is to shift the refining industry's supply curve to the right, most likely to a position such as S_2S_2.

The final result in the petroleum product market is that there is no change in product prices (such as motor gasoline prices), with the effects on the quantity supplied domestically and the volume of imports undetermined. The most likely outcome is the one shown in Figure 2-2; that is, a *slight* increase in the volume of imported petroleum products being the final consequence of decontrol (Q_3-Q_2).

FIGURE 2-3. World Market for Crude Oil

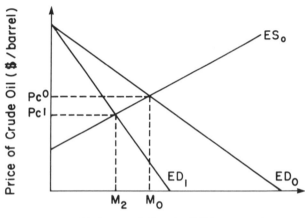

Volume of Crude Oil (barrels)

It is possible to subject this hypothesis to an empirical evaluation. As I have noted earlier, the process of decontrol of crude oil prices began in June 1979 and was completed on January 28, 1981. Over the period June 1979 to February 1981, imports of refined products remained basically unchanged. For example, in the April-June 1979 period, petroleum-product imports averaged about 1.73 MMb/d, during the November-December 1980-January 1981 period, they averaged about 1.8 MMb/d, up slightly, as our analysis predicted. In the interim, monthly imports fluctuated within the 1.4-2.3 MMb/d range. Thus, basically, imports of petroleum products have been quite steady during the decontrol period. Since the first of the year (1981) petroleum product imports have declined from about 1.85 MMb/d (January-February 1981) to about 1.40 MMb/d (in May-June-July 1981). The most likely explanation of this reduction is based on the weak overall demand for petroleum products, due to the onset of the recession in the United States (that is, in Figure 2-2 the demand curve for petroleum products has shifted downward and to the left).

Decontrol of U.S. crude oil prices brought about a sharp reduction in U.S. import demand for crude oil and also some decrease in the world price of crude, as is predicted in Figure 2-3.

Between May-June 1979 and November-December 1980 imports of crude oil have declined from an average of 6.4 MMb/d to 4.65 MMb/d, a reduction of 27 percent. This trend has continued since controls were terminated on January 28, 1981. By June-July 1981 imports of crude oil fell to 3.9 MMb/d, a decline of about 40 percent since full decontrol began.

Recent developments in the world market for crude oil are well known; in 1981, the average world price of crude oil has fallen from \$35.5 per barrel to just below \$34 a barrel, a decline of about 4.4 percent. Clearly it would not be correct to attribute the entire fall in the world price of crude oil to the decontrol of U.S. petroleum prices. In addition, there has been a sustained and sizable reduction in the demand for petroleum products in the major oil-importing industrial countries over the 1980-81 period.[40] However, the impact of the reduction in U.S. demand for imported crude oil of about 2.5 MMb/d in the period May-June 1979 to June-July 1981 must have been an important factor contributing to the fall in the price of oil in 1981.

In sum, the regime of federal price controls, in effect until February 1981, encouraged an excessive level of petroleum consumption, discouraged U.S. energy production, and subsidized the use of imported petroleum. Under price controls, the U.S. import subsidy automatically increased with the rise in the world price of crude oil, thereby offsetting roughly one half of the impact of higher import prices on the average cost of oil to refiners.[41] (See Table 2-5.)

This misguided program not only ensured our growing dependence on foreign sources of petroleum but also made it easier for OPEC to raise petroleum prices and make these higher prices stick. U.S. imports of crude petroleum and refined petroleum products have expanded particularly rapidly ever since the implementation of comprehensive federal energy regulations in 1973. (See Table 2-6.)

The inexorable rise in U.S. imports of petroleum has been reversed since the process of oil price decontrol began in June 1979, finally ending with President Reagan's executive order eliminating all price controls on crude oil and refined petroleum products on January 28, 1981. The share

TABLE 2-5. Entitlement Subsidy to Crude Oil Producers

	(dollars/bbl.)
Dec. 1978	1.27
March 1979	1.80
June 1979	3.01
Sept. 1979	3.92
Dec. 1979	4.71
March 1980	5.05
June 1980	5.44
Sept. 1980	3.52
Dec. 1980	1.52

Source: Department of Energy, Energy Information Administration, Monthly Energy Review, January 1981.

of imports in U.S. demand for petroleum products peaked in 1979, and has been steadily declining ever since, reaching its lowest level since the early 1970s in the first three quarters of 1982. By the third quarter of 1982 U.S. imports of petroleum and petroleum products dropped to just below 5 MMb/d and the ratio of imports to demand was reduced to the level experienced in the 1972-1973 period. When the process of decontrol of oil prices started in June 1979, oil imports stood at the 8.3 MMb/d level; two years later they amounted to 5 MMb/d, a drop of 40 percent.

Between the second quarter of 1979 and the second quarter of 1981, crude oil imports fell by 2.5 MMb/d—a two-fifths reduction—as we noted, a decline of this magnitude is bound to make a difference in the world market for crude oil. And indeed, between January 1981 and February 1982, the world price of crude oil declined by $1.50 per barrel, and by the end of 1982 the world price of crude oil averaged $33 per barrel.

To attain a better understanding of the effect of U.S. energy policies on the world market, one should note the sharp production (and export) adjustments that OPEC countries had to undergo to prevent an even greater erosion in petroleum prices. (See Table 2-7.)

During the 1960s and early 1970s OPEC supplied an ever growing share of the world's output of petroleum. This share reached its peak in 1973 at which time it amounted to 55.7 percent of total world production.

TABLE 2-6. U.S. Imports and Total Demand for Petroleum and Petroleum Products, and Share of Imports in U.S. Demand

	(1) U.S. Imports (thousands barrel/day)	(2) U.S. Demand for Petroleum Products (thousands barrel/day)	1/2 x 100 (percent)
1970	3,419	14,697	23.3
1971	3,926	15,213	25.8
1972	4,741	16,367	29.0
1973	6,256	17,308	36.1
1974	6,112	16,652	36.7
1975	6,056	16,322	37.1
1976	7,313	17,461	41.9
1977	8,787	18,431	47.7
1978	8,202	18,847	43.5
1979	8,389	18,513	45.3
1980	6,865	16,056	40.3
1981	5,264	15,983	32.9
1982*	4,026	15,250	26.4

*Average for the first ten months of 1982.

Sources: American Petroleum Institute, Basic Petroleum Data Book, vol. II, no. 2, section IX, May 1982, Table 1. U.S. Department of Energy, Energy Information Administration, Monthly Petroleum Statement, December 1981, p. 1. U.S. Department of Energy, EIA, Petroleum Supply Monthly, December 1982, p. 31.

Following OPEC's first major price increase in 1973-74, OPEC's output fell in both 1974 and 1975. Their production rose moderately over the next few years, growing at an annual rate of 3.2 percent from 1975 to 1978. The period of relative oil price stability that prevailed since 1974 was abruptly halted in 1979. The immediate cause of the turbulence in world oil markets was the disruption of oil exports from Iran in late 1978 and the subsequent sharp drop in the country's production in early 1979. The production cutbacks, combined with the fact that world inventories were already reduced below their normal level during 1978, caused the market for crude oil to tighten. Prices began to rise sharply in the spot market, with spot shortages developing in some industrial countries and especially in the United States.

TABLE 2-7. World Crude Oil Production Annual and Monthly Data
(thousands b/d)

			Annual		
Year	OPEC	OPEC Share(%)	Non OPEC	Non OPEC share(%)	World Output
1973	30,989	55.7	24,685	44.3	55,674
1974	30,729	55.0	25,123	45.0	55,852
1975	27,155	51.4	25,725	48.6	52,880
1976	30,738	53.7	26,574	46.3	57,312
1977	31,278	52.4	28,407	47.6	59,685
1978	29,805	49.6	30,252	50.4	60,057
1979	30,928	49.5	31,607	50.5	62,535
1980	26,890	45.2	32,648	54.8	59,538
1981	22,624	40.6	33,164	59.4	55,788
			Monthly		
6/78	29,260	48.9	30,535	51.1	59,795
9/78	32,086	51.5	30,199	48.5	62,285
12/78	30,504	49.1	31,631	50.0	62,135
3/79	30,515	49.3	31,355	50.7	61,870
6/79	31,115	49.8	31,405	50.2	62,520
9/79	30,895	49.3	31,815	50.7	62,710
12/79	30,430	48.6	32,190	51.4	62,620
3/80	29,100	47.1	32,645	52.9	61,745
6/80	27,175	45.5	32,565	54.5	59,740
9/80	25,955	44.3	32,670	55.7	58,625
12/80	25,050	43.2	33,010	56.8	58,060
3/81	25,190	43.1	33,220	56.9	58,410
6/81	22,945	41.1	32,920	58.9	55,865
9/81	20,385	38.1	33,235	61.9	53,620
12/81	21,230	39.3	32,870	60.7	54,100
3/82	18,615	35.7	33,585	64.3	52,200
6/82	18,845	35.5	34,355	64.5	53,200
8/82	17,895	34.3	34,305	65.7	52,200
9/82	18,515	34.9	34,560	65.1	53,075

Source: DOE Monthly Energy Review, July 1980, January 1981, August
1981, and February 1983.

As a result of these developments the world petroleum market was subjected to the second major energy price shock of the decade. The average price of crude oil exported by OPEC rose sharply from approximately $13 per barrel on December 31, 1978 to $28.30 per barrel on January 1, 1980, an increase of 113 percent, with further price increases taking place during 1980. At the same time, oil inventories were being replenished to the point where at the end of 1979 they were equivalent to more than three months' consumption compared to some 80-82 days of consumption at the end of 1978. Just as the world petroleum market was adjusting to these new developments, the war between Iraq and Iran broke out.

In 1978 the combined output of the two warring nations was about 7.8 MMb/d, roughly one fourth of OPEC's total production. During the fourth quarter of 1980, their combined production plummeted to about 0.62 MMb/d. Thus the world petroleum market was faced with a potential loss of output in excess of 7 MMb/d. In the interim, several countries stepped up their production thereby offsetting these losses to some extent. Saudi Arabia's output increased by about 2 MMb/d, with additional production of 0.9 MMb/d and 0.66 MMb/d respectively provided by Mexico and the United Kingdom.[42]

The following production changes took place: On balance OPEC output fell by about 5.3 MMb/d; this was partially offset by increased production in the rest of the world of about 2.5 MMb/d, resulting in a potential reduction in supply of roughly 2.8 MMb/d. To complete the analysis, we must consider the changes that took place on the demand side of the petroleum market. The continuing impact of higher petroleum prices, together with a pronounced economic slowdown in the major industrial countries, had a depressing effect on world oil consumption in 1980. Between 1978 and 1980 petroleum consumption of IEA member countries declined by about 2.9 MMb/d, a fall of 8 percent.[43]

U.S. oil consumption and the consumption of petroleum products in the major industrial countries has continued to decline in the first half of 1981. (See Table 2-8.) The largest decline was experienced in Western Europe, where economic activity has been weakest and oil prices have risen the most, largely because of the appreciation of the dollar in the foreign exchange market since July of 1980.[44]

As a result of these developments the world petroleum market was distinctly soft in 1981, as evidenced by the weakening of crude oil prices, particularly in the spot market, but also in the longer-term contract market.

TABLE 2-8. Oil Consumption in Major Industrial Countries (percentage change from comparable period in previous year)

	1980	Mid-year 1981
U.S.	- 8.2	- 5.2[a]
Canada	- 2.8	- 5.9[b]
Japan	- 9.1	- 7.0[c]
France	- 6.1	-12.9[b]
Germany	-10.8	-15.2[d]
Italy	- 2.2	0.2[d]
U.K.	-14.8	-11.5[d]

[a] January-July 1981
[b] January-May 1981
[c] January-April 1981
[d] January-June 1981
Source: Morgan Guaranty Trust, World Financial Markets, August 1981, p. 5.

Moreover, world oil inventories were reduced only moderately in the first half of 1981, and as of early July 1981, were about 600 MMb above the normal level of 5.4 billion barrels.[45]

Considering the circumstances likely to prevail in the world oil market in 1981-82 and given the existence of high interest rates, oil companies continued to pare the level of their crude oil inventories during the rest of 1981 and into 1982.

As a result, several OPEC members were forced to cut their production levels sharply--most significant were the cutbacks by suppliers of high-priced (and high-quality) crudes--such as Libya, Algeria, and Nigeria, but sharp production cutbacks have been also undertaken by Kuwait and the United Arab Emirates. By the end of 1982 OPEC production was down to less than 18 MMb/d.[46]

Absent a further sharp cut in Saudi Arabia's petroleum production the world oil market is likely to remain soft in 1983 and perhaps even into 1984. In fact, some analysts flatly predict that declining real oil prices will prevail through the mid 1980s. This conclusion is based on sharply reduced energy consumption levels in OECD countries, resulting from the delayed impact on energy users, of the 1973/74 oil price hikes, as well as the impact of the more recent--1979/80 price increases.[47]

CONCLUDING REMARKS

As a result of the move toward a market-oriented energy policy under the Reagan administration, there has been a remarkable turnaround in the petroleum prospects of the United States.

In fact, I am afraid that the good tidings brought about by recent developments in the petroleum market have been somewhat overstated in the popular press to the point of giving the American public the misleading impression that our problems and worries are over.

For example, William Tucker, in a recent issue of *Harper's* in effect was writing OPEC's obituary. To quote him: "Few people seem to realize that OPEC's monopoly of the (petroleum) market lasted only about three years," and later on in the same article he exclaims: "Without our support, OPEC would have been defunct by 1977. Now it is falling apart anyway."[48]

Now, it is true that these times are not the happiest of times for OPEC, yet, to paraphrase Mark Twain, the rumors of the oil cartel's demise have been somewhat exaggerated.

The difficulties facing the oil cartel are clearly in evidence all around us. The declining consumption of petroleum in the industrial countries, increasing competition from non-OPEC suppliers of oil, greater substitution of non-oil energy resources for petroleum, all of these factors have caused a decline in the price of crude oil since 1981.

Also in recent months, there have been persistent reports of "chiseling" by OPEC members of the cartel's price, through hidden discounts, favorable credit terms, and other special deals. An accusing finger was pointed directly at Nigeria, Iran, and Venezuela, whose sale of oil has fallen dramatically, and their foreign exchange reserves have been severely depleted. These developments represent the classic response of a cartel faced with a shrinking demand for its product. Yet one must caution against any premature gloating because I believe that it is within the capacity of OPEC to weather the current crisis and prevent the collapse of the cartel.

The crucial question remains whether Saudi Arabia, the United Arab Emirates (UAE), and Kuwait are willing to cut back production sufficiently, in line with the reduced demand for OPEC's oil. Nobody can predict with confidence how much the Saudis will be willing to reduce their output in order to support the oil cartel's price structure. Even under the most favorable circumstances, given OPEC's huge excess capacity, the cohesion and resilience of the cartel will be sorely tested in the years ahead. Nevertheless, these developments should not lull the United States and other oil-importing nations into a false sense of security, given that future oil price shocks will continue to pose a serious threat to the economic well-being and security of the West.

NOTES

1. U.S. Department of Energy, *Securing America's Energy Future*, National Energy Policy Plan, July 1981, p. 5.

2. Production data are taken from American Petroleum Institute, *Basic Petroleum Data Book* and Department of Energy, *Monthly Energy Review*, December 1982, p. 30. Projections of U.S. oil supply are taken from U.S. Department of Energy, *Energy Projection to the Year 2000*, *July 1982 Update*, August 1982, p. 5-3.

3. Congress of the United States, Office of Technology Assessment, *World Petroleum Availability, 1980-2000*, October 1980, p. 36.

4. The Department of Energy and the low estimates (by Exxon) are taken from Department of Energy, *Energy Projection to the Year 2000*, July 1981 (DOE/PE-0029), p. 5-4. The high estimate is from Sam H. Schurr et al., *Energy in America's Future* (Baltimore: Johns Hopkins University Press, 1979), pp. 228-29.

5. "U.S. Activity Is Unprecedented," *World Oil*, August 15, 1981, pp. 62-72; and U.S. Department of Energy, *Monthly Energy Review*, December 1982, p. 56.

6. "Six New Fields Make List of U.S. Oil Giants," *Oil and Gas Journal*, January 26, 1981, p. 153.

7. The information related to EOR is taken from Department of Energy, *Energy Projections to the Year 2000*, section 5, pp. 10-11.

8. This wide range is in part explained by the great uncertainty related to future world oil prices and the costs of development and commercialization of the EOR techniques.

9. The effects of price controls on crude oil production are described and analyzed in a number of recent studies on which this section draws in part; see, for example, Kenneth J. Arrow and Joseph P. Kalt, *Petroleum Price Regulation* (Washington, D.C.: American Enterprise Institute Studies in Energy Policy, 1979) and Paul Bennett, Harold Cole, and Steven Dym, "Oil Price Decontrol and Beyond," *Federal Reserve Bank of New York Quarterly Review*, Winter 1980-81, vol. 5, no. 4.

10. Yvonne Levy, "Crude Oil Price Controls and the

Windfall Profit Tax: Deterrents to Production?" *Federal Reserve Bank of San Francisco Economic Review*, Spring 1981.

11. Ibid., pp. 17-19.

12. For an excellent description of President Carter's energy initiatives including the windfall profit tax see Joseph A. Yager, "The Energy Battles of 1979," in Crawford D. Goodwin (ed.), *Energy Policy in Perspective* (Washington, D.C.: Brookings Institution, 1981), pp. 613-29.

13. Ibid., p. 628.

14. For additional details consult Stephen L. McDonald, "The Incidence and Effects of the Crude Oil Windfall Profit Tax," *Natural Resources Journal*, April 1981, vol. 21, no. 2, pp. 331-39.

15. For a general discussion of the effect of excise taxes consult Micha Gisser, *Intermediate Price Theory* (New York: McGraw-Hill Company, 1981), pp. 317-23.

16. See Philip K. Verleger, Jr., "OPEC's Threat to Mr. Reagan's Balanced Budget," *Wall Street Journal*, October 15, 1981, p. 28.

17. This is based on an International Energy Agency's estimated drop in the weighted average price of OPEC crude oil from $35.45 in January 1981 to $33.45 per barrel in October 1981. Taken from Y. M. Ibrahim, "OPEC Oil Minister's Signal Effort to End Group's Bitter Disagreement over Prices," *Wall Street Journal*, October 15, 1981, p. 4.

18. See, Levy, "Crude Oil Price Controls," pp. 19-23.

19. For an excellent historical narrative regarding the oil quota under Eisenhower consult William J. Barber, "The Eisenhower Energy Policy: Reluctant Intervention," in C. D. Goodwin (ed.), *Energy Policy in Perspective* (Washington, D.C.: Brookings Institute, 1981), pp. 229-61.

20. Douglas Bohi and Milton Russell, *Limiting Oil Imports: An Economic History and Analysis* (Baltimore: Johns Hopkins University Press, 1978). Also see James W. McKie, "Oil Imports: Is Any Policy Possible?" *Natural Resources Journal*, VIII, 4 (October 1978):731-45; and more recently Walter J. Levy, "Oil: An Agenda for the 1980s," *Foreign Affairs*, LIX, 5 (Summer 1981):1079-1101; and also David Stockman, "Needed: A Dual Resurrection," *Journal of Energy and Development* V, 2 (Spring 1930):171-81.

21. The Ford Foundation *Energy: The Next Twenty Years* (Cambridge, Mass.: Ballinger Publishing Company, 1979), p. 202.

22. American Petroleum Institute, *Basic Petroleum Data Book*, vol. 1, no. 3, section IX, table 1.

23. An alarming note was sounded by reports that

Saudi Arabia itself is planning a *1.5* billion barrels oil storage facility near the Red Sea port of Yanbu. The project is intended to help protect the Saudis from possible disruptions in the flow of oil from the country's huge Persian Gulf oil production facilities. This report comes on the heels of the completion of a 2 MMb/d pipeline from the Persian Gulf to Yanbu. In addition, the Saudis have given their consent for Iraq to build its own pipeline to the Red Sea parallel to the one built by Saudi Arabia. Incidentally, the planned Saudi storage facility will be twice the size of the one that the United States is creating. Y. M. Ibrahim, "Saudi Arabia to Store Oil near Red Sea to Avoid Vulnerable Persian Gulf Area," *Wall Street Journal*, October 13, 1981, p. 2.

24. In that category I included *all* oil imports from the Middle East plus imports from Algeria, Angola, Libya, and Zaire.

25. R. Stobaugh, "After the Peak: The Threat of Imported Oil," R. Stobaugh and D. Yergin (eds.), *Energy Future* (New York: Random House, 1979), p. 47.

26. The then Congressman David Stockman suggested that a 2 billion barrel stockpile for all OECD members would be appropriate. Stockman, "Needed: A Dual Resurrection?" p. 180.

27. U.S. Department of Energy, *Securing America's Energy Future: The National Energy Policy Plan*, July 1981, p. 19.

28. Thomas C. Lowinger, "U.S. Energy Policy: A Critieal Assessment," *MSU Business Topics*, Winter 1980, pp. 17-20.

29. If a duty of $2/barrel were levied on imports of crude oil, such a tax given the *current* levels of imports of about 4 MMb/d, would generate about $3 billion in added revenue. Based on a world price of $33 per barrel, this would enable the government to purchase an additional 90 million barrels of oil for the SPR. Of course imports are likely to fall some as a result of the higher price.

30. M. A. Adelman, "Constraints on the World Oil Monopoly Price," *Resources and Energy*, vol. 1 (1978), pp. 2-4.

31. Douglas R. Bohi and W. David Montgomery, *Oil Prices, Energy Security, and Import Policy* (Baltimore: Johns Hopkins University Press, 1982), p. 132.

32. For further details consult: James L. Cochrane, "Carter Energy Policy and the Ninety-fifth Congress," in C. D. Goodwin (ed.), *Energy Policy in Perspective* (Washington, D.C.: Brookings Institute, 1981), pp. 556-77.

33. Stockman, "Needed: A Dual Resurrection?" pp. 177-78.

34. Lester C. Thurow, *The Zero-Sum Game Society* (New York: Basic Books, 1980), ch. 2.

35. This is the average price paid by refiners for domestic crude oil compared to their acquisition cost of imported oil. U.S. Department of Energy, *Monthly Energy Review*, April 1981, p.76.

36. The task force also estimated the oil import quotas cost U.S. consumers about $4.8 billion in 1969. U.S. Cabinet Task Force on Oil Import Control, *The Oil Import Question* (Washington, D.C.: Government Printing Office, 1970), pp. 259-63.

37. The factual information is culled from a number of sources including K. J. Arrow and J. Kalt, *Petroleum Price Regulation* (Washington, D.C.: American Enterprise Institute for Public Policy Research, 1979); P. Bennett, H. Cole and S. Dym, "Oil Price Decontrol and Beyond," *Federal Reserve Bank of New York Quarterly Review*, vol. 5, no. 4, Winter 1980-81, pp. 36-42.

38. For technical details of the estimates of the social cost of price controls and entitlements, see Arrow and Kalt, *Petroleum Price Regulation*, ch. 3, pp. 9-22.

39. It is important to note that this analysis assumes no action on the part of OPEC to reduce the supply of crude oil to counteract the effect of decontrol on world oil demand.

40. Consumption of petroleum products in the industrial countries remained unchanged in 1979 and declined by about 7.5 percent in 1980. It is likely that further decreases will take place in 1981. IMF, *World Economic Outlook* (Washington, D.C., June 1981), p. 97.

41. Under price controls, foreign and uncontrolled domestic oil constituted about half of the oil used by refiners. P. Bennet, H. Cole, and S. Dym, "Oil Price Decontrol and Beyond," *Federal Reserve Bank of New York, Quarterly Review*, V, 4 (Winter 1980-81):38.

42. The comparison here is between average crude oil production in 1978 (a "normal" year) and the average of the IVQ1980 and IQ of 1981.

43. This information is available from: IMF, *World Economic Outlook*, pp. 91-96.

44. The effective exchange rate of the U.S. dollar vis-a-vis the currencies of 15 other major countries has appreciated by 15 percent between July 1980 and August 1981. Morgan Guaranty Trust, *World Financial Markets*, September 1981, p. 14.

45.   Youssef M. Ibrahim, *Wall Street Journal*, July 16, 1981.

46.   Petroleum Intelligence Weekly estimate, reported by Y. M. Ibrahim, in *Wall Street Journal*, July 16, 1981.

47.   For further details consult M. Radetzki, "Falling Oil Prices in the 80s," *Scandinaviska Enskilda Banken Quarterly Review*, nos. 1-2, 1981, pp. 20-28.

48.   William Tucker, "The Energy Crisis Is Over!" *Harper's*, November 1981, pp. 33-34.

Natural Gas
— 3 —
The Future Belongs to the Efficient?

In an introduction to a recent study of natural gas prospects to the year 2000, the International Energy Agency stated: "Natural gas has the potential to play an *increasingly* important role in the energy systems of industrialized countries over the next two decades, as a clean-burning fuel that can substitute in many uses for limited supplies of oil."[1] (Emphasis added.)

The modern era of natural gas utilization in the United States started at the beginning of the nineteenth century when in 1821 a 27-foot-deep well was drilled in Fredonia, New York. The first industrial application commenced in 1841 in the Kanawha Valley of West Virginia.

The use of natural gas as an important fuel was enhanced by large number of discoveries of gas either in association with oil or separately, and also when it became practical to transport it through pipelines from producing areas to the location where it was consumed. Perhaps the most important factor behind the rapid rise of NG was that its use offered several technical and economic advantages to industry.

Many have sung the praises of this premium fuel, which has been called the "prince of hydrocarbons," to wit: "unlike coal, natural gas burns clean, without soot and sulphur emissions; nor does its extraction and transportation cause the environmental damage associated with the black solid. Finally, unlike nuclear power, natural gas poses no waste disposal problem."[2] Indeed the virtues of

NG have not been overstated, and it is in fact a clean and environmentally benign source of energy. Gas-drilling activities do not have a major detrimental impact on the environment, and the release of gas in the event of a blow-out creates only minor pollution problems that can be disregarded if it takes place in relatively unpopulated areas. The environmental impact of pipelines that carry the gas to consumers is generally also minimal, and data available on pollutant emissions and on land use show that the use of NG is more advantageous than that of other fossil fuels. The advantages of using NG compared to other fuels from the point of view of reducing pollutant emissions from fuel combustion are illustrated in Table 3-1.

TABLE 3-1. Emissions from Different Fuels in Domestic Appliances
(grams/Gcal)

Pollutant	Coal 7,000 kcal/kg sulphur content 1%	gasoil sulphur content 0.8%	natural gas 7,580 kcal/m
Aldehyde (HCHO)	0.36	28	--
Carbon monoxide	3,570	28	0.7
Hydrocarbons	715	42	--
Nitrogen dioxide (NO)	572	1,000	209
Sulphur dioxide	2,710	1,750	0.7
Sulphur trioxide	--	22	--
Solid pollutants (dust)	600	167	34

*net caloric value
Source: International Energy Agency, Organization for Economic Cooperation and Development, Natural Gas Prospects to 2000 (Paris: OECD, 1982), p. 162.

Such risks that do exist--for example, the risk of explosion--can be minimized through careful design, planning, and monitoring activities. Furthermore, NG can be used in all energy sectors; it has a wide range of applications in industry, especially in plastics, chemicals, and fertilizers. Its use in the commercial and the household sectors for the purposes of heating and cooking is expanding in many countries.

Thus, it is not surprising that in the United States, NG provides slightly less than half of all the energy used by households, and it is a leading source of energy in industry and commerce. (See Table 3-2.)

TABLE 3-2. U.S. Consumption of Natural Gas by End-Use Sector, Selected Years   (percentage of total)

	Residential	Commercial[a]	Industrial	Electric Utilities	Transportation[b]
1951	21.6	6.8	57.4	11.2	2.8
1961	26.0	8.6	47.7	14.7	3.0
1971	22.8	11.5	44.0	18.2	3.4
1981	23.7	13.5	40.8	18.7	3.2

[a]Includes deliveries to municipalities and public authorities for institutional heating purposes.

[b]Pipeline fuel.

Source: U.S. Department of Energy, Energy Information Administration 1981 Annual Report to Congress, vol. 2, Energy Statistics, May 1982, p. 107.

In fact, of the total of 71 quads of energy consumed in 1982, NG accounted for 18.3 quads, or about 26 percent of the total, as compared to 30 percent in 1973. The total consumption of NG by the residential and commercial sectors was 7.5 quads, which amounted to about 49 percent of net energy consumed by those two sectors in 1980.[3]

A more detailed perspective on the consumption of NG in OECD countries is provided in Table 3-3. The use of NG is more pervasive in North America as compared to Europe, accounting for more than one fourth of total primary energy (TPE) used since 1960. Natural gas, though, could expand its share in future energy balances since it is technically substitutable for other energy sources. More immediately as a substitute for oil, NG could replace almost all the fuel oil used in industry and power generation, and it could be used instead of gasoil in industry and the residential/commercial sector.

As will be explained in greater detail further on in this chapter, the limits on the "technical" demand for NG are formed by its price relative to alternative fuels, and by government policies. For example, in some countries, the

TABLE 3-3. Natural Gas Use in OECD Countries, 1960-80.

Region	Gas Use				Avg. Annual % Change		
	1960	1973	1979	1980	1973/60	1980/73	1980/79
OECD Countries							
Total gas use (Mtoe)[a]	314.4	697.2	741.5	737.0	6.3	0.8	(0.6)
Share of TPE (%)[b]	16.9	19.5	19.3	19.7	--[c]	--	--
Sectoral distribution (Mtoe)							
Electricity	50.0	115.9	127.2	129.8	6.7	1.6	2.0
Industry	118.5	252.7	234.8	232.5	6.0	(1.2)	(1.0)
Residential/commercial	115.1	241.3	295.9	293.5	5.9	2.8	(1.0)
Share of sectoral energy use[d]							
Electricity	15.9	17.5	10.3	10.3	--	--	--
Industry	23.2	25.5	23.3	22.2	--	--	--
Residential/commercial[e]	25.1	27.9	32.2	33.7	--	--	--
North America							
Total gas use (Mtoe)	303.3	565.5	532.4	526.2	4.9	(1.0)	(1.2)
Share of TPE (%)	27.3	28.5	25.4	25.8	--	--	--
Sectoral Distribution (Mtoe)							
Electricity	48.0	89.9	84.5	88.7	4.9	(0.2)	5.0
Industry	110.4	194.4	158.5	157.8	4.4	(2.9)	(0.4)
Residential	104.1	190.0	208.3	201.7	4.7	0.9	(3.2)
Share of sectoral energy use[d]							
Electricity	29.3	23.3	12.5	12.7	--	--	--
Industry	37.6	41.8	29.8	31.3	--	--	--
Residential/commercial[e]	38.1	40.2	42.6	43.7	--	--	--

[a] Million tons of oil equivalent

[b] Total primary energy

[c] Not applicable.

[d] The percentage shares shown for sectoral distribution refer to the percentage of total energy use in the sector accounted for by natural gas. For electricity, this is measured on a fuel input basis.

[e] Including agriculture.

Source: International Energy Agency, Organization for Economic Cooperation and Development, Natural Gas Prospects to 2000 (Paris: OECD, 1982), pp. 44-45.

overall effect of government pricing and taxation is to
encourage the use of NG through price controls and/or
higher taxes on competing fuels.

In the near term, NG use in electricity generation will
continue to decline as nuclear power and coal are likely to
be used more widely instead of gas. On the other hand in
the industrial and residential sectors, NG will continue to
provide an increasing share of total energy consumption if
competitively priced supplies are available.

AVAILABILITY OF NG RESOURCES[4]

This section presents a brief overview of the availability of
NG resources worldwide and especially in the United States.

Based on the information contained in Table 3-4, at
current production rates, the world's NG reserves could
last at least another 46 years. However, other estimates
suggest that additional conventional gas reserves, perhaps
four times as large as current known reserves, remain to
be discovered.

It is significant though that the OECD area--which is
currently the major consuming area--contains less than one
fourth of the remaining recoverable NG reserves in the
world. North America contains 11 percent of the world's
proven reserves, of which the United States alone has only
8 percent, as compared to 28 percent in 1967. The resource base nowadays is concentrated in the developing
countries, OPEC being especially prominent, with one third
of the world total. Equally important is the role of the
centrally planned economies (the socialist countries), where
41 percent of the global reserves can presently be found.

The same basic pattern emerges when one examines
future reserve additions, with the largest additions expected to come from the Middle East, Africa and the Soviet
Union.[5]

Table 3-5 shows OECD estimates of NG production
potential for the year 2000 and beyond; these figures are
not forecasts but rather represent production capacity that
is *technically* achievable under favorable economic conditions. An interesting point to note with respect to Table
3-5 is that even under high production levels the life of
recoverable NG reserves is a long one indeed. For example, given the production levels indicated in Table 3-5,
there still would be nearly 50 years of gas available *beyond*
the year 2020. The inescapable conclusion is that the
worldwide natural gas resource base can support a considerable expansion of world output and trade in NG--we are

TABLE 3-4. Natural Gas Reserves, Production and Production Ratios

	Reserves January 1, 1981					
	Proved[c] bcm	%	Additional[d] bcm	%	Total bcm	%
OECD total	13,472	17	49,275	26	62,747	24
North America	8,188	11	41,077	22	49,265	19
OECD Europe	4,246	5	5,223	3	9,469	4
OECD Pacific	1,038	1	2,975	1	4,013	1
Developing countries	32,353	42	76,308	40	108,661	41
Geographical distribution						
Middle East	18,396	24	29,332	16	47,728	18
Africa	5,906	8	26,253	14	32,159	12
Latin America	4,830	6	10,234	5	15,064	6
Far East/ Pacific	3,221	4	7,289	4	10,510	4
Antarctic	--[f]	--	3,200	2	3,200	1
Political distribution						
OPEC	25,585	33	28,531	15	54,116	20
Non-OPEC	6,768	9	47,777	25	54,545	21
Centrally planned economies	31,752	41	63,011	33	94,763	35
Total world	77,577	100	188,594	100	266,171	100

[a] Billion cubic meters.

[b] Gross production.

[c] CEDIGAZ, "Quelques Elements Statistiques Concernant la Situation du Gaz Naturel dans le Monde en 1980," June 1981; and IEA Secretariat.

[d] World Energy Conference 1980, based on 80 percent recovery of reserves in place. Reserve estimates as of January 1, 1979 were adjusted by the secretariat to approximate additional reserves as of January 1, 1981.

Production 1980 (bcm)[a]			Reserve/Prod. Ratio[b]	
Gross [e]	Flared or lost	Net	of proved	of total
849.7	29.9	819.8	16	74
634.6	18.8	615.8	13	78
202.0	10.4	191.6	21	47
13.1	0.7	12.4	79	306
338.4	158.3	180.1	96	321
121.9	74.5	47.4	151	392
71.7	51.7	20.0	82	449
86.0	20.0	65.5	56	175
58.8	11.6	47.2	55	179
--	--	--	--	--
223.0	125.3	97.7	115	243
115.4	32.9	82.5	59	473
507.6	13.0	494.6	63	187
1,695.7	201.2	1,495.5	46	157

[e] Excluding reinjected gas.

[f] Not available.

Note: Some subtotals do not add due to rounding.

Source: International Energy Agency, OECD, Natural Gas Prospects to 2000, Paris, 1982, p. 66.

TABLE 3-5. Estimated Natural Gas Production Capability
(billion cubic meters)

	1980[a]	2000[b]	2020[c]
North America	635	818	278
	(37)	(28)	(9)
OECD Europe	202	187	57
	(12)	(6)	(2)
OECD Pacific	13	57	120
	(1)	(2)	(4)
OECD Total	850	1062	455
	(50)	(36)	(14)
OPEC	223	600	1647
	(13)	(20)	(51)
Non OPEC-LDCs	115	200	250
	(7)	(7)	(8)
Total free world	1188	1862	2352
	(70)	(63)	(72)
Centrally planned	508	1100	900
economies	(30)	(37)	(28)
Total world	1696	2962	3252
	(100)	(100)	(100)

[a]CEDIGAZ, "Quelques Elements Statisques Concernant la Situation du Gaz Naturel dans le Monde en 1980," June 1981; and IEC Secretariat. Actual production minus quantities reinjected. Numbers in parentheses indicate percent share of world production.

[b]IEA Secretariat estimate.

[c]From the 1977 World Energy Conference. These numbers were not altered for WEC 1980. Converted from exajoules at 1 EJ=26.0 bcm.

Source: International Energy Agency, OECD, Natural Gas Prospects to 2000 (Paris: OECD, 1982), p. 72.

not running out of the "prince of hydrocarbons" any time soon.

But what are the prospects of future production of NG in the United States based on actual and prospective reserves? The natural gas industry in the United States has been under the yoke of regulation for a long time, and this has resulted in "decreased system flexibility, delayed projects, and restrained price increases, thereby deterring both conservation and exploration."[6] The effects of regulation on the natural gas industry will be examined in detail in following sections of this chapter. Table 3-6 presents estimates of U.S. NG reserves ranging from a low estimate

Natural Gas / 49

TABLE 3-6. Potential Conventional United States Gas Reserves,
January 1, 1980

(trillion cubic feet, including Alaska)

	Year of Est.	Proved Reserves	Additional Reserves*	Total Remaining Reserves
United States Geological Survey	1981	200	621-885	861-1085
Rand	1981	200	196	396
Exxon	1976	200	342	542
Shell	1979	200	326	526
Potential Gas Committee	1981	200	913	1113

*Estimates of inferred and undiscovered gas resources.

Source: U.S. Department of Energy, Energy Projections to the Year 2000, July 1981, p. 6-4.

by the Rand Corporation to a highly optimistic forecast by the Potential Gas Committee.

Twenty years of steady increases in proven gas reserves ended in 1967; since that year annual production has exceeded annual reserve additions, the only exception being 1970, when the Prudhoe Bay reserves were added to the U.S. total. By 1973 the reserve situation in the lower 48 states reached the point wherein production levels actually began to decline. Although, in 1979, a small increase in production was registered as a direct result of a much intensified drilling effort. Yet, despite the increased drilling activity, reserve additions have not reached the levels attained in the early 1960s (See Figures 3.1 and 3.2.).

The American Gas Association maintains that the bulk of exploratory drilling took place in areas that have already been extensively explored and as a result hold little promise for new "giant" discoveries. If exploration activity is redirected to deeper strata and to the Outer Continental Shelf, the production decline could be slowed down in time.

Another area of obvious promise is Alaska, where proven reserves amount to 35 TCF (trillion cubic feet) with

FIGURE 3-1. Proved Reserves of Liquid and Gaseous Hydrocarbons, Year-end

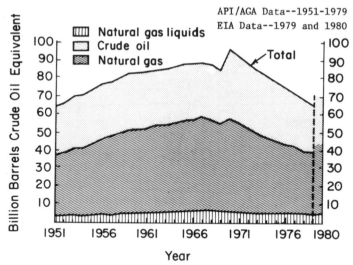

Source: U.S. Department of Energy, *1981 Annual Report to Congress*, vol. II, May, 1982, p. 42.

additional, as yet undiscovered, reserves put at 100 TCF.[7] There is a widespread belief within the industry that Alaska warrants further exploration and development. A caveat is in order, because it has become apparent to several observers of the industry that the exploration, development, and transportation of Alaskan gas all face major obstacles today. Some of these obstacles are due to the harsh physical environment of Alaska, others are man-made, and yet others are economic in nature.

Natural gas production from conventional sources in the United States (including Alaska) is expected to range from 11.2 to 17.8 TCF in the year 2000, according to projections prepared by the Department of Energy. The mid-range projection is 14.4 TCF. When unconventional and synthetic gas is added to the total, the projections range from 15.8 to 22.4 TCF. A more optimistic projection of 28 TCF in 2000 is provided by the American Gas Association, as compared to the mid-range projection of about 18 TCF, by the Department of Energy.[8] For the sake of comparison we note that in 1981 U.S. natural gas production amounted to 19.4 TCF. Thus even when unconventional sources of gas are included, NG production in the United States in the year 2000 is expected to be below the level of production in 1980 and 1981.

FIGURE 3-2.   Exploratory Wells Drilled for Oil and Gas

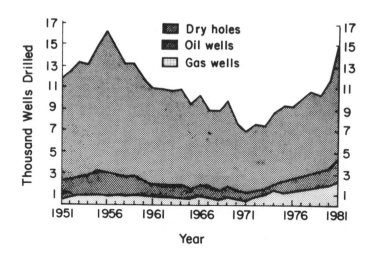

Source: U.S.   Department   of   Energy,   *1981   Annual Report to Congress*, vol. II, May 1982, p. 36.

While over the longer haul NG production depends on the amount of resources trapped underground, other factors that will influence future supplies are prices, drilling activity, the future of price controls, the extent of leasing activity, and the speed with which new areas are opened up for exploration and later on for development.

Conventional onshore and offshore production in the lower 48 states and in the Gulf of Mexico is expected to decline at a 3 percent per year rate between now and the year 2000. On the other hand, the coastal areas in the Atlantic and the Pacific remain essentially unexplored. In those areas, new acreage is expected to be offered for lease in the coming years and drilling activity is expected to pick up. As we have noted Alaska's contribution to our nation's NG supplies depends crucially on the completion of the Alaskan Natural Gas Pipeline in the mid-1980s.

Finally, for the OECD countries as a whole, when one compares the projected demand for NG with the likely indigenous production, it becomes apparent that the potential for increased imports of NG is indeed large. By 1990 imported NG could amount to as much as one fourth of the total consumption of OECD countries, as compared to only six percent in 1980. In the United States, imports of NG from Canada and Mexico could amount to 10 percent of total supply by 1990 as compared to less than 5 percent in 1980.

The actual level of NG imports ten to twenty years from now is unknown, of course, but it will depend on the price of imported gas relative to the prices of alternative energy supplies; on the return to gas exports available to non-OECD suppliers as compared to the return for the domestic use of gas; and on OECD countries' views as to the security of supply of imported NG. This last issued I would like to address briefly.

As was pointed out earlier in this chapter, certain members of OPEC (primarily Algeria, Iran, Indonesia, and Nigeria) and the Soviet Union will tend to dominate world trade in NG in the late 1980s and beyond.

OPEC members have in the past imposed sudden huge oil price increases on oil importers and some have even embargoed crude oil exports based on political consideration. The Soviet Union has in the past curtailed gas supplies for technical reasons and has suspended shipments for apparent political reasons. Thus there is a definite cause for concern as regards security of supply from both sources.

It is true though, that the United States with a substantial production base and an extensive pipeline system is less prone to sudden supply interruptions than is Western Europe, where there is less flexibility built into the NG supply system, and where the ratio of imports to total domestic consumption is already higher than in the United States.

It seems paradoxical to say the least, that Western Europe and Japan, concerned as they are with their excessive dependence on *imported oil* should actively pursue certain non-OECD suppliers of NG, whose dependability as a steady supplier of gas is questionable. This issue, of course, has come to a head as regards the so-called Yamburg pipeline project that would link the gas fields of Western Siberia (USSR) with Western European markets. This project when completed could more than double Soviet gas deliveries to Europe by the 1990s. The argument has been advanced recently that the Soviet Union has good reasons to seek to become a dependable supplier of NG to Western Europe.[9] The argument presented by Greer and Russell is that the Soviet Union supposedly is attempting to diversify its domestic energy base, and furthermore that the Soviets are always in need of large amounts of Western currencies. Be that as it may, this still does not guarantee that the Soviet Union at some future date will not interrupt the flow of NG to Western Europe, thereby putting the

Western Alliance under great political pressure. This kind of political leverage on the West would be just too tempting for the Soviets to resist, should the opportunity arise.

As the British weekly *The Economist* has recently put it in somewhat more veiled terms: "It would have been better if most of Western Europe had not chosen to make itself dependent on Russia for a worrying amount of its future energy consumption, thereby providing Russia with a large annual hard-currency income."[10]

Furthermore a number of disturbing questions have been raised concerning the economic aspects of this huge project. The contract signed with West Germany, the largest customer among the Western Europeans, entails a base price and a floor price for Soviet gas, with both prices specified in German marks. Given the exchange rate that prevailed at the time the contract was signed, the base and floor prices were roughly equal to $4.70 to $5.70 per million Btus (c.i.f. at the German border).[11] At a base price of $4.70 per million Btus Soviet gas is *apparently* competitive when considered on fuel-equivalent basis. But is it really? Probably not, when one adds the additional costs of extending the present European gas grid network to add a degree of security against supply disruptions. Given the risk inherent in the Soviet gas deal, it is incumbent upon the Western Europeans to enlarge their emergency storage facility and construct an extended gas grid system.

At this time the Groningen field in the Netherlands constitutes the backbone of Western Europe's strategic NG reserve; in the future the possibility of an expanded role for North Sea gas should also be considered. This point has been underscored by the recent discovery of a huge NG field in the North Sea of the Norwegian Coast. The so-called Troll field contains by far the largest NG deposits in Europe and possibly in the world outside of Western Siberia. The field covers about 300 square miles and up till now only ten exploratory wells have been drilled by the Royal Dutch Shell Group. The proven reserves based on these limited drillings are put at 17 TCFs, but the estimated total reserves are thought to be about four times as much. The Troll field undoubtedly will be difficult and costly to develop, because of its size and the geological characteristics of the reservoir.[12]

The Norwegians do not expect production drilling to start in earnest until 1985, although the Royal Dutch Shell Company and its partners will be ready with proposals for the commercial development of the field by mid-1983.

Production from the Troll field at the rate of about 875 billion cubic feet could commence toward the late 1980s and continue for forty years. Thus it appears that strictly from an energy supply standpoint the Soviet gas deal seems superfluous.

But then how is one to interpret the Western European willingness, nay eagerness, to proceed with the Siberian gas deal, a project that is not required from an energy standpoint and one that is highly suspect from a security point of view. I believe the most useful way of looking at this project is as an expensive European make-work project. Note the following comment by Pitt Treumann, a top official of the Amsterdam-Rotterdam Bank: "The whole point of the pipeline was to give work to European exporters, and the gas itself was less important."[13]

Or observe the action of the French government, which in early 1980 entered into an agreement with the Soviets that involved an open-ended line of credit given through December 1985 that could be used for *any* French exports to the Soviet Union, at a subsidized rate of interest. By the middle of 1981 with French interest rates at around 16 percent, the Soviets were able to persuade the French government to extend a 7.8 percent rate of interest to NG pipeline contracts as well. A Belgian government official estimates that with financing extended over about twelve years, direct and indirect French government subsidies could reach 50 percent of the contract's value.[14] Thus what is involved here is a very costly effort by the Europeans to save a few thousand jobs through exports to the Soviet Union paid for to a large extent by the governments of the Western European countries. Finally, having made the largely political decision to rely to a much greater extent on non-OECD sources of gas, the Western Europeans must, for the sake of their security, take the necessary steps to reduce their future vulnerability to possible large-scale disruptions in NG supplies from abroad.[15]

AN OVERVIEW OF U.S. NATURAL GAS MARKETS

In this section we provide a brief overview of the natural gas market in the United States as a convenient backdrop to the forthcoming discussion of the impact of government regulation on this industry.[16]

From 1950 to 1972, growth of gas consumption has generally paralleled the expansion of the capacity of the NG pipeline network. NG consumption peaked in 1972 at 22.1 TCF, declined between 1972 and 1975, and has stabilized in recent years at about 20 TCF per year. The use of NG since 1972 has remained relatively stable in the residential sector, although gas use *per customer* has declined. The total number of households using NG has increased, as a result of the construction of new houses that were heated by gas, and also due to conversion of existing furnaces to NG.

Industry consumes more NG than any other sector, although its share of total consumption has been declining since 1950. The decline in the consumption of gas by industry since 1973 was initially caused by decreasing industrial production and spot shortages of NG. However, in more recent years, energy conservation by industry has resulted in declining demand for gas on their part.

The growth of natural gas production parallels the pattern of consumption, although production has grown less rapidly. Marketed production of dry natural gas has grown from 7.5 TCF in 1951 to a peak of 22.7 TCF in 1973, but it has declined since then, with the 1981 figure being put at 20.4 TCF.[17]

Additions to reserves have been below production levels for almost every year since 1967, the only exception being 1970 when large amounts of gas were discovered in Prudhoe Bay, Alaska. Recently there has been an upturn in reserve additions. A record number of 15,700 wells were drilled in 1980, and drilling has continued to increase through 1982 with the number of wells drilled climbing to yet another high of 19,000. The increased drilling activity since 1973 is closely associated with the higher price of oil and gas received by producers in the 1973-81 period. (See Figure 3-3.)

Although presently more wells than ever are being drilled, the productivity of drilling has been declining since the mid-1960s. This is measured by a statistic known as the "finding rate"--gas reserves added per successful exploratory well. Early explorations tend to discover the biggest reservoirs of natural gas, but as exploration proceeds, successively smaller targets are usually found. A large number of smaller finds tends to lower the finding rate; however, one way to increase it is to explore successfully in heretofore unexplored areas. This is indeed taking place in offshore areas such as the Gulf of Mexico and in an area known as the Overthrust Belt in the Rocky Mountain region, as well as in previously developed areas where the drilling now is going much deeper than in the past.

The natural gas industry in the United States can be divided into three broad categories: the field market, the pipelines, and the distribution markets.[18] The field market

FIGURE 3-3.   Natural Gas Wellhead Prices

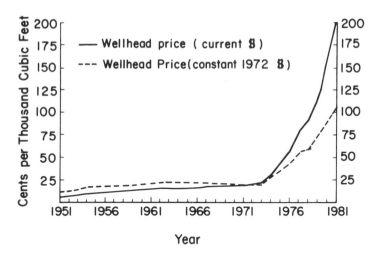

Source: U.S. Department of Energy, 1981 Annual Report to Congress, vol. II, *Energy Statistics*, May 1982, p. 114.

for NG revolves around contracts in which petroleum companies agree with a pipeline company to deliver gas during a prespecified period of time.   The field market is the market for gas at the wellhead.   Petroleum companies bring the gas to the surface through the wells they have drilled and deliver the "dry" gas into the buyers' pipelines.   Next enter the pipeline companies, which purchase the gas from the "field" companies, transport it to market, and sell it generally through a distribution network for resale to the ultimate users.   The companies involved in distribution of the gas are usually the local utilities that sell the gas to a variety of customers.

NG reserves of the producing companies are accumulated through a complex and lengthy process.   First, the producer typically undertakes a geophysical survey to establish the presence of underground hydrocarbon reservoirs.   Second, wells are drilled into the reservoir to determine the existence of oil, gas, or water.   These activities can be thought of as an investment in information gathering, and they are, of course, subject to a great deal of uncertainty.   Undoubtedly as the expected rate of return on such activities rises, so does the intensity of the exploratory effort. Profitability depends on future (expected) prices and costs, and these are known only with uncertainty. Typically, though, higher expected prices or lower costs should lead in time to expanded exploratory effort in general, and additional drilling of exploratory (wildcat) wells in particular. Technical progress may to some extent keep down the cost of finding the ever diminishing deposits of hydrocarbons as the exploration effort proceeds.

After deposits of NG are discovered the producers "dedicate" or commit them in long-term contracts to the pipeline companies. Gas producers attempt, as best as they can, to estimate the size of newly discovered deposits and provide sufficient documentation to support contractual commitment to pipeline companies for a period of time that may be as long as 25 years. Since reserves are not known with certainty, these contracts are, in effect, *promises* to deliver an expected volume of NG on a specified date in the future.

The gas pipeline companies in turn provide NG under long-term contracts to their customers--retail public utilities and industrial buyers. Wholesale prices of gas depend on prices at the wellhead and on transportation charges for delivering the gas from the field to the eventual consumers. The pipelines can offer their customers immediate deliveries of NG as it is being burned, and at a price that includes a markup over the wellhead prices. Markups in the past were determined based on historical average costs of transmission and by the transportation profit margin allowed by Federal Power Commission (now the Federal Energy Regulatory Commission).

Average wellhead price change only slowly as prices on new field contracts increase, because new contracts constitute only a small percent of all gas under contract in any given year. Since typically there exists a lag between changes in wellhead prices and changes in wholesale prices, this attenuates the impact of large increases in new contract prices on the users of NG.

Normally, the field and wholesale markets operate to provide the pipelines with sufficient gas so that these companies will be able to meet the demand of their residential, industrial, and commercial customers. Price increases would act to guarantee that no shortages of NG should arise. However, when prices are set by a regulatory agency such as the FPC or its successor the FERC, there is no presumption that the price arrived at will be a market clearing one. The economic impact of natural gas regulation is the subject of the next section.

THE PERFORMANCE OF THE NATURAL GAS INDUSTRY UNDER REGULATION

Brief Historical Sketch of NG Regulation[19]

The passage of the Natural Gas Act of 1938 gave the Federal Power Commission (FPC) the authority to regulate interstate pipeline rates and the terms and conditions associated with NG sales. The essential responsibility of the FPC was to set interstate rates and to issue certificates of public convenience and necessity.

Although the act specifically exempted the production and gathering of NG from federal regulation, the U.S. Supreme Court in its 1954 *Phillips Petroleum* v. *Wisconsin* decision, specifically required that the FPC regulate wellhead gas prices for gas delivered into *interstate* pipelines. The commission initially attempted to respond to this ruling by applying to NG producers the same standards and practices that were associated with public utilities--that is, setting their rates based on historic costs plus an allowed rate of return.

This regulatory attempt by the FPC turned out to be an unmanageable task, due to the very large number of producers to be regulated on the basis of their historic costs, and it was further complicated by the problem of allocating costs in cases where gas was produced in association with oil. Given the time-consuming requirements of this process, by 1960 only 10 cases have been completed, while more than 2,900 applications for rate reviews were pending before the commission at that time.

Thus, in the 1960s the FPC turned to a simpler regulatory method: First, it set maximum prices based on regional average historical costs, and then it adopted a national price structure for new reserves committed to interstate NG pipelines. This procedure served the FPC's apparent aim of preserving the price structure of the late 1950s, and in fact it resulted during the 1960s in a constant price level on new contracts for gas going into interstate pipelines. The FPC was able to hold down gas prices while prices of other fuels went up by as much as 10 to 25 percent during the same period.[20]

The FPC's policies were modified in 1971 in a series of decisions that allowed for substantial increases in the field prices of natural gas. In fact, the end result of this policy switch has been a significant rise in new contract prices for gas in the early 1970s.

In addition to the regulated interstate market there also existed an intrastate market that was not subject to FPC regulation. During the 1970s, prices in intrastate markets rose relative to regulated prices. Furthermore, production for the unregulated market became attractive for yet another reason: Once reserves were "dedicated" to the interstate market, they had to remain there from then on and be therefore subject of FPC's price regulation for an indefinite future. Consequently, commitments to the interstate gas market started to decline about 1966-67.

By 1968, signs of an impending NG shortage in the interstate market started to appear. Reserves committed to interstate markets over the next ten years declined steadily, while the level of intrastate and uncommitted reserves remained roughly constant.[21] By the winter of 1972, actual shortages started to materialize in the interstate market, wherein the demand for gas exceeded the supply of gas made available to the pipeline companies.

These shortages were caused by both institutional and political factors.[22] The technical circumstances of NG production result in long lags between new discoveries of gas reserves, and the production of that gas for the ultimate user. FPC regulation, by preventing price increases over most of the decade of the 1960s, created the essential preconditions for the emergence of NG shortages in the interstate market in the 1970s. At the time that the rate of reserve additions was declining (see Figure 3-4), gas pipelines were faced with increased demand on the part of consumers of NG. To meet the expanded demand, the companies were drawing down their inventories of old, already committed reserves. The alternative would have been for the pipeline companies to deny new customers access to reserves.

According to MacAvoy and Pindyck, price controls imposed by the FPC together with the long lags that exist between price increases and expanded production had a two-pronged effect on the NG market. First, the frozen prices led to a reduction in the amount of new reserves added in the second half of the 1960s. Second, additional demand was met by coaxing more production out of the "old" stock of reserves.[23] In turn consumption was encouraged by the relatively low wholesale prices that resulted from the frozen field prices.

Finally, can one say anything at all about who gained and who lost from this type of regulation? Obviously, those consumers not having to pay the higher "unregulated" prices for the amount of gas actually received have clearly gained. On the other hand, those customers that were unable to increase their gas use without taking a reduction in reserve backing were losers, and of course, producers

FIGURE 3-4. Reserve Additions of Natural Gas in the Lower 48 States, Excluding the Gulf of Mexico

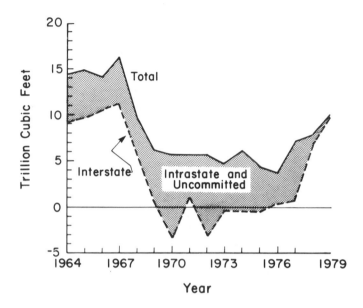

Source: U.S. Department of Energy, Energy Information Administration, *Intrastate and Interstate Supply Markets under the Natural Gas Policy Act* (Washington, D.C., October 1981), p. 3.

of NG were clear losers due to the maintenance of price ceilings below a market clearing level.

On the whole, consumers as a group gained from regulation of NG prices while producers were the clear losers from this effort by the FPC. Price stability has been achieved but at the expense of reduced additions to NG reserves *and* periodic shortages of gas supplies.

The Economic Effects of the
Natural Gas Policy Act of 1978[24]

At this time, natural gas is the only major energy resource subject to federal price controls. In this section the most important provisions of the Natural Gas Policy Act (NGPA) of 1978 will be discussed and their economic effects evaluated.

The NGPA altered the structure of NG regulation in a number of important ways. First, the Federal Energy Regulatory Commission as a successor to the FPC was granted jurisdiction over virtually *all* NG production in the United States--interstate and intrastate. Second, a complex schedule of ceiling prices at the wellhead was put in place by the act. The maximum prices producers could receive were tied to the physical characteristics of the well, to its proximity to other wells, to whether the gas was sold in the interstate market before November 8, 1978, to the date the well started producing gas, and to the type of deposits from which the well produced. Finally, the NGPA established a set of rules for allocating the costs of certain high-priced gases to industrial users served by interstate pipelines (these provisions are defined by Title II of the NGPA).

Clearly though, the heart of this legislation lies in its pricing provisions, which will occupy us in the remainder of this section. The NGPA sets price ceilings at the wellhead for a number of different categories of NG, in general permitting higher prices for gas from newer sources and lower prices for gas from older reservoirs. On November 1, 1979, high-cost NG--gas produced from wells deeper than 15,000 feet and drilled after February 19, 1977--was deregulated. Also, gas produced from geopressured brine, coal seams, and Devonian shale was deregulated at the same time.

Production from reserves can roughly be categorized as follows: old interstate, old intrastate, and new gas. As a rule, gas from older sources qualifies for a lower range of ceiling prices.

Most old reserves--those discovered prior to 1977--are produced under price ceilings governed by sections 103, 104, 105, and 106 of the act. Those price ceilings change through time depending on the section of the act, on contract provisions, and on the depth of the well. Section 104 of the act covers all NG produced from properties that were dedicated to interstate commerce on or before November 9, 1978. Prior to the enactment of the NGPA, this gas was priced in accordance with decisions taken by the FERC pursuant to the provisions of the Natural Gas Act. Under section 104 of the NGPA, the so-called just and reasonable gas prices are to be continued with monthly adjustments for inflation factored in; under the provisions of the act such gas is never to be decontrolled.

The NGPA allows for the gradual lifting and partial elimination of wellhead price ceilings. On January 1, 1985 price ceilings on gas from most new sources will be eliminated. However, the conditions for lifting the price ceilings differ as between interstate and intrastate gas. Almost all development and extension wells, begun after February 19, 1977, qualify for section 103 price ceilings. The price ceilings for wells under 5,000 feet will be removed on July 1, 1987. In order to qualify for section 102 status, an onshore well sunk after February 19, 1977, must be producing from a new reservoir, or be at least 2.5 miles from or 1,000 feet deeper than a marker well.[25] Offshore gas qualifies for section 102 if production is from new leases or from reservoirs discovered on or after July 27, 1976. And if all this is not crystal clear, have your lawyer or accountant, or better both, contact the FERC immediately!

It is rather difficult to estimate with any degree of precision how much gas will in fact be decontrolled, come 1985. A reasonable estimate is that between one half and two thirds of all domestic gas will be freed from the yoke of regulation at that time.[26]

Title II of the NGPA also contains pricing provisions for allocating a portion of the costs of certain high-priced NG directly to industrial users. In fact though, only large industrial boilers are affected by these incremental pricing provisions of the NGPA, and in practice the FERC has set the regional price of high-sulphur No. 6 fuel oil as the ceiling price to those users.

In sum, the *intent* of the NGPA was to decontrol prices in a manner "that would not disrupt the market." Under the phased decontrol provisions of the NGPA, some gas always remains under controls until it is exhausted.

However, the sad story of this legislation does not end here; in accompanying legislation several kinds of demand restrictions on NG use were also put into effect. For example, through the Power Plant and Industrial Fuel Use Act of 1978, the amount of gas (and oil) that electric utilities may burn in existing power plants is limited, and construction of new large industrial boilers and power plants fired by gas (or oil) is prohibited where coal is a feasible alternative. These restrictions and other provisions of this legislation that have not been spelled out here constitute a set of allocational rules that guarantee preferred access to residential consumers of gas, and provide for the worst access, or give the lowest priority, to large industrial users and to electric utilities. The large industrial users in particular are made to bear a disproportionate share of wellhead costs in the prices they pay and their supplies are most vulnerable to curtailment.

Having provided a capsule description of the major provisions of the NGPA, we now turn to a closer examination of their economic effects. As we have noted earlier, during the mid-1970s, many industrial users and electric utilities were affected by NG curtailments, and also by the restrictions on new residential hookups.[27]

During the 1970s the price of NG rose but not sufficiently to allocate available supplies among current and *potential* (future) customers. In the years following the passage of the NGPA in 1978 the shortage atmosphere that sometimes bordered on panic has largely disappeared and the restrictions on new residential hookups have been eliminated by 1980. In part this change in the market fortune of NG represents the delayed reaction of producers to the sharp increases in wellhead prices during the early and mid-1970s. The surge in drilling that resulted from the aforementioned price increases stabilized gas production and led to a reversal in the steady decline in NG reserve additions that had begun in the late 1960s.[28]

The impact of higher NG prices, together with the constraints on gas usage during the 1970s, had caused many potential users of NG to switch to alternative sources of energy. One result of the restrictions on residential gas hookups has been the increased use of electricity for home heating, and as was noted earlier, industry and electric utilities, were encouraged to look elsewhere to meet their energy needs.

The large oil price hikes engineered by OPEC during 1978-79 have once again caused NG to appear increasingly attractive to potential users. Between 1955 and 1972 the price of NG to residential customers averaged from 80 to 90 percent of the energy-equivalent price of home heating fuel. After falling sharply in 1974, this price ratio was restored to about 70 percent in 1978; however by mid-1981 it was once again only at the 50 percent level. In addition the ratio of gas-to-oil prices for use by industry and electric utilities fell to about 60 percent during the most recent time period.[29] Furthermore, there exists evidence to indicate that consumers are starting to respond to the price advantage of gas relative to oil. For example, the number of residences that converted to gas heat rose sharply in 1980 as did the total number of new gas customers.[30] Thus, if home construction recovers from its present slump, and overall economic activity picks up in 1983-84 and beyond, we could once again see excess demand (that is, shortages) materialize at the regulated price of NG.

In addition, one should not labor under the illusion that under partial decontrol consumers are, as if by some magic, protected from price increases. It has been correctly pointed out that the fact that pipelines use average cost rather than marginal cost pricing does not guarantee that prices will be held down for users of NG.[31] The point being that if due to average cost or "rolled-in" type pricing, the blending of controlled and uncontrolled gas resulted in prices to users *lower* than the market clearing price, then pipelines would bid for additional supplies to satisfy the existing excess demand and in the process the price of decontrolled gas would inevitably rise high enough so as to clear the *overall* gas market.

Earlier (than 1985) decontrol would inevitably lead to higher prices in the near term, but in turn it would keep shortages from materializing. Furthermore, starting the transition to a *fully* decontrolled NG market now when the NG is in a state of rough balance (although not equilibrium) means that sharper price increases down the line could possibly be avoided.

There are several other economic effects, some obvious and others somewhat more subtle that result from *partial* decontrol, but would not arise under *full* decontrol. The present partial decontrol scheme results in an inefficient allocation of resources, because it leads to higher prices of uncontrolled gas than would otherwise be the case. The higher prices of "free" gas attract additional resources (manpower and capital equipment) into the exploration, development, and production of uncontrolled NG. The end result is that production of some "older" gas is foregone and far too many resources are devoted to the exploitation of "new," higher cost sources of gas. It is also possible and even quite likely that current pricing arrangements under the NGPA result in less exploration and development activity than otherwise would be the case, because of expectations of higher prices in the future. The petroleum industry may also show a tendency to drill for the now decontrolled oil and the higher-cost (also decontrolled) gas and leave other gas exploration and development that is made less profitable under the NGPA for the future.

From 1971 through 1980 successful exploratory drilling for gas has grown at an annual rate of 18 percent while oil drilling has risen at an 11 percent annual clip during the same time. In the post-1978 period the growth rate of drilling for *gas* has fallen off to 12 percent per year, while drilling for *oil* has risen by 20 percent per annum.[32] During the same period well completions that qualify for new or high-cost gas treatment under Title I of NGPA has risen at an astounding rate. There has also been a noticeable upsurge in deep drilling, that is, wells drilled below 15,000 feet. Some onshore areas where deep drilling is taking place are: the Gulf Coast region and the Anandarko basin in Oklahoma and Texas.

A Department of Energy study has concluded that federal price ceilings on NG have indeed been *binding* and that prices paid for new gas cluster closely around the ceiling prices. The DOE has reluctantly concluded that "the effects of the NGPA violate the efficiency properties of a market without price ceilings."[33] I have noted previously that as a result of the perverse pricing incentive implicit in this act, gas projects with higher costs per MMBtu are being developed before lower-cost projects are undertaken, with the lamentable result of *not* obtaining any given amount of gas at the lowest cost possible. The nation's scarce resources--of workers, material, and capital--are being unnecessarily and foolishly wasted.

There are other undesirable and inefficient aspects of the federal regulatory mechanism that should be briefly mentioned. For one, gas sold to pipelines is priced on the basis of rolled-in pricing, wherein all acquisition costs of NG are averaged and recovered uniformly from the pipeline company's customers. Since the acquisition costs of older, less expensive gas supplies are averaged or "melded" into the cost of newer supplies, the price paid by the consumer is *less* than the cost of purchasing and delivering the incremental unit of gas. These circumstances are clearly portrayed in Figure 3-5, which depicts domestic NG supply in 1980. Most "old" gas (sections 104, 105, and 106 of the NGPA) is priced below the national average price, which in 1980 was $1.50 per MMBtu. Newer gas (under sections 102 and 103 of the NGPA) is currently priced substantially above the national average. The combined effect of binding price ceilings *and* average cost pricing results in wealth transfers from producers to consumers of lower-priced gas, and in intraindustry transfers of rents to high-cost gas producers.

Higher gas prices attendant on complete deregulation of the NG industry would inevitably result in the adoption of additional cost-effective energy-saving measures by homeowners and commercial establishments. The gas conserved would be available to meet the energy requirements of current oil users. As a case in point, industrial users of gas and electric utilities would be able to cut back on the use of oil in their operations.

FIGURE 3-5. Natural Gas Supply Market, 1980

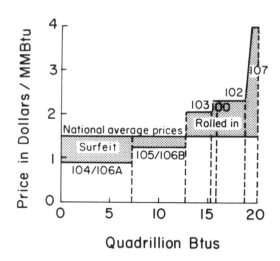

Quadrillion Btus

Source: U.S. Department of Energy, Energy Information Administration, *The Current State of the Natural Gas
Market* (Washington, D.C., December 1981), p. 46.

It is difficult to estimate precisely the additional amount
of energy conservation that would be undertaken under
complete NG deregulation. One study suggested that a 10
percent increase in real NG prices will induce conservation
of gas equivalent to about 2 percent of consumption in the
short run, rising perhaps to about 5 percent in the longer
run when further adjustments become feasible.[34]

In addition to encouraging more economic usage of NG
(that is, conservation), complete deregulation would bring
about greater production of gas in the United States and
further reduction in the imports of NG and oil.[35] A
Federal Reserve Bank of New York study estimated that if
full decontrol were to take place early in 1983, enough gas
conservation could be induced to reduce oil imports by
about half a million barrels per day by late 1984.[36] Be
that as it may, it is evident that complete and prompt
deregulation would encourage economically desirable conservation measures, and lead to further reduction in both gas
and oil imports. In addition, as we have noted, the existing regulatory maze holds down gas exploration and development due to perverse price expectations, thus retarding
the search for new domestic gas resources.

The superiority of full price deregulation as far as the
efficient allocation of resources goes is so obvious that on

the face of it there would seem to be little reason to continue the present course of incomplete and piecemeal
deregulation.[37] However, one must be very clear in
emphasizing that a policy of complete deregulation would
result in substantial income gains to some groups in our
society and losses to others.

On the whole, consumers that have been weaned artificially on cheap gas would lose, while producers of "old" gas
would reap substantial benefits from decontrol.[38] Natural
gas price decontrol would have an impact on other energy
products as well; for example, deregulation of NG is likely
eventually to lead to smaller demand for distillate and
residual fuel oil.

With complete and immediate wellhead price decontrol,
producers' revenues are likely to rise substantially. A
windfall profits tax on gas could of course be devised so as
to siphon some of these added revenues from producers and
into government coffers. The overall net impact on federal
revenues of a tax that is assumed to be similar to the one
currently in place on crude oil has been estimated. In one
case, in which gas prices are allowed to adjust upward
gradually, the net impact of decontrol would be to raise
federal revenues by $1 billion in FY 1983 and $7 billion in
FY 1984.

In another case, in which NG prices are allowed to rise
instantaneously to parity with residual oil prices, the effect
on federal revenues would be more dramatic: An additional
$12 billion in FY 1983 and FY 1984 would be garnered by
the United States Treasury.[39] This is not to say that one
would necessarily recommend that a windfall tax on producers' revenues be put into effect. What would seem least
objectionable is a *one-time genuine excess profit tax* on NG
producers in the event of complete deregulation of NG
prices. A genuine excess profit tax rather than a tax on
revenues would not discourage gas production and most
likely would have a negligible impact on future exploration
for new gas resources. On the other hand, it would not
raise a great deal of tax revenue for the United States
Treasury either.

SYNTHETIC GAS: A GLIMMER OF OUR ENERGY FUTURE?

Deposits of NG are found in coal mines, in geopressured
hot brine deposits along the Gulf Coast, and in tight
Devonian shale formations in the central United States.[40]
Of these unconventional gas sources the largest deposits
exist in the Gulf Coast geopressurized zone, where as much

as 100,000 TCF are thought to be trapped in hot brine at depths from 10,000 to more than 50,000 feet. However, only a small fraction of this total is thought to be recoverable because of geological, technical, and economic problems. On the other hand some gas *is* being produced from the extensive tight-formation Devonian shales in the central states. However, production from single wells is low because of the low permeability of the shale.

Degassing of coal seams has a well-known technological base, but it is rarely used today because of its short supply life. The National Petroleum Council has studied extensively the U.S. potential for the recovery of natural gas from the unconventional sources mentioned above. The council has volunteered the following caveat: "The resource estimates depend heavily on the extrapolation of limited data."[41] In other words, the reliability of such estimates are questionable in the extreme, or, as the council prefers to put it, the estimates are "optimistic." Potential production rates based on just such "optimistic" assessments are presented in Table 3-7. These projected production rates are based on certain assumed parameters, such as gas prices, *real* (after tax) rates of return, and certain projected advances in the state of technology. They also assume a high rate of exploration and development. While the estimates presented in Table 3-7 were based on a 10 percent after-tax *real* rate of return, the study wryly notes: "Because of the difficulty of properly assessing risk, anticipated rates of return higher than 10 percent may be required to attract investment at least initially."[42] On the whole, the geological and technical uncertainties attendant on such estimates of unconventional gas sources are so large that all information regarding reserve additions and/or production potential must be taken with the largest grain of salt, and really amounts to no more than an informed guess. A more recent study prepared by the Department of Energy projected incremental gas production from unconventional sources to exceed 1 TCF per year by 1990, and it could be in excess of 2 TCF per year by 2000. Even these more modest and thus more believable projections are no more than rough guesses.[43]

Of the four unconventional gas sources, western tight sands appear to be the most promising. In fact, tight sands at this time are already producing about 0.8 TCF per year; however, the high cost of producing gas from these relatively impermeable structures has discouraged further investment and drilling activity in those areas. Recent softening of world oil prices, together with high interest rates, has undercut private sector investment and raises

TABLE 3-7. Potential Production Rates for NG from Nonconventional Sources,
10 Percent Rate of Return for Gas Price of up to $9/MMBtu
(TCF/yr)

Source	1990	2000
Coal seams	0.6	2.4
Devonian shale	0.6	1.0
Geopressured brines	0.05	0.08
Tight gas reservoirs	2.5	10.5
Total	3.8	14.0

Source: National Petroleum Council, Unconventional Gas Sources,
December 1980, p. 5.

serious questions as to whether the higher end of the
projected range for unconventional gas supplies will be
reached.

Coal gasification, on the other hand, has been in
commercial operation now for more than 150 years. It took
place in various metropolitan areas in the United States
until after World War II. With the advent of cheap natural
gas transported in pipelines across the country, the domestic industry basically ceased to exist by the mid-1950s.

None of the gasification technologies currently available
for commercial use produce gas with a heating value
equivalent to that of NG. The gases produced by the
process of converting coal into gas are a mixture of carbon
monoxide and hydrogen with small amounts of methane.
These gases (called low-Btu gases), have heating values
that are one fifth to one third less than an equivalent
amount of NG, which is practically pure methane. The
low-Btu gas has a heating value too low to make it
worthwhile to transport, although it could be used to power
on-site industrial boilers and/or electric power generating
equipment.

On the other hand, high-Btu gas, equivalent in heating
value to NG, could serve as direct replacement for NG in
existing pipelines and distribution systems. A high-Btu
coal gasification technique that is currently ready for use
involves the methanation of medium-Btu gas. There is room

though for more efficient gasification processes than the currently available Lurgi process. Of the second-generation processes now under investigation a few have reached the pilot plant test stage. One of the objectives of current research is to produce raw gases of high methane content and thereby reduce the need for oxygen in the gasifier.

More advanced processes with prospectively greater thermal efficiencies are being studied based on feasibility studies and experimental techniques. Two techniques that are emphasized in the federal R&D programs are hydro-gasification, which produces high-Btu gas by direct reaction of coal with hydrogen, and catalytic gasification, which eliminates the shift reaction and methanation steps altogether.

The only synthetic gas project actually under way that will produce pipeline-quality synthetic gas is the Great Plains Coal Gasification project, sponsored by a consortium of five U.S. companies with gas pipeline subsidiaries. The plant being built in Mercer County, North Dakota, is designed to produce 125 million cubic feet per day (about 20,000 barrels per day oil equivalent) or roughly 45 billion cubic feet of synthetic gas annually; its expected date of completion is December 1984.[44]

The process used by Great Plains Gasification Associates brings together 14,000 tons/day of lignite coal with 2,850 tons/day of oxygen and 13,650 tons/day of steam, into a fixed-bed Lurgi gasifier. Part of the crude gas obtained in this manner then goes through a catalytic shift conversion process to increase the hydrogen-to-carbon-monoxide ratio. The remaining crude gas is cooled and purified and finally catalytically methanated, to result in a gas equivalent of NG. This high-Btu synthetic gas is then compressed and dried and moved through a pipeline to its destination.

The ash handling, coal handling, and cooling water systems are of the same order of magnitude as those used in large coal-fired electric power plants. The process uses very large amounts of both electricity (600,000 megawatt hours/year) and water (7,000 acre feet/year), and of course, its prime input is an abundantly available local resource--lignite coal.[45] The financing of this coal gasi-fication project depends crucially on a federal loan guaran-tee of up to $2.02 billion that was required in order to finance the debt portion of this project. The loan guaran-tee will provide $1.552 billion of the total financing required while the Great Plains consortium itself will chip in with $561 million in equity financing. Clearly, this is a major financial, engineering-construction, and energy production undertaking, one that probably would not have been undertaken without the government loan guarantee.[46]

The gas, when it becomes available, will be sold to the pipeline companies that sponsored this project under a complicated pricing formula that calls for a base price of $6.75 per MMBtu, *plus* quarterly price escalation starting in April 1981, based on the producer price index and the price of no. 2 oil. The price of this gas will be "rolled in" or melded as part of the pipeline companies' gas acquisition costs.

The economic viability of such plants can certainly be questioned. Of course there are no operating plants that produce high-Btu gas at this time; the one in North Dakota is only about 50 percent completed. However, a Resources for the Future study estimated that the cost of gas produced based on the Lurgi technology will be *at least* $3 per MMBtu. The study noted, "Costs at the lower end of those scales would be competitive with other sources, *but the achievement of such low costs would depend on apparently optimistic assumptions about technical success as well as on stable real price of coal.*"[47] (Emphasis added.)

Department of Energy projections of synthetic gas production for the year 1990 are very modest--0.2 TCF per year, which lies somewhere in the mid-range of projection provided by other sources.

The DOE also has kindly provided the key assumptions that lie behind those projections; in particular, one should note that the range of *minimum* "acceptable" prices goes from $40 to $75 (in 1981 dollars), per barrel of crude oil equivalent.[48]

Thus the near-term prospects of synthetic gas appears murky at best with serious questions being raised regarding the economic viability of such projects and of prospective demand for synthetic gas in the near term. Finally, mention should be made of the federal government's role in synthetic fuels developments. The Reagan administration's intent is that the synthetic fuels program rely more on private sector investments and initiative and less on government largess. The role of the Synthetic Fuels Corporation (SFC), according to the administration's energy plan, would be to provide financial assistance for the development of the synthetic fuels industry, on a modest scale, through minimal outlays of "up front" money. Thus, the growth of this industry will be largely determined by the pace of investment by the private sector, with the SFC definitely playing second fiddle. In the current economic climate of high interest rates and falling real prices of oil, this probably implies a snail-pace development for synthetic fuels in this decade, and probably a not too bright future in the years leading up to the twenty-first century.

A FEW CONCLUDING COMMENTS

In this chapter the NG industry's current economic prospects under the NGPA have been closely scrutinized and the appropriate conclusions based on recent experience were drawn. Besides the problems attendant on the regulation of the industry under federal legislation, there are other more fundamental issues that confront the industry. Current and past regulation of the NG industry has resulted in a cost of gas to the user that is an average of the historical prices of past contracts from which that gas was obtained. The result is that the price that the customer pays for gas is often much less than the incremental cost to the utility of obtaining or generating new gas (see for example the pricing arrangements associated with the Great Plains Coal Gasification Project). This in effect provides a subsidy to the users of NG, and such a subsidy discourages consumers from conserving the "prince of hydrocarbons" to the most economically desirable (optimal) degree. Furthermore, artificially cheap NG provides an incentive to use more NG in lieu of other alternative energy sources that could be supplied at a lower *real resource cost*. Energy sources that could be negatively affected by this are the so-called alternative energy resources, such as solar collectors, heat pumps, thermal storage, insulation, and others as well.

Another controversial issue in the current debate over the regulation of the NG industry concerns the impact of increases in NG prices on existing long-term contracts. In today's NG market, one finds pipeline companies that are leaving in the ground gas that costs $2 to $3 per thousand cubic feet, while paying three or four times as much for other sources of NG.

For example, the El Paso pipeline company is refusing to buy NG for $2 to $3 per thousand cubic feet from small producers in the San Juan Basin of New Mexico for delivery to users in Southern California. The same company is paying around $8 per thousand cubic feet for gas it purchases in the Anadarko Basin of Oklahoma. It is also paying its own producing subsidiary as much as $10.35 per thousand cubic feet for gas coming from the Anadarko Basin, which amounts to twice the price for an equivalent amount of oil.[49] The fact is that in spite of the partial decontrol that is taking place under the NGPA, gas prices could be significantly lower if the pipelines were to use the ample reserves of cheaper, so-called shut-in gas. In Ohio, many small producers of gas have been releasing into the air "cheap" gas they are unable to sell to the pipelines.

These absurdities arise from a combination of two factors; the first is the existence of long-term--so-called take-or-pay type contracts in the wellhead gas market--and the second is the drastic change both in oil prices and in federal gas price policy of the past decade.[50] Consequently, the pipeline companies are arguing that they are forced to cut all gas wells back as close as possible to the "take-or-pay" levels. Whatever the merits of their *argument*, the results of their *actions* are economically wasteful and lead to gas prices that are unnecessarily high.

An obvious solution to such problems would be a full and immediate decontrol of the NG industry combined with a gradual shift to *marginal cost pricing*--that is, charging NG customers the full cost of the gas that they use.[51] Undoubtedly, objections will be raised to such a "simple" approach to dealing with the NG problem. In particular the argument will be made that such a move would leave the utilities with excessive profits. But we have already argued previously that this can be remedied by levying a genuine excess profit tax or a franchise fee to be paid by the utility. Then if one so desires, these levies could be "recycled" to consumers of NG through lower taxes.

NOTES

1. International Energy Agency, Organization for Economic Cooperation and Development, *Natural Gas Prospects to 2000* (Paris: OECD, 1982), p. 11.

2. I. C. Bupp and Frank Schuller, "Natural Gas: How to Slice a Shrinking Pie," in Robert Stobaugh and Daniel Yergin (eds.), *Energy Future* (New York: Random House, 1979), p. 56.

3. A "quad" stands for quadrillion or 10^{15} Btus. U.S. Department of Energy, Energy Information Administration, *Monthly Energy Review,* November 1981, p. 6.

4. Much of the factual background material in this section has been obtained from: International Energy Agency, OECD, *Natural Gas Prospects to 2000* (Paris: OECD, 1981).

5. Natural gas reserves come in either associated or non-associated form. Non-associated gas is found in reservoirs where it could come in contact with water, but not oil. Associated gas is produced in conjunction with the

production of oil. Unless there is a market for it, associated gas must be either reinjected to maintain reservoir pressure, or flared. The amount of gas now flared in Saudi Arabia alone is about equal to the annual volume of expected deliveries through the controversial new Soviet pipeline to Western Europe. About 10 percent of world gas output in 1980 was flared, mainly in the Middle East and Africa. This is a wasted energy resource if there ever was one.

6. International Energy Agency, OECD, *Natural Gas Prospects,* p. 80.

7. The total of undiscovered yet recoverable NG reserves in the United States is put at about 600 TCF. Of that total about 20 percent is likely to be found in Alaska (both on and off shore) and about 30 percent would come from offshore formations. Delivery from Alaska to the lower 48 states is not likely to take place until 1985. By 1990 it could amount to about 1 TCF if the Alaskan Natural Gas Transportation System is ever completed. See U.S. Department of Energy, *1981 Annual Report to Congress,* vol. II, May 1982, Table 15, p. 33.

8. AGA Gas Supply Committee, *The Gas Energy Supply Outlook: 1980-2000,* Arlington, Virginia, 1980. U.S. Department of Energy, Office of Policy, Planning, and Analysis, *Energy Projection to the Year 2000,* February 1981, p. 6-2.

9. Boyce I. Greer and Jeremy L. Russell, "European Reliance on Soviet Gas Exports: The Yamburg-Urengoi Natural Gas Project," *Energy Journal* III, 3 (1982): 15-37.

10. "Life with an Andropov," *The Economist,* October 9, 1982, p. 12.

11. This information was taken from Wilfried Prewo, "The Pipeline: White Elephant or Trojan Horse," *Wall Street Journal,* September 18, 1982.

12. For further details see "Huge Gas Field off Coast of Norway," Seattle *Times,* November 5, 1982, p. A3.

13. See David Brand, "Energy Enigma: Europeans Subsidized Soviet Pipe-line Work to Save Jobs," *Wall Street Journal,* November 2, 1982, p. 1. Along the same line also see Ed A. Hewett, "The Pipeline Connection: Issues for the Alliance," *Brookings Review,* Fall 1982, p. 19.

14. David Brand, "Energy Enigma: Europeans Subsidized Soviet Pipeline Work to Save Jobs," *Wall Street Journal,* November 2, 1982, p. 20.

15. As Wilfried Prewo has noted, it isn't as if satisfactory alternatives cannot be found. Gas can be obtained from a wide variety of sources, including the North Sea, the South Atlantic, the Canadian Arctic, the Persian Gulf

area, and Western Africa. Such diversification of import sources would sharply reduce the inherent risk of supply disruptions. It also would obviate the need for a greatly expanded exploration program in any *one* country. Finally, it would give rise to a much expanded European pipeline grid system. Wilfried Prewo, "The Pipeline: White Elephant or Trojan Horse," *Wall Street Journal,* September 18, 1982.

16. Much of the factual information in this section has been obtained from the following sources: F. H. Murphy, R. P. O'Neill, and M. Rodekohr, "An Overview of the Natural Gas markets," *Monthly Energy Review,* U.S. Department of Energy, December 1981, pp. I-VIII; R. P. O'Neill, "The Interstate and Intrastate Natural Gas Markets," *Monthly Energy Review,* U.S. Department of Energy, January 1982, pp. I-VIII; and R. P. O'Neill, "Natural Gas Drilling and Production Under the Natural Gas Policy Act," *Monthly Energy Review,* U.S. Department of Energy, February 1982, pp. I-VIII. Much of the statistical information presented in this section is taken from U.S. Department of Energy, *1981 Annual Report to Congress,* vol. II, Energy Statistics, May 1982.

17. Natural gas as it rises from the well is a mixture of gaseous hydrocarbons--primarily methane, but also present are other gases such as carbon dioxide and hydrogen sulfide. These nonmethane gases (called natural gas liquids) are separated from methane at processing plants. The product after the separation process is completed is known as "dry" natural gas. The term "marketed production" refers to the difference between gross withdrawals of NG from production reservoirs, less gas used for reservoir repressuring and quantities vented and flared. U.S. Department of Energy, *1981 Annual Report to Congress,* vol. II, May 1982, p. 105.

18. This section draws on the following studies of the NG industry: Robert B. Helms, *Natural Gas Regulation an Evaluation of FPC Price Controls* (Washington, D.C.: American Enterprise for Public Policy Research, July 1974); Paul W. MacAvoy and Robert S. Pindyck, *Price Controls and the Natural Gas Shortage* (Washington, D.C.: American Enterprise Institute for Public Policy Research, May 1975).

19. This historical sketch of NG regulation draws primarily on the following sources: Keith C. Brown (ed.), *Regulation of the Natural Gas Producing Industry* (Washington D.C.: Resources for the Future, 1972), chs. 4, 5, 7, 9, and 10; Helms, *Natural Gas Regulation and Evaluation of FPC Price Controls;* P. W. MacAvoy and R. S.

Pindyck, *The Economics of the Natural Gas Shortage (1960-1980)* (Amsterdam: North-Holland, 1975); see also U.S. Department of Energy, Energy Information Administration, *The Current State of the Natural Gas Market,* December 1981.

20. For further details see MacAvoy and Pindyck, *Economics of Natural Gas Shortage,* chs. 1 and 2.

21. O'Neill, "The Interstate and Intrastate Natural Gas Market," p. II, Figure 1.

22. For further details for the reasons behind the NG shortage consult MacAvoy and Pindyck, *Economics of Natural Gas Shortage,* chs. 1 and 2.

23. Ibid., pp. 21-22.

24. Most of the factual information was obtained from the following sources: U.S. Department of Energy, Energy Information Administration, *Intrastate and Interstate Supply Markets Under the Natural Gas Policy Act* (Washington, D.C., October 1981); U.S. Department of Energy, Energy Information Administration, *The Current State of the Natural Gas Market* (Washington, D.C., December 1981), Part I; U.S. Department of Energy, "Natural Gas Drilling and Production under the Natural Gas Policy Act," *Monthly Energy Review,* February 1982, pp. I-VIII; also see U.S. General Accounting Office, *Changes in Natural Gas Prices and Supplies Since Passage of the Natural Gas Policy Act of 1978* (Washington, D.C., June 4, 1981); Paul Bennett and Deborah Kuenstner, "Natural Gas Controls and Decontrols," Federal Reserve Bank of New York, *Quarterly Review,* Winter 1981-82, pp. 50-60.

25. A "marker" well is one that was producing gas in commercial quantities any time between January 1, 1970 and April 20, 1977.

26. See Bennett and Kuenstner, "Natural Gas Controls and Decontrols," p. 51.

27. Full analysis of the NG shortage, its causes, and consequences is available in P. W. MacAvoy and R. S. Pindyck, *The Economics of the Natural Gas Shortage (1960-1980),* chs. 1 and 2. For added insights consult Henry D. Jacoby and Arthur M. Wright, "The Gordian Knot of Natural Gas Prices," *The Energy Journal,* vol. 3, no. 4 (1982): 1-25.

28. For example, in both 1978 and 1981 total discoveries of NG plus net revisions of existing reserve estimates exceeded by 0.6 TCF and 2.7 TCF, respectively, the production of NG during those two years. See U.S. Department of Energy, Energy Information Administration, *Monthly Energy Review,* September 1982 (highlights).

29. This information is taken from Bennett and

Kuenstner, "Natural Gas Controls and Decontrols," p. 55.

30. The total number of gas customers rose by half a million in 1980. Over the longer period from 1976 to 1980, the number of customers rose by about 2 million, or by 4.5 percent. See American Gas Association, Department of Statistics, *Gas Facts 1980 Data,* 1981, p. 73.

31. See Bennett and Kuenstner, "Natural Gas Controls and Decontrols," p. 56.

32. U.S. Department of Energy, *Current State of Natural Gas Market,* pp. 21-36.

33. Ibid., p. 45.

34. See Douglas Bohi, *Analyzing Demand Behavior: A Study of Energy Elasticities* (Baltimore: Johns Hopkins University Press, 1981), ch. 4.

35. The major source of NG imports into the United States are Canada and Mexico; further imports come from Algeria in the form of liquefied natural gas (LNG). The combined total of pipeline and LNG imports was 0.99 TCF in 1980 compared to 1.25 TCF in 1979, a decrease of 21.4 percent. Of the total 1979 gas supply of 12.7 TCF to interstate pipeline companies, 7.6 percent was from Canada, while LNG imports amounted to 1.8 percent of the total. Although gas imports do not constitute a large part of U.S. gas supply, they are quite important in meeting *regional* gas needs. For example, the Northwest Pipeline Corporation imported 63.8 percent of its gas in 1979 from Canada. About 24 percent of California's gas also came from Canada. See, U.S. Department of Energy, Energy Information Administration, *The Current State of the Natural Gas Market,* pp. 53-58.

36. For further details consult Bennett and Kuenstner, "Natural Gas Controls and Decontrols," p. 59.

37. Jacoby and Wright agree with the statement that immediate and full decontrol would be the preferred "policy option" and would in their words "untie the Gordian knot" of natural gas regulation. But while cogently arguing the merits of *immediate* decontrol they appear to bow to political "reality" by calling this best option "impractical as it is ideal" and by raising the specter of unspecified yet "substantial" short-term adjustment costs. Henry D. Jacoby and Arthur W. Wright, "The Gordian Knot of Natural Gas Prices," *The Energy Journal,* III, 4 (1982): 19 and 24.

38. The valid point has been made by MacAvoy and Pindyck that those consumers who were unable to obtain gas during the recurring market shortages that developed in the 1970s would benefit from deregulation of NG. For further details of this argument see MacAvoy and Pindyck, *Economy of Natural Gas Shortage,* pp. 49-56.

39. For details on these figures consult "Combining Decontrol of Natural Gas with a New Tax on Producer Revenues, *Federal Reserve Bank of New York Quarterly Review,* Winter 1981-82, vol. 6, no. 4, pp. 61-66.

40. Some of the factual information on synthetic and unconventional gas was obtained from the following sources: National Petroleum Council, *Unconventional Gas Sources,* Executive Summary, December 1980. Also see National Academy of Sciences, National Research Council, *Energy in Transition 1985-2000* (W. H. Freeman and Co., 1980), pp. 173-178.

41. National Petroleum Council, *Unconventional Gas Sources (Executive Summary),* December 1980, p. 3.

42. Ibid., p. 5.

43. U.S. Department of Energy, *Energy Projections to the Year 2000 July 1982 Update,* Washington, D.C., August 1982, pp. 5-17.

44. The plant being constructed at an estimated cost of $2.1 billion is based on the well-known Lurgi coal gasification technology, which has been further developed by the South African company Sasol. Sasol has built two large coal conversion facilities based on the Lurgi process in Secunda, South Africa, and it has been retained as a consultant for the U.S. coal gasification project.

45. Much of this detailed information has been culled from a number of publications and documents provided to me by John A. Graham, manager, legislative relations, Great Plains Gasification Associates.

46. As of June 1, 1982, the U.S. Synthetic Fuels Corporation has received 37 proposals for government support of synthetic fuels projects; of the total, nine were coal gasification projects. The projects are currently being evaluated by the staff of the Synfuels Corporation.

47. Sam H. Schurr et al., *Energy in America's Future* (Baltimore: Johns Hopkins University Press, 1979), p. 262.

48. The "minimum acceptable price" is based on economic costs of production, including capital costs, feedstock costs, and adjustment for risk. Department of Energy, *Energy Projections to the Year 2000 July 1982 Update,* Washington, D.C., August 1982, Tables 5-7 and 5-9.

49. This information comes from "Gas Consumers Say Pipelines Are Paying More than Necessary for Their Supplies," *Wall Street Journal,* November 11, 1982, p. 52.

50. "Take-a-pay" contracts require the buyer to pay for the gas irrespective of whether he takes delivery or not, as long as the seller is willing to supply the contracted for amounts. For further details consult Jacoby

and Wright, "The Gordian Knot of Natural Gas Prices," p. 17.

51.   For further details consult Frank A. Camm, Jr., *Average Cost Pricing of Natural Gas: A Problem and Three Policy Options* (Santa Monica: Rand, July 1978).

The Economics of Nuclear Power
— 4 —
Current Issues and Future Prospects

This chapter describes and analyzes the current state of
the nuclear industry and the policies advocated by the
Reagan administration to attain a "political and institutional
climate in which the full potential of nuclear power can be
attained."[1]

The future of the "nuclear option" in the United States
is under a cloud these days, and the call for restoring the
light-water-reactor (LWR) industry to health may sound a
bit hollow. No place in the United States is this situation
more apparent than in the Pacific Northwest (PNW). Thus,
it is entirely appropriate to start this chapter with a brief
perspective on the problems of nuclear energy in the PNW,
specifically focusing on the current financial and public
confidence crisis, confronting the Washington Public Power
Supply System (WPPSS). It is evident that the significance
of the problems confronting WPPSS extends far beyond the
regional boundaries of the Pacific Northwest. While report-
ing on the difficulties confronting WPPSS several major
newspapers underscored the national significance of what is
taking place there. After describing the current predic-
aments of WPPSS, the *Wall Street Journal* noted: "If the
trouble [with WPPSS] persists the economic growth of the
Northwest and the survival of nuclear power in the U.S.
could be in serious jeopardy."[2]

The serious nature of the PNW's financial and energy
problems is underscored in a *Washington Post* story that
stated in part: ". . . the Pacific Northwest is on the

brink of an unprecedented financial disaster because of a nuclear building program that may quadruple electric bills, bankrupt several local communities and trigger one of the biggest bond defaults in U.S. history."[3]

Clearly, the significance of the future of the five nuclear facilities planned for the PNW is national in scope, and their problems have repercussions that extend well beyond the geographic boundaries of the region.

In the summer of 1981 a special three-man panel was appointed by Governors John Spellman of Washington State and Victor Atiyeh of Oregon to investigate the economic consequences to the PNW region of the various options open with respect to WPPSS's nuclear plants numbers 4 and 5. The governors' panel concluded that "the enormity of the financial problems associated with WPPSS 4 and 5, if not properly managed and controlled, could inject serious harm on the region's economy."[4]

WPPSS: BRIEF HISTORY AND ANALYSIS OF CURRENT PROBLEMS

The Washington Public Power Supply System was established in 1957 as an organization of 16 publicly owned utilities in Washington State. A municipal corporation and a joint operating agency of the state, WPPSS was established for the purpose of "acquiring, building, operating and owning power plants and systems for the generation and trans- mission of electricity."[5]

In 1968, the Joint Power Planning Council--an or- ganization consisting of 108 Pacific Northwest electric utilities and the Bonneville Power Administration--adopted a ten-year hydro-thermal program to meet the projected growth of electricity demand in the PNW over the 1970-90 period. Under this program, the federal government agreed to develop the remaining hydroelectric power potential of the region to meet the growth of peak demand, and nonfederal utilities agreed to construct and operate additional thermal (coal and nuclear) plants to meet the growth of baseload electrical requirements.

In the late 1960s, on the basis of perceived power needs of the region, WPPSS decided to proceed with the construction of three nuclear power plants. In 1974, the supply system ordered two more reactors; thus by the mid-1970s, WPPSS had embarked on an ambitious program of constructing five nuclear power plants in Washington State. Three of the five plants are located on the Department of Energy's Hanford Reservation (these are WNP-1, WNP-2 and

WNP-4), while two others are located near Satsop, Washington (WNP-3 and WNP-5). Plants WNP-1/WNP-4 and WNP-3/WNP-5 are "twins"--in the sense that the nuclear reactors and generators are of substantially identical design, and they also share some common facilities for using water in their cooling system.

As of July 1981, the construction of WNP-1 and WNP-4 was approximately 41 and 23 percent complete, respectively. The WNP-3 and WNP-5 plants were 32 and 14 percent complete as of the same date.[6] All five projects have suffered from lengthy delays, ranging from 32 months (on WNP-5) to 72 months (on WNP-2). An internal study prepared by WPPSS indicates that the probability of completing these plants according to the official timetable (inclusive of "official" delays) is extremely low. Schedule delays have had a direct impact on the overall cost of the five nuclear plants, primarily because additional financing was required as construction schedules were extended. These delays have exposed construction costs to the impact of higher interest rates, during a period where such rates have risen sharply. The total estimated cost of building the five plants rose from an initial estimate of $6.6 billion to a more recent WPPSS estimate of $23.8 billion. WPPSS 1981 budget reveals that the cost of completing WNP-4 and WNP-5 alone increased by $4.2 billion since the 1980 estimates were prepared. Fully 65 percent of the additional costs were attributed to higher financing costs (both higher interest rates and the additional financing required).[7]

In the final analysis, the higher costs of these plants, whether they are completed or not, will be borne by the consumers of electricity in the Pacific Northwest. Based on WPPSS official cost estimates, which of course continue to be revised upward, electric power rates by 1990 are projected to increase by 50 percent for some utilities and by as much as 500 percent for others.[8] The average electric power rates paid by PNW customers will increase sharply in the coming years. These increases will be the result of two factors; first, the participating utilities buy most of or all of their power from the Bonneville Power Administration, which will be raising wholesale rates to reflect the costs of WNP-1, 2, and 3, and second, the utilities have to start paying off their WNP-4 and 5 financial obligations as of January 22, 1983.

Figure 4-1 displays the average residential rates of the PNW from 1960 to the present and projected rates through the remainder of the century. Roughly one-third of the rate increases projected for 1990 were attributed to the costs of WNP-4 and 5.[9]

FIGURE 4-1. Average Residential Electricity Rates in Pacific Northwest

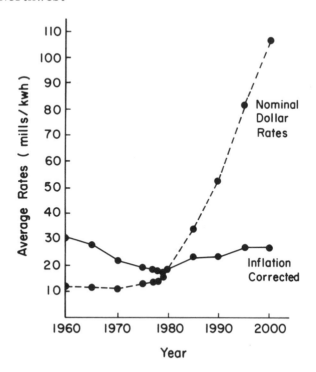

Source: Office of Applied Energy Studies, Washington Energy Research Center, *Independent Review of Washington Public Power Supply System Nuclear Plants 4 and 5, Final Report to the Washington State Legislature,* Washington State University, March 1982, p. 22.

The PNW Regional Power Act and the Role of Bonneville Power Administration

The Bonneville Power Administration (BPA) was created in 1937 through an Act of Congress in order to market and transmit electric power from the Bonneville and Grand Coulee dams. Subsequently, its role was greatly expanded to the point where in 1980 BPA sold power from 30 federal hydroelectric projects with a firm energy capability of 7,583 average MW. BPA is a wholesale supplier of electricity whose principal customers are publicly owned utilities--those owned by municipalities, cooperatives, and public utility districts--and also to some degree private utilities and the direct service industries (DSI).[10] The publicly owned utilities, federal agencies, and the DSIs obtained the bulk (88 percent in fiscal 1980) of the relatively inexpensive hydropower supplied by BPA.

The Regional Power Act, enacted by Congress in 1980, has recognized that any new power capacity in the Northwest will have to come from nonfederal sources, either private or public.[11] The Regional Power Act calls for the creation of the Pacific Northwest Electric Power and Conservation Planning Council, whose primary task is to develop by April 1983 a long-range power and conservation plan for the Pacific Northwest, including a twenty-year electricity demand and supply forecast.

Under the provisions of the Regional Power Act, the council, when planning future resource acquisitions, must consider all "cost-effective" sources of power in the following order: conservation, renewable resources, cogeneration resources utilizing waste heat, and finally, "all other" resources. The last category also includes power generated by new nuclear plants, such as WNP-4 and WNP-5. The term "cost effective" refers to resources that are deemed to be reliable and available to meet future power demand at an estimated *incremental* system cost no greater than that of the least-cost available alternative. The Power Act further mandates that the costs of new energy resources must include all quantifiable environmental costs and benefits. The act also requires that the future cost of transmissions and acquisitions of power be recouped by BPA through rates charged to its customers. BPA is to continue to meet the power needs of its firm electric preference customers (that is, public utilities and rural electric cooperatives) as well as the expanded load growth of private utilities, federal agency loads, and the fixed loads of the aluminum companies.

Finally, the act in an attempt to avoid regional conflict over the allocation of low-cost federal power provides a formula for the sale and cost distribution of the region's power. Bonneville's traditional preference customers will still have first call on the power generated by the Federal Base System.[12] In addition, though, residential and rural customers of private utilities will be phased gradually, over the 1981-1985 period, into the relatively cheaper power available from Bonneville. The Direct Service Industries will pay rates based on the higher cost of electricity generation experienced by the region's private utilities, rather than the cheaper hydropower rates they had access to in the past. Given these new provisions, rates charged the aluminum companies have tripled in the past two years.

Factors Behind WPPSS Cost Overruns
and Scheduling Delays

The decision to build five nuclear power plants in the State of Washington was based on the belief that the Northwest's consumption of electrical power would continue to grow at rates comparable to those experienced in the 1950s and 1960s (5 to 7 percent a year). In recent years it has become apparent that future load growth will be well below those historical rates. By the end of the 1970s, public concern regarding large-scale cost overruns and their effect on the Washington Public Power Supply System became widespread and pervasive. A combination of escalating construction costs, high interest rates paid during construction periods, and protracted schedule delays led the WPPSS into its present predicament.

The supply system's difficulties are illustrated in Table 4-1. WPPSS estimates of the dates on which the five nuclear plants were expected to start generating electricity on an ongoing basis have been pushed back by approximately 27 years, when compared to the original schedule. Consequently, a cost overrun of at least $17 billion is projected by the supply system. Several developments have taken place during 1981-82. In June 1981 the supply system announced a construction slowdown of nuclear plants WNP 4 and 5. This led to the eventual cessation of construction at these two sites as the financial crisis facing the supply system worsened during the summer of 1981.

During the fall and winter of 1981, WPPSS tried to develop and implement a plan to mothball the two ill-fated nuclear plants; this effort was unsuccessful because of the resistance of participating utilities that jointly "own" shares in the project. Finally, on January 22, 1982, the supply system's board of directors voted to terminate WNP-4 and WNP-5. It should be noted that at the time of termination, WNP-4 was about 23 percent complete and WNP-5 was about 14 percent complete. The termination of these two plants meant that the rate payers of the region will have to assume the costs of the two terminated facilities, which includes $2.25 billion already spent on the two nuclear plants, an additional $750 million (approximately) in termination costs, and the extra costs to be borne by the "twin" plants (WNP-1 and 3) for the shared facilities with WNP-4 and 5--for a total cost of termination of about $4.3 billion.

As has been noted in the report of Governors' Panel, the crisis related to WNP 4 and 5 and the resulting climate

TABLE 4-1. Washington Public Power Supply System Nuclear Projects Status According to Independent Review

Project	Estimated Date of Commercial Operation		Slippage	Estimated Cost (in millions)		Estimated Cost Overrun (in millions)
	Original	1982 Estimated[a]		Original	1982 Estimated	
WNP 1	9/80	6/86	69 months	$1,204	$4,268	$3,064
WNP 2	9/77	2/84	77 months	$ 504	$3,216	$2,612
WNP 3	7/81	12/86	63 months	$1,402	$4,532	$3,130
WNP 4 [b]	3/81	6/87	63 months	$1,610	$5,510	$3,900
WNP 5 [b]	3/83	12/87	57 months	$1,951	$6,261	$4,410
Totals			329 months	$6,671	$23,787	$17,116

[a]WPPSS, "Construction Budget Summary: 1982 Estimate at Completion," May 1981.

[b]Commercial operation dates and cost estimates given do not take into account the construction slowdown plan begun in June 1981.

Note: Dollar figures are considered to be "as-spent dollars."

Source: Office of Applied Energy Studies, Washington Energy Research Center, Independent Review of Washington Public Power Supply System Nuclear Plants 4 and 5, Final Report to the Washington State Legislature, Washington State University, March 1982, p. 32.

of uncertainty endangers the timely completion of the remaining three nuclear plants, which in turn could create a situation wherein the region will be faced with "an economic and energy crisis of serious proportions."[13]

The Financing of the Supply System's
Nuclear Power Projects

Figure 4-2 vividly illustrates the financial burden of financing the five projects in a municipal bond market that was severely strained to begin with. Since WPPSS is a municipal corporation of the State of Washington, its debt issues are tax-free revenue bonds. Thus, it's possible to identify a niche in the financial market for bonds issued by

FIGURE 4-2. The Burden of Financing WPPSS's Five Nuclear Projects

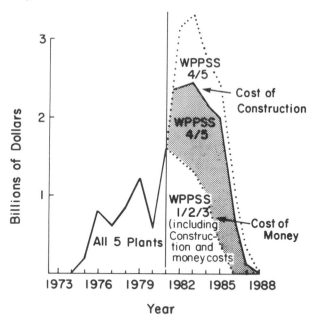

Source: Edward E. Carlson, John Elorriaga, and George H. Weyerhauser, "A Report on the Economic Impacts of the Alternatives Facing the Region on Washington Public Power Supply System Units 4 and 5," September 1981, p. I-2.

the supply system, although the debt issued to finance WNP 1, 2, and 3 should be treated separately from the bonds issued to pay for the construction of WNP 4 and 5.

Financing of the first three nuclear plants has an indirect federal government guarantee by virtue of an ingenious financial arrangement known as "net billing." Net billing is an accounting device whereby the participating public utilities assigned their shares of the capacity of the first three nuclear plants to BPA. In return BPA gives the participants an "offset" or credit, based on the cost of that power, against any amounts the participants owe for power currently being purchased from Bonneville.

There are two primary economic effects of the "net billing" arrangement. First, it places the costs of these three plants in BPA's rate structure by "melding" or combining the supply system's high cost of nuclear power generation with BPA's much cheaper hydropower so that Bonneville's wholesale and retail customers are not immediately confronted with the full cost of the resources required to supply this new block of baseload power.

Second, BPA's commitment to purchase the capacity and/or output of the three nuclear plants amounts to a firm federal guarantee that these projects will be paid for even if they are never completed, thus practically eliminating any risk of default on debts issued to pay for the construction of WNP 1, 2, and 3 and consequently lowering the interest rates that the supply system has to pay on such borrowings. The construction of WNP 4 and 5 is also financed with revenue bonds, albeit without BPA's guarantee or the distinct advantage of a net billing arrangement.

Bonds issued to finance the construction of WNP 4 and 5 were to be repaid with revenues raised by the 88 participating utilities from the sale of electricity to their customers. Principal and interest due on these bonds must be paid regardless of whether the two nuclear plants are ever completed and operated by WPPSS.[14] For these and other reasons, these bonds are considered more risky by the investment community, and they have been rated one or more grades below the debt issued to finance the construction of WNP 1, 2, and 3.

A survey of the financial community conducted in October 1981, by the Independent Review concluded that additional bonds for the construction of WNP 4 and 5 can no longer be marketed.[15] In the view of the bond dealers and investors that "make" the market in WNP-4 and WNP-5 debt, the risk attendant on such issues was simply too high relative to other comparable tax-free securities.

WPPSS Management's Responsibility for
Schedule Delays and Cost Overruns

The Washington State Senate's WPPSS inquiry did not mince words in stating its conclusion that "WPPSS mismanagement has been the *most* significant cause of cost overruns and schedule delays on the WPPSS project."[16]

The "WPPSS inquiry" identified eight specific instances of errors and deficient management practices on part of the supply system. In reviewing the methods that WPPSS's management has used to prepare its budgets and completion schedules, the investigator noted that these were not being used as tools for the control of costs and schedules. The supply system's preparation of cost estimates lacked sufficient detail to assure their accuracy, and thus made them unsuitable for such purposes. Furthermore, some of the assumptions used in preparing the costs of construction and financing estimates were unrealistically low. WPPSS's management has been especially lax in the management and control of the architects-engineers and construction contractors on the projects. The senate inquiry stated: "The architect-engineers and major construction contractors have taken advantage of the fact that WPPSS has not effectively managed their extremely complex projects involving management of hundreds of contractors, billions of dollars and more than a hundred million man-hours of craft labor."[17]

Another critical area identified by experts involved the effective management of change. Because the five nuclear plants were being constructed on a fast-track basis, frequent contract changes became necessary, along with other changes stemming from new or revised regulatory requirements.[18] The lack of an effective management system is thought to be a "direct and principal" cause of construction schedule delays and cost overruns. In a fast-track project contracts are awarded and construction begins *before* the design is complete. Fast-track scheduling is commonly used in the nuclear industry where long construction times can lead to greatly increased costs. The price paid for this is the increased complexity of problems management must be able to handle. Furthermore, since the design is unfinished at the time the original contracts are awarded, contracts are constantly being revised as work specifications change. For example, one contractor agreed to install some concrete and reinforced steel for $40 million, but an "avalanche" of modifications pushed the price tag to well over $200 million.

In one instance the NRC found so many defects that it

ordered WPPSS to stop work for several months on major parts of one plant. WPPSS management responded to the criticism of its management practices by attributing virtually all cost increases and schedule problems to causes and circumstances beyond their immediate control. The supply system's officials have specifically stated that in their estimation as much as 50 percent of the cost overruns were due to new or revised regulatory requirements by state and federal agencies. This figure has been vigorously disputed by the Washington State Senate investigators. Furthermore, WPPSS has stressed in its presentation the effects of escalating inflation and low labor productivity as important causes of cost increases and schedule delays. Undoubtedly such factors as inflation, low labor productivity, and unanticipated regulatory requirements--contributed to the problems experienced by the supply system, but it is unlikely that in this case they can be assigned *primary* responsibility for the financial difficulties of WPPSS. After considering the reliability and the self-serving nature of the supply system's explanations one has to agree with the senate inquiry that "WPPSS' mismanagement, a controllable factor, has been the most significant cause of cost and schedule problems."[19]

In conclusion, the WPPSS experience, while more dramatic and far-reaching in its economic implications, is not unique and has been replicated in other parts of the country. The economic and regulatory environment within which all electric utilities operate today has caused other nuclear power projects to be delayed or terminated.[20] Such factors as the increasing cost of capital combined with escalating construction costs and project delays have plagued all utilities to one degree or another. However, as shown by the Washington State Senate's investigation, WPPSS's schedule performance, when compared to other nuclear plants begun about the same time, leaves much to be desired. WPPSS's financial woes have been made even worse by the common practice of issuing bonds that not only pay for the cost of construction but also for interest costs incurred on money borrowed during the period the plants are being built. When interest rates are high, the capitalizing of interest charges causes the ultimate cost of the project to rise dramatically because high debt service charges during the period of construction are added to the principal on which the high interest rates must be paid. Because WPPSS capitalized a higher proportion of such costs than most utilities, it is ultimately faced with a much larger amount of debt and higher debt service charges when a plant eventually starts producing power.[21]

The financial problems of the supply system have been compounded by the low public esteem and lack of confidence that it suffers from. An indication of the public's attitude has been the passage in 1981, by Washington State voters, of Initiative 394. The initiative, requiring voter approval of bonds issued by WPPSS after July 1, 1982, is indicative of the widespread concern and apprehension of PNW residents over the future financing of the supply system's activities and more fundamentally about the energy prospects for the entire region.[22]

CURRENT STATE OF THE
NUCLEAR POWER INDUSTRY

During the 1950s and 1960s, electricity consumption and generating capacity in the United States grew at a steady rate of about 7 percent a year. Many electric utilities based their expansion plans on a continuation of that trend into the future. Encouraged by governments, utilities enthusiastically placed orders for nuclear plants, which appeared to be the cheapest way to meet the anticipated growth of demand for electricity. The late 1960s and early 1970s were the boom years for nuclear power, with orders for new nuclear plants peaking at 20 in 1973.

The dramatic increases in the world price of petroleum following the 1973 oil embargo only acted to reinforce the utilities' faith in the future of nuclear power. Official estimates envisaged growth in U.S. nuclear capacity from about 21 gigawatts (one gigawatt equals 1,000 megawatts or one million kilowatts) at the end of 1973 to 1,100-1,200 gigawatts by the year 2000, a sixtyfold increase in capacity. As of June 30, 1982, there were 77 reactors licensed for operation in the United States with a combined net maximum dependable capacity of 58.6 gigawatts. Since 1978 no orders were placed for new nuclear plants, while about 30 gigawatts of nuclear power plant capacity were canceled since 1979.[23]

As shown in Table 4-2, as of March 1982, there was a total of 122 Gigawatts electric (GWe) of nuclear capacity accounted for by plants that were either operating or had "significant" construction completed. However, U.S. Department of Energy nuclear power projections have dropped precipitously since the heady days of the early 1970s. Based on varying assumptions for GNP and electricity demand growth, nuclear capacity is projected to range from 116 to 124 GWe in 1990, and from 145 to 185 GWe by the year 2000.[24]

TABLE 4-2. Status of Nuclear Power Plants[a] (March 1, 1982)

Status	Capacity (gigawatts)
Existing capacity on line[b]	57
Significant construction complete	65
Subtotal firm or committed capacity	122
Construction permit granted but construction not started or not significantly complete	16
Plants ordered or under construction permit review	10
Total surveyed capacity	148

[a]Based on Energy Information Administration, U.S. Commercial Nuclear Power, DOE/EIA-0315, March 1982, p. 17.

[b]Fully operable or in power ascension. Does not include Indian Point 1 (265 MWe), Humboldt Bay (65 MWe), Three Mile Island 2 (906 MWe), and Dresdan (200 MWe)--all of which are currently shut down indefinitely.

Source: U.S. Department of Energy, Office of Policy, Planning and Analysis, Energy Projections to the Year 2000 July 1982 Update, August 1982, p. 7-2.

Since presently in the United States it is virtually impossible to bring a plant on line in less than ten years, one can obtain a reasonably accurate estimate of nuclear capacity for the early 1990s by simply adding the capacity of those plants to which a significant commitment has been made to those already in commercial operation at this time. On that basis, U.S. nuclear capacity is projected to grow at best to 122 GWe in the early 1990s.

Much the same is true for OECD countries as a whole. Estimates for installed nuclear capacity in the OECD area in 1990 have been reduced sharply to 319 GWe from the more than 1,000 GWe projected in 1973. Of the OECD's current operating capacity of 132 GWe, three countries--the United States, France, and Japan--account for over 70 percent, a share that is projected to remain essentially unchanged through 1990.[25]

In the early 1960s, the planning, siting, construction, and licensing of nuclear power plants involved relatively simple and straightforward procedures and steps. But in the 1970s, concerns about the environment, regional considerations, health and safety issues, and technical factors combined to extend the average time required for the planning, permitting, and construction of nuclear power plants. Particularly discouraging for the industry has been the practice of changing prescriptive requirements during the design, engineering, and even construction phases of nuclear power plants. Some delays have also been caused by unforeseen technical problems and management errors.

All these factors are responsible for lengthening lead times for bringing nuclear plants on line. In the United States current lead times average 11 years compared to 6 years, the norm in the early 1970s. In Japan and France, two countries with major nuclear programs, lead times now average from six to eight years.[26] Such long lead times are especially burdensome for the relatively capital-intensive nuclear industry. This, combined with protracted public hearings and even litigation, has seriously eroded the confidence of the managers of public utilities in the future of the nuclear option, as is evidenced by the cessation of new orders and increasing frequency of cancellations.

The current acute predicament of the nuclear power industry can be observed in the Tennessee Valley Authority (TVA) region. In the late 1960s and early 1970s, when power consumption was expected to double every ten years, TVA set on an ambitious course to build 17 nuclear power-generating units with capacity of about 21,500 MWe. As of January 1982, TVA has deferred or is considering for deferral 8 of these 17 nuclear units, representing almost half of the planned addition to capacity. TVA's power loads have grown at an average annual rate of only 1 percent from 1973 to 1981, and even TVA's latest "high" (or most optimistic) forecast expects consumption of electricity to grow only 2.4 percent per year from 1981 to 2000. The sluggish growth in electricity consumption occurred while the region's gross product expanded at a 3.3 percent per annum in the late 1970s.

Recent experience nationwide indicates that the growth of electricity consumption is not as closely linked to economic activity as was once thought to be the case. This so-called decoupling of the relationship between electricity consumption and economic growth resulted principally from improved efficiency in the use of electricity. The resulting conservation of energy can be measured in terms of KWH of electricity consumed per unit of output. Between 1973 and

1979, the consumption of electrical power per unit of output fell by 8 percent in the TVA region alone. Conservation, while evident among all classes of customers, was especially notable in the residential sector.[27] The impressive reduction in the average use of electricity in the TVA region is largely attributable to the rising price of electricity and to TVA's own conservation programs. Due to combination of factors the cost of electricity rose 19 percent per annum and the *real* (inflation adjusted) wholesale price of electricity throughout the decade of the 1970s has increased 8.8 percent annually.

The improved efficiency in the use of electricity and the enhanced prospects for conservation in the area served by TVA have resulted in a reduced need for new generating capacity equivalent to *eight* nuclear units. TVA's most recent forecast expects peak loads to grow from 0.7 to 2.5 percent annually, for the period 1981 to 2000.[28] For the United States as a whole Department of Energy projections show the demand for electricity delivered to final consumers growing at about 2.8 percent annually to the year 2000. Thus, the option chosen by TVA--to defer construction of up to eight nuclear units--would, according to TVA's own analysis, provide an adequate power supply to meet future demand based on TVA's *high* load growth forecast, while at the same time reducing costs and minimizing risks to the region's rate payers.

THE ECONOMICS OF NUCLEAR POWER

The principal argument of nuclear power advocates has been that it would produce cheaper electricity compared to alternative energy sources. Like many other aspects of the nuclear debate, the comparative economics of nuclear power and other sources of electricity have become embroiled in controversy. Given the limited role that oil, natural gas, and hydropower can be expected to play in the near-term expansion of electrical power, it is possible to limit our discussion to two alternative sources of electrical power generation--nuclear and coal.

Not until 1963 were nuclear reactors sold in th United States under what may be described as "free" market conditions; subsidies of one type or another were granted for reactors being built in the United States.[29] Starting in 1963 the General Electric and Westinghouse corporations offered to build nuclear plants with generating capacity of more than 400 MWe. These manufacturers agreed to construct such plants for fixed prices--the so-called turnkey

plant contracts. Such contracts reflected the then prevailing assumption that in selected locations the cost of
electricity generated by nuclear plants will be competitive
with fossil fuel plants and that the capital costs of nuclear
plants were as predictable as comparable fossil fuel plants.
Alas, by the mid-1960s when the first 25 plants were completed, it turned out that their capital costs were about
twice the projected levels. In the event, coal prices rose
sharply around that time and nuclear plants started to look
somewhat more attractive on the basis of cost comparisons.
Also in the ensuring years, as the environmental movement
gathered momentum, the nuclear option may have gained
converts due to its promise to deliver clean power, especially when compared to coal.

   Although construction delays were experienced as soon
as the first few commercial nuclear plants were built, they
did not significantly affect the pace of commercialization
until the late 1960s. But as the light-water reactor plants
ordered by utilities increased in sophistication and size, so
did the inevitable delays in their construction. In fact,
with the important exception of safety considerations, no
pervasive technological difficulties have affected the
development of the LWR.[30]

   By 1976 more than 70 percent of all the operating power
reactors worldwide were LWR of either the pressurized
water (PWR) or the boiling water (BWR) variety. In the
BWR, water boils in the core of the reactor and the resulting steam is piped directly to the generating turbine. In
the PWR, water is heated in the primary high-pressure
circuit in the reactor core, and then pumped through a
heat exchanger and returned to the core. A separate
circuit uses the steam produced in the heat exchanger to
drive a turbine.

   In the course of 20 years, nuclear power plants have
grown in size from 100 MWe to 1,250 MWe and the fuel they
use--uranium dioxide clad in zircalloy--evolved into a
successful commercial product. The Rand study noted that:
"Despite technical and institutional problems, the operational
history of large nuclear plants was as good [as] or better
than large modern fossil fuel plants."[31]

   The principal causes of the sharp increases in the cost
of nuclear power generation since its commercial introduction have been the subject of considerable controversy but
not of adequate objective examination. One of the major
findings of a Rand study was that capital costs of LWR
power plants were increasing at a rate of $158 per KWe per
year (in 1978 dollars) over a five-year period and that
there were no indications that such cost escalation was

leveling off. [32]

The study also found that the average construction time of LWRs was increasing at a rate of about four months per year. A subsequent update of the study, based on a larger sample (55 plants compared to 39), essentially confirmed the former results and found the average annual increase in capital costs to be $140 per KWe (in 1978 dollars). Statistical analysis of capital cost escalation yields several important insights:

1. The major driving force behind capital cost increases is a pervasive temporal trend, which for a variety of reasons contributes to longer construction times and subsequent higher capital costs. This temporal trend, which contributes to longer construction times, could have resulted from changes in plant designs occasioned by growing safety and environmental concerns, or from the growing technological complexity of larger nuclear plants.

2. Economies of scale were found to be of limited statistical significance, leading the author to conclude that costs "appear to increase linearly with the size of the plant, with no sizable diminution in unit costs as the size increases." [33]

3. Cost reductions due to learning by the architect/engineers have been observed, but the overall impact on costs is not very large. In other words, if the previously noted temporal trends will continue into the future the prospects of reducing costs through learning curve effects appear to be meager.

4. Finally, significant regional differences in the cost of building plants were noted. Specifically plants built in the Northeast appear to cost $221/KWe more than plants built elsewhere in the United States. This is attributable to higher labor costs and possible lower labor productivity in that region.

The Rand study warns against rosy scenarios that frequently assume that LWR capital costs are either fixed (and low) or declining. Mooz's study shows that capital costs of plants coming on line in 1978/79 averaged $1,200 (in 1978 dollars) per kilowatts of installed electrical capacity, and every indication exists that costs are still rising. Furthermore, one cannot count on learning effects or economies of scale to bring down costs sufficiently so as to offset the cost increases due to temporal factors. The observed cost increases resulted in part from growing safety and environmental requirements, and also from greater design complexity, larger buildings, and more exacting inspection and quality assurance programs.

Finally the study warns that "continued increase in capital costs may dry up the market for LWR power plants."[34]

As our discussion of Pacific Northwest energy situation emphasized, the costs of constructing nuclear plants have generally exceeded early estimates and often by huge margins, while on the other hand, the capacity factor has been significantly lower than expected.[35] Charges against capital invested in a nuclear power plant constitute a substantial proportion of the cost of generating electricity. Capital charges are equal to the capital costs of a plant times a fixed-rate charge. These fixed charges represent the sum of the cost of borrowed money, depreciation, federal income taxes, state and local taxes, and insurance premiums. Such charges are related to the initial decision to invest in the asset (the power plant) and are independent of its actual usage.

Because these charges are independent of the number of kilowatt hours of electricity produced, their contribution to average generation costs decreases as the number of KWh generated increases. Thus, to lower their average cost, utilities will try and squeeze as much output as possible from their nuclear plants.

Until the late 1960s capacity factors of 80 to 90 percent were routinely assumed in making cost estimates for nuclear plants. A detailed study done for the Council on Economic Priorities found that 48 commercial-size nuclear plants had an average capacity factor on only 57.5 in 1976. As regards future performance, the study noted that "size-related reliability problems, no clear improvements for recent reactors, and only modest age improvement--pointed toward future capacity factors less than current industry averages for the very large reactors now being planned."[36] A caveat is in order; there is no agreement on a generally acceptable method for calculating the capacity factor on the basis of actual operating experience; this reflects differences based on the exclusion of certain units from the data base, on some ambiguity about the capacity factor of individual LWR units, and on different methods used in obtaining averages.

Nonetheless, several sources have suggested that the performance of nuclear plants may deteriorate with size. For example, data of the Nuclear Regulatory Commission

(NRC) show that in 1975 the average capacity (using an unweighted average) of plants greater than 800 MWe was 51.1 percent as compared to 65.3 percent for units of less than 800 MWe. [37]

Table 4-3 reveals several important operating trends. In the first place, smaller units have been more reliable than larger units, as evidenced by significant differences in capacity factors, availability, and forced outage rates. Second, nuclear power plants greater than 800 MWe have been operated at capacity factors that are significantly lower than plant availabilities would permit; this probably reflects the daily and seasonal peaking patterns of domestic electricity demand.

Since capital charges are directly proportional to construction costs and inversely related to capacity factors, and since such charges are a major (about two-thirds) component of the total cost of generating electricity, it is not surprising that actual costs per KWh generated by nuclear plants ended up being much higher than projected costs based on earlier estimates.

The total investment costs of nuclear plants include all costs associated with their design, engineering, and construction. The costs of nuclear power plants have tended to escalate as manufacturers have been forced to revise earlier cost estimates, and also as more stringent safety requirements have been put into effect by government regulation, and as safety and environmental reviews have become lengthier.

The trend of capital costs for nuclear and coal power-generating plants has been moving up relentlessly. Estimated total investment costs for LWR nuclear power plants have increased from about $134/KWe in 1967 to over $700/KWe based on the 1974 estimate, and finally to $4,307/KWe in a recent estimate (for a plant that is expected to be in operation in 1993). During the same period the share of total cost attributable to the nuclear steam supply system and the turbine-generator declined from 40 percent in 1967 to only 6 percent in 1980.

On the other hand, escalation costs incurred during the construction period plus interest charges on funds used during construction increased their share from 17 percent in 1967 to over 68 percent in 1980. Clearly it is those time-related factors that were primarily responsible for the upward surge in capital costs of nuclear power plants, rather than the cost of the hardware itself. A recent DOE study concluded that other than general cost escalation factors related to the design, licensing, and construction of nuclear power plants, the "most significant contributors to

TABLE 4-3. Nuclear and Coal-Fired Power Plant Performance, 1971-80

Size Category (MW)	Number of Units	Unit Years	Cumulative Capacity Factor	Equivalent[a] Availability	Equivalent[b] FOR	Scheduled Outage
Nuclear Plants						
400-599	11	82	72.3	79.6	8.0	13.3
600-799	8	62	68.1	71.0	11.5	23.4
800-999	30	160	56.1	63.5	22.4	19.3
1,000-and above	13	72	56.2	64.9	23.3	17.2
Coal-Fired Plants						
300-499	93	746	56.8	70.2	18.9	14.5
500-699	97	618	57.6	70.0	19.6	13.9
700-899	34	241	59.1	65.4	26.2	12.8
900-and above	16	115	60.6	69.9	20.9	12.8

[a]The equivalent availability factor is defined as the fraction of a given operating period (one year) that a unit is available for service less the time the unit is out of service for scheduled or forced (unanticipated) outages.

[b]The forced outage rate (FOR) represents that fraction of total time the unit was unavailable due to unanticipated equipment failure (hours the unit was in service plus hours the unit was out of service, not including scheduled maintenance time).

Source: U.S. Department of Energy, Energy Information Administration, Office of Coal, Nuclear, Electric and Alternate Fuels, Projected Costs of Electricity from Nuclear and Coal Fired Plants, Vol. 1, August 1982, p. 20.

the increase in U.S. nuclear and coal-fired power plant construction costs are more stringent and greater quantities of regulations, codes, and standards."[38]

Construction schedules have been delayed by the longer time required to obtain regulatory approval and by the increasing number of local, state, and federal agencies, whose approval is required to get a plant on line. Government regulatory agencies have expanded their requirements in the areas of safety and the environment leading to additional plant features and design requirements. Thus the emergence of longer design and construction schedules due to the increasing detail and complexity of plant construction, as well as due to lengthier permitting and licensing stages, has led to ever increasing time-dependent costs. For instance, in 1978, just a one-year delay in the construction schedule of a two-unit 2,000-MWe nuclear power plant added $170 million to the total cost of the plant.

The 1970s and especially the time interval from 1973 to 1979, witnessed a veritable explosion of regulatory requirements issued by the NRC, the Environmental Protection Agency (EPA), and the Occupational Safety and Health Administration (OSHA). This in turn has led to a very sharp growth in the number of standards for nuclear power applications--the full impact of which will be keenly felt over the coming years. Estimated costs of nuclear plants will continue to escalate as these new standards are actually applied to plants being designed and constructed in the first half of the 1980s (see Figure 4-3).

Construction schedule slippages, caused by more stringent and greater volume of regulations, codes, and standards, as well as by strikes and other problems, have sharply increased interest and escalation costs during the decade of the 1970s. A nuclear plant that went into commercial operation in 1973-75 would take about seven and a half years to complete. It took about one and a half years to prepare, and for the NRC to review, the application for a construction permit and another six years for actual construction and power ascension. For plants completed in 1978-82 the overall nuclear project schedule has been extended to 13 years, of which the construction and power ascension phase took about 10 years. A total of three years were required for the preparation and review of various licensing documents. In 1974, less than one third of the time required for the completion of a nuclear project was devoted to preparation, public hearings, and review of licensing documents; by 1981, almost one half of the project's duration was spent on such activities. Overall

FIGURE 4-3. Impact of Regulations, Codes, and Standards on Capital Costs

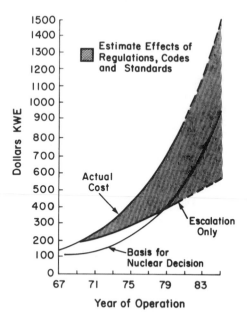

Source: U.S. Department of Energy, *A Review of the Economics of Coal and Nuclear Power*, September 1981, p. III-24.

schedule delays whether due to regulatory-, engineering-, or construction-related causes, are of increasing importance in causing cost escalation of nuclear power plants.

The overall length of nuclear plant schedules increased by about 70 percent between mid-1974 and 1980. An important consequence of the above-noted delays has been to shift the cost sensitivity of nuclear plant construction from the cost of equipment to the cost of credit--that is, to interest rates. The pressure to lower costs on time-related factors, rather than on hardware, will continue to be a major concern for the industry in the future.

A Comparison of Total Generating Costs
for LWR and Coal Plants

The following tables contain estimates of power-generating costs for both nuclear and coal-fired electricity-generating plants. The data reported in Table 4-4 indicate that nuclear plants show slightly lower average generating costs than coal-fired plants. However, given the uncertainties in cost projections inherent in such comparisons, one can conclude that the cost of power generation from these two sources is roughly of the same order of magnitude.

A more recent study by the Department of Energy examines the comparative economics of nuclear and coal-fired generating plants for new plants expected to begin commercial service in 1995.[39] The choice of the year 1995 is crucial because it roughly coincides with the time horizon

TABLE 4-4. Projected Base Load Generating Costs for Plants Coming on Stream in 1990 (mills/KWh, 1978 dollars)

Cost Factors	Nuclear	Coal
Capital charges[a]	15.4 ± 3.3	12.9 ± 2.9
Operations and maintenance	2.0 ± 0.6	3.5 + 2.5
Fuel		- 1.5
U_3O_8	3.2 + 3.0	12.0 ± 3.0
Conversion to UF_6	0.1 ± 0.02	
Enrichment	2.0 + 0.5	
	- 1.5	
Fabrication	0.5 ± 0.1	
"Back end" costs (i.e., spent fuel storage and waste management and, in the event of reprocessing, including credit for recovered Pu and U)	0.8 ± 1.5	
Decommissioning	0.02 + 0.10	
	- 0.015	
Total[b] (U.S. average)	24 + 5	28 ± 5
	- 4	

[a]Based on costs of 730/KWe and 610KWe for nuclear and coal generation respectively, assuming in the nuclear case two 1,150 MWe units and in the coal case three 800 MWe units with flue gas desulfurization. Capacity factors of 0.65 for both coal and nuclear and a capital charge of 12 percent are assumed.

[b]These are bus-bar costs. The charge to the consumer could be 50 to 200 percent higher, because of distribution costs and the need for high cost peak power.

Source: Hans M. Landberg et al., Energy: The Next Twenty Years, (Cambridge, Mass.: Ballinger, 1979), p. 419.

required to bring a new nuclear plant (with its lead times of 11-13 years) on line, starting with an initial investment decision taken in 1982-83.

The comparison is in terms of "levelized bus-bar costs," which represents the average cost of producing electricity over the 30 years assumed life span of a nuclear or coal-fired plant, but it does not include the cost of transmission or distribution to final users.[40]

The levelized bus-bar cost of electricity includes the following:

1. *Capital-related costs*, which in turn are subdivided into the following:

--plant construction costs, including allowance for interest on funds used during the construction period;

--the investments required for refurbishing the plant's major components during its economic life;

--the sum of income taxes, property taxes, and insurance paid throughout the plant's economic life; and

--the end-of-life disposal cost of the plant.

2. *Operation and Maintenance (O&M) Costs.* O&M costs consist primarily of the largely fixed salaries and wages paid to on-site personnel. Other O&M costs are "variable," that is, they are a function of the plant's output and they consist primarily of materials, lubricants, and certain equipment required for continuous operation of the plant. Federal Energy Regulatory Commission data show that O&M costs have been increasing at 12 percent per year in *real* terms, since 1975.[41] These trends are the result of the increase in equipment size, the complexity of the newer and larger generating units, and the associated reduction in plant availabilities. The largest increase in nuclear O&M costs occurred in 1979 and 1980 as a direct result of the aftermath of the Three Mile Island (TMI) accident.

3. *Fuel costs.* Fuel accounts for most of the *variable* cost for both nuclear and coal-fired plants. The fuel cost of a coal-fired plant consists of the costs of purchasing coal and then transporting it to the site of the power plant. For a nuclear plant, fuel costs are those expenses associated with the purchase of uranium oxide, of processing it into fabricated fuel, and finally the management of spent nuclear fuel. The cost of

nuclear fuel is projected to increase at a modest 0.8 percent per year through 1995, while the price of coal delivered to electric utilities is expected to rise by 3.3 percent per year in real terms.

Table 4-5 summarizes the comparative cost estimates for a single 1,200-MWe nuclear power plant and a competitive coal-fired power plant as projected by EIA for the ten federal regions of the country. All bus-bar costs are represented in levelized constant 1980 dollars based on 30 years of plant life.

These projections indicate that nuclear plants enjoy a small cost advantage over a comparable coal-fired plant in New England (8 percent) and in the South Atlantic Region (6 percent). On the other hand, coal-fired plants have a significant cost advantage over nuclear plants in the Southwest and the North Central Region (of 27 percent).

Finally, for most of the country, coal-fired and nuclear power costs are projected to be within 5 percent of each other. For example, total generating costs in the Central Region (consisting of Iowa, Kansas, Missouri and Nebraska) are very close--42.5 mills per KWh for nuclear and 42.9 mills per KWh for coal.

The large cost advantage enjoyed by coal-fired electrical plants in the Southwest and the North Central Region is attributed to the very low coal prices projected for these two regions. In all regions of the country, oil- and gas-fired plants are not economically viable alternatives to nuclear or coal-fired plants operating at baseload. The Department of Energy study concluded: "Nuclear power can assure its place as a competitive generating option in all regions of the nation, except in the areas where coal fields are closely situated to demand centers, *given* a more favorable regulatory environment, stabilized construction requirements, and lower interest rates."[42]

Given that new baseload generating stations cost billions of dollars to construct and hundreds of millions of dollars to operate each year, it is essential that they produce as much electricity as possible during their operating lifetime. This is especially important for nuclear power plants. At plant capacity factors above 65 percent, nuclear plants would remain competitive with coal-fired plants in most regions of the country.

Finally, electrical utilities are presently at a critical juncture in this country. In addition to high inflation and high interest rates, their problems are compounded by their

TABLE 4-5. Comparative Costs for Nuclear and Coal-Fired Power Plants

	Region I		Region II		Region III		Region IV		Region V	
	Nuclear	Bit Med* Coal (1.3)	Nuclear	Bit Med Coal (1.3)	Nuclear	Bit Med Coal (1.3)	Nuclear	Bit High Coal (3.0)	Nuclear	Bit High Coal (3.0)
Construction cost (dollars/KWe)	1,575	930	1,660	965	1,505	930	1,445	900	1,585	960
Fixed charge rate (percent/year)	10.71	10.46	10.71	10.46	10.71	10.46	10.71	10.51	10.71	10.51
Fuel price (dollars/million Btu)	0.79	2.61	0.79	2.27	0.79	2.03	0.79	2.26	0.79	1.98
Levelized cost (mills/KWh)										
Capital	29.6	17.1	31.2	17.7	28.3	17.1	27.2	16.6	29.8	17.7
O&M	4.9	4.0	5.3	4.0	5.1	4.0	4.9	5.3	5.2	5.3
Fuel	8.5	25.7	8.5	22.4	8.5	20.0	8.5	22.2	8.5	19.4
Total	43.0	46.8	45.0	44.1	41.9	41.1	40.6	44.1	43.5	42.4

	Region VI		Region VII		Region VIII		Region IX		Region X	
	Nuclear	Lig Med Coal (1.3)	Nuclear	Sub Low Coal (0.3)	Nuclear	Lig Med Coal (0.8)	Nuclear	Bit Low Coal (0.3)	Nuclear	Bit Low Coal (0.3)
Construction cost (dollars/KWh)	1,445	950	1,530	920	1,520	995	1,635	990	1,640	955
Fixed charge rate (percent/year)	10.71	10.00	10.71	10.45	10.71	10.00	10.71	10.48	10.71	10.48
Fuel price (dollars/millions Btu)	0.79	0.83	0.79	2.26	0.79	0.93	0.79	2.39	0.79	2.63
Levelized cost (mills/KWh)										
Capital	27.2	16.7	28.8	16.9	28.6	17.5	30.8	18.2	30.8	17.6
O&M	4.9	4.4	5.2	3.6	5.2	3.9	5.5	3.5	5.5	3.5
Fuel	8.5	8.4	8.5	22.4	8.5	9.6	8.5	9.6	8.5	25.4
Total	40.6	29.5	42.5	42.9	42.3	31.0	44.8	44.8	44.8	46.5

*Figures in parentheses represent pounds of sulfur per million Btu as indication of coal quality. Coal types are indicated as bituminous ("bit"), subbituminous ("sub"), or lignite ("lig"), with relative sulfur content of low ("low"), medium ("med"), or high ("high"). The heat rates (Btu/KWh) assumed for nuclear and coal-fired power plants are as follows: nuclear, 10,700; coal-fired Bit Low, 9,652; Bit Med, 9,857; Bit High, 9,817, Sub Low, 9,856; Lig Med (0.8), 10,276; Lig Med (1.3), 10,156.

Notes: All costs in equivalent 1980 constant dollars levelized over 30 years of plant operation beginning in 1995 at an average annual capacity factor of 65 percent.

	Region	States
I	New England	Connecticut, Maine, Massachusetts, New Hampshire, Rhode Island, Vermont
II	New York	New Jersey, New York
III	New Jersey	
III	Middle Atlantic	Delaware, District of Columbia, Maryland, Pennsylvania, Virginia, West Virginia
IV	South Atlantic	Alabama, Florida, Georgia, Kentucky, Mississippi, North Carolina, South Carolina, Tennessee
V	Midwest	Illinois, Indiana, Michigan, Minnesota, Oklahoma, Wisconsin
VI	Southwest	Arkansas, Louisiana, New Mexico, Oklahoma, Texas
VII	Central	Iowa, Kansas, Missouri, Nebraska
VIII	North Central	Colorado, Montana, North Dakota, South Dakota, Utah, Wyoming
IX	West	Arizona, California, Hawaii, Nevada
X	Northwest	Alaska, Idaho, Oregon, Washington

Source: U.S. Department of Energy, Energy Information Administration, Office of Coal, Nuclear, Electric and Alternate Fuels, Projected Costs of Electricity from Nuclear and Coal-Fired Power Plants, vol. 1, August 1982, p. 30.

inability to get new plants into service, and by state regulation of electricity rates, which is causing utility revenue increases to lag behind cost increases, resulting in earned rates of return that are less than the current cost of capital. In many instances state regulators do not allow the costs of new plants (while still under construction) to be reflected in the rate base until the plant is actually commissioned. Given those financial constraints utilities have a difficult time in providing the necessary cash flow to finance large nuclear construction programs.

As we have noted earlier, since 1978 no new domestic orders for nuclear plants have been placed; furthermore, 91 nuclear plants have been canceled over the last decade. The reasons for these developments are complex, but they include a projected reduction in the growth of electricity demand, a decision by utilities to reduce the resulting surplus of reserve generating capacity, and the increasing costs of new plant construction combined with the financial squeeze utilities find themselves under. The lengthening of construction lead times must be avoided if nuclear power is to remain cost competitive. While economic factors are not the sole criteria for nuclear power development, higher construction costs associated with longer lead times are a substantial obstacle and unless they are controlled the outlook for a resurgence in nuclear plant orders is not favorable.

A recent report noted that each time actual coal and nuclear construction experience is reviewed there is the hope that costs have finally stabilized, and that future increases will broadly reflect the overall inflation rate. The authors go on to interject the following cautionary note: "The economic viability of the nuclear option in the United States is threatened by uncontrolled regulatory and institutional factors as opposed to insolvable technical issues. Pursuit of the unattainable goals of zero risk and legal proof of perfection has had a paralyzing effect on effective engineering and construction management."[43]

NUCLEAR REACTOR SAFETY ISSUES:
THEIR IMPACT ON THE FUTURE OF NUCLEAR POWER

Most prominent among the factors that will determine the future viability of nuclear power in the United States are safety, environmental, and nuclear proliferation issues. In the aftermath of the TMI accident there has been increased concern and awareness of the safety aspects of nuclear reactors. The accident itself has been unquestionably the most thoroughly investigated and reported (by the media) nuclear accident in history.[44]

The nuclear reactor at TMI, and other LWRs, use the nuclear fission process as a source of heat to generate steam used to operate turbines, which then spin the generators. LWRs use slightly enriched uranium dioxide as fuel and water as coolant and moderator. The uranium dioxide is in the form of ceramic pellets sheathed in twelve-foot long zircalloy tubes. The core is contained within a steel pressure vessel, which itself is housed in a large containment structure. If a fuel rod melts because of inadequate cooling, all the gaseous and volatile fission products would be released from the UO_2 pellets. The release of substantial amounts of radioactive materials into the environment would imply the melting of fuel elements. Such an event can occur only after the water coolant that removes heat from the core has been lost.

Potential cooling problems could range from small leaks in the primary cooling system's piping to a rupture of the reactor pressure vessel--the structure that contains the twelve-foot-high nuclear core. A "loss of coolant" accident typically begins with a rapid loss of system pressure and ejection of coolant from the reactor pressure vessel. At some point, the burning of the fuel cladding in water would itself become a significant heat source as temperatures rise above 2,100° F. The core heats up rapidly and if no emergency cooling is provided, temperatures could quickly increase from 600° F to 3,000° F. The melting point of the uranium oxide fuel is about 5,200° F.

Therefore, if the loss-of-coolant is not contained in time by effective injection of emergency cooling water, an uncontrolled meltdown could take place within minutes of the accident. If the safety provisions engineered into the system fail and the core melts, rupture of the containment vessel would take place for a number of reasons including steam explosion. In a commercial LWR, the explosive power that would be unleashed if the heat of the entire molten core were instantaneously transferred to the surrounding water is equivalent to about 10 tons of TNT.

The Shadow of TMI

The Three Mile Island accident began in the early morning hours of March 28, 1979, when several water pumps shut off in the TMI Unit-2 power plant. Thereafter, pressure from expanding hot water built up in the reactor. A relief valve promptly opened to release the pressure, and the fission process was thereby automatically halted. But then, instead of closing after reactor pressure had decreased, the relief valve remained open for more than two hours. Radioactive water flowed out of the reactor and was inadvertently pumped into an auxiliary building. The emergency core cooling system, as it was designed to do, started pumping water into the reactor core, about two minutes after the accident began. The operators of the TMI plant did not know that water was escaping from the stuck valve and proceeded to shut off most of the water flowing from the emergency cooling system. They were unaware that the loss of reactor cooling water would expose the core and cause it to overheat to the point where the uranium fuel could melt through the reactor vessel and under the worst circumstances, could release large amounts of radioactive materials into the environment. Radiation levels rose in the containment and auxiliary buildings, and three hours after the accident started were increasing throughout the plant.

Experts investigating the mishap were in agreement that most of the air-borne radioactivity released into the environment came from the water that flowed into the reactor coolant system and then continued to flow from the containment building into the auxiliary building. From the beginning of the accident, plant operators did not fully understand what was taking place and consequently were not able to gain control of the situation as it was developing. Furthermore, there were delays in informing local and state officials about developments at the plant; and the public was given confusing and at times erroneous reports regarding the existence of a potentially explosive "hydrogen bubble" in the reactor system.

Just now, more than three years after the accident, the extent of the damage to the reactor core is becoming apparent.[45] While no appreciable amount of radioactive materials actually escaped from the plant and into the surrounding environs, an accident that started as a minor mishap, threatened to cause very serious damage indeed. The various studies of the TMI accident concluded that the radioactive releases occasioned by the accident will have negligible or no effect on people's physical health.

Population dose estimates and the potential health effects resulting from the TMI accident based on four different studies are summarized in Table 4-6. The president's commission investigating the accident (chaired by John Kemeny) and the utility's contractor, using different methods of inquiry, both concluded that the radioactive materials released at TMI were minute and posed a minimal risk to people who live and work around TMI. The maximum dose that any individual located near TMI could have been exposed to was estimated to be 100 millirems. By way of comparison, an individual living in Harrisburg, Pennsylvania, receives routinely about 116 millirems each year from natural background radiation. Thus the most serious health effect observed was the severe mental distress, which was short-lived in all groups except TMI workers themselves.[46]

Several investigations conducted in the aftermath of TMI concluded that the accident resulted from a sequence of events more severe than the system was designed to handle. Specific design deficiencies were identified, and most significantly it was discovered that the NRC did not have an adequate plan in place to identify and address such design problems. Specifically, it was recommended that the NRC require additional power plant features to mitigate the effects of core-meltdown accidents.[47]

NRC's licensing review places primary emphasis on those items labeled "safety related." However, a clear distinction between "safety" and "non-safety" related systems is hard to make since the interaction between the two is extensive. For example, the TMI accident was triggered by a failure of a "non-safety" item, and it was made worse by a relief valve that became stuck open and by misleading instrumentation.

Since TMI, the Nuclear Regulatory Commission has expressed greater interest in the safety-related interaction among various plant systems, and in identifying these supposedly "non-safety"-related items that should be given higher priority than was the case in the past. The TMI studies found that both the nuclear industry and the NRC failed to consider the needs of reactor operators and other personnel, in the design of present day reactors. Rather, the NRC chose to believe that *designed* safety systems could be relied on for the safe operation of reactors, without the need to depend on human performance and judgment. The NRC placed greater emphasis on ensuring that accidents do not happen, and if one did, seeing to it that the design could handle it with little or no operator intervention.

The analysis of the TMI accident identified control room design and instrumentation-related problems as major factors in the accident. Besides requiring the addition of specific TMI-related instrumentation, the NRC has directed utilities to review and upgrade their control room design and instrumentation. As a condition for receiving new operating licenses, the NRC now requires utilities to perform a full design review of the control room itself.

TABLE 4-6. Estimated Offsite Doses and Potential Health Effects as Result of TMI Accident

Study Group	Maximum Dose to Individual[a] (millirem)[b]	Maximum Thyroid Dose[a] (millirem)[b]	Total Population Dose[c] (person-rem)	Non-Fatal Cancers	Fatal Cancers	Genetic Ill Health	Total Health Effects	Normally Expected Cancer Cases in TMI Population
Ad hoc inter-agency dose assessment	100[d]	5	3,300	1[d]	1[d]	1[d]	2	541,000
Presidential commission	70	6.9	2,000[e]	1[de]	1[de]	1[d]	1.5[f]	541,000
NRC special inquiry	100	--[g]	2,000	1[de]	1[de]	1[d]	1.5[f]	541,000
Utility	76	9.8	3,500	--	--	--	--	--

[a] The maximum radiation dose which could have been received by a hypothetical individual from the accident.
[b] A rem is a unit of radiation dose. A millirem is 1/1,000 of a rem.
[c] The total population dose is the sum of the individual doses received by the population in a given area. It is calculated by multiplying the average dose per person by the number of persons in the population. ("Collective dose" is a synonym for "Population dose.") The unit of population dose is the person rem.
[d] Less than.
[e] Includes a correction for the protection afforded by shelter.
[f] Zero not excluded.
[g] Not available.

Source: U.S. General Accounting Office, Three Mile Island: The Most Studied Nuclear Accident in History (Washington, D.C., September 9, 1980), p. 7.

The accident also raised serious questions regarding the ability of utilities to ensure the safe operation of nuclear power plants and their reactions when emergency conditions arise. These concerns arose from the operators' seeming inability to cope with the unexpected events that unfolded at TMI. As has been widely reported, the qualifications and training of TMI personnel were deficient and thus contributed to the seriousness of the accident.

In general, both the NRC and the nuclear industry have neglected and underestimated the importance of having well-trained plant operators during an accident. To solve these problems, a number of steps were recommended and adopted to upgrade the qualifications of plant operators and to improve the quality of utility training programs in general. In addition, the nuclear industry itself has taken steps to improve the quality of plant operators and of utility training programs. The industry, cognizant of the fact that it has the most to lose should another serious accident take place, is attempting to play a greater role in determining safety-related criteria. It has formed an organization to monitor nuclear operations, to review and analyze all existing training programs, and to establish educational and training requirements for all plant personnel.

Overall, operator performance has improved since TMI as a result of extra training and more stringent federal licensing tests. The NRC and the industry now stress the importance of well-trained and properly motivated people to the safe operation of nuclear power plants.[48]

The accident also brought to the public's attention some of the organizational, managerial, and regulatory problems that have plagued the NRC for quite some time.[49] The NRC has the final authority in certifying the safety of U.S. nuclear power plants. As part of this process, the NRC has to weigh the benefits and the costs (risks) of nuclear power. However, no clear guidelines exist as to how much weight ought to be given to the benefits as compared to the risks.

One of the major criticisms of the NRC concerns its refusal (or perhaps inability) to determine what constitutes a desired level of safety in nuclear power plant design and operation. For example, it may be possible to use probabilistic risk assessment methods to establish an acceptable safety standard and then set actual reactor designs and performance against those standards. It appears reasonable that the NRC, subject to congressional and public review and oversight, should be the *principal* body responsible for establishing an acceptable level of safety for nuclear plants, but this task still remains undone.

The president's commission that investigated the TMI accident found "serious inadequacies" in both the licensing and the inspection and enforcement functions of the NRC. As regards safety issues, the Kemeny commission noted, "NRC's primary focus is on licensing and insufficient attention has been paid to the ongoing process of assuring nuclear safety." An important example of this is the case of "generic problems"--that is, problems that apply to a number of different nuclear power plants. Once an issue is labeled "generic," the individual plant being licensed is not responsible for resolving the issue prior to licensing. That, in itself, would be acceptable if there were a strict procedure within NRC to assure the timely resolution of generic problems, either by its own research staff or the utility or its suppliers. However, the evidence indicates that labeling of a problem "generic" may provide a convenient way of postponing decision on a difficult question.[50] The report went on to criticize the NRC for not applying new safety standards to previously licensed plants; for relying "too heavily" on the industry's own records for its inspection and enforcement activities; and for being too heavily equipment-oriented as opposed to being people-oriented and for overall poor management. As a result of its analysis, the Kemeny Commission concluded that fundamental changes were necessary in the NRC's organization, procedures, practices, and most importantly, its attitude.

President Carter, while not proposing a total restructuring of the NRC, did implement a number of changes that substantially strengthened the role of the NRC chairman, while maintaining the overall authority of the commission for policy formulation, rule making, and adjudication.

Consequently the commission is now free from day-to-day management tasks and at least in theory can concentrate its efforts on safety issues and on overseeing and directly participating in major licensing decisions--an area that has been somewhat neglected in the past.

Since TMI, the Nuclear Regulatory Commission has undertaken to implement the numerous recommendations that have been made after the accident. At the outset the priorities of the agency have been reset with much greater emphasis being placed on finding and correcting deficiencies in the regulatory process and in the design and operation of LWRs. The recommendations pursuant to the various investigations of the accident have been transformed into a workable course of action that is included in a document titled "TMI Action Plan." This plan consists of about 175 discrete tasks along with their schedules and expected costs of implementation. A significant number of these specific actions are behind schedule, some by more than a year. There is also some evidence that the NRC is placing more emphasis on the licensing of new reactors at the expense of safety modification on already operating plants. This might be a short-sighted and counterproductive strategy.

The most important single task facing the NRC, following the setting of its own house in order, is to restore public confidence in the safe and reliable operation of nuclear power plants across the country.[51] This in turn calls for close adherence and good performance with respect to the steps outlined in the NRC's "TMI Action Plan." An internal NRC investigation by its Office of Inspector and Auditor found a ". . . lack of attention to the implementation of the plan. . . . No one seems to be really managing or coordinating the NRC's efforts."[52]

By careful attention to plant design, operator training, and effective enforcement of safety-related rules and standards, and through the cooperative effort by both the NRC and the nuclear industry, the probability of a TMI-like accident can be significantly reduced. If the country is to maintain nuclear power as a safe and environmentally acceptable energy option, it is essential that the measures included in the "TMI Action Plan" be implemented in a timely and cost-effective fashion, thus enabling the industry to get from under the TMI shadow.

At this point mention should be made of the cost--both direct and indirect--associated with the TMI accident. First, there is the direct cost of the TMI-2 cleanup, estimates of which range from $1.1 to $1.6 billion.[53] Second, if the plant is not restored to its pre-accident conditions and is never operated again, there is a large cost of writing-off this asset, minus its scrap or recovery value. Third, there is the added financial burden of replacing the power that was lost not only due to the accident at TMI-2, but as a result of having to shut down the undamaged TMI-1 plant. And last but certainly not least, there is the cost in human lives related to the replacement of the lost generating capacity with power generated from fossil fuels, principally coal. One source estimates that this action alone will result in four additional deaths a month.[54]

The final effect of the TMI accident has been to lower confidence in the nuclear industry on part of the general public. Furthermore, utilities that operate nuclear plants adopted a cautious approach and either shut down or derated their nuclear reactors while the investigations were being conducted. An analysis conducted recently showed that the TMI accident had a pronounced effect on the operation of pressurized water reactors all throughout the Western world. [55]

The argument advanced by the Reagan administration that the root cause of the nuclear industry's difficulties lies in "excessive and unpredictable government regulatory procedures" in this instance appears to be misplaced and dogmatic. This is not to say that room does not exist for streamlining the regulatory process, but it must be done in a way that does not increase the likelihood of serious accidents of the type experienced at TMI while at the same time boosting public confidence in the safety and reliability of nuclear power.

The licensing process has been under attack by the nuclear industry itself, which claims that several finished or almost finished plants are caught in a regulatory bottleneck costing the utilities and their customers dearly. [56] One major proposal for reform would result in the licensing process being changed from a two-stage review to a one-step procedure. The two-stage review requires that before the plant is constructed, the utility submit preliminary plant design and safety information, while final designs are reviewed by the NRC during the second, or operating-license phase of the process. A single-stage licensing process would enable the NRC to review the application and resolve all outstanding safety issues *before* construction begins.

Under the present two-step review process, safety issues are often left unresolved by the NRC until the final stages of the review. A one-step licensing procedure combined with a policy of standardizing plant designs could result in a significant reduction in the time--currently 11 to 13 years--that it takes to get a nuclear plant through the licensing process and into commercial operation.

A one-step licensing procedure would focus on the granting of the initial construction permit to the utility intent on building a nuclear power plant. This streamlined licensing procedure could also involve the standardization of nuclear plant designs, which would cut costs without sacrificing safety. Nuclear power plants would no longer be custom-designed according to utility specifications, but rather utilities would select from among two or three previously approved standardized designs that incorporate in them the safety lessons learned from TMI and from operating experience in general.

The nuclear industry's development in this country involved an unusual degree of variability and diversity. Basically each and every nuclear power plant has been custom-designed and built to unique specifications.[57] The fact that almost every reactor is unique has led to difficulties in verifying the safety of individual plants and in transferring the safety lessons from one reactor to another. It may also have something to do with the long lead times and with sharp cost escalation of nuclear power plants construction.

Some of nuclear industry's problems could be alleviated if the industry, with the active support of the NRC, should move toward a greater degree of standardization in its design, construction, operation, and licensing practices. A minimal level of standardization would entail the adoption of common criteria for performance, reliability standards, and general design principles.

The NRC is presently devoting little time to the issue of nuclear power plant standardization. If this concept is to catch on, the NRC ought to start planning for it now, during a lull in nuclear power development. Presently, the NRC could develop plans for future standardization, including the implementation of one-step licensing.

The adoption of a national safety goal would help the NRC to arrive at consistent and more predictable decisions regarding design changes. As things stand now, the NRC has not issued standards that systematically address the question of an acceptable level of risk for overall plant operation. The absence of a well-defined safety goal-- which might be either qualitative or quantitative--has been identified as a major constraint to an orderly decision-making process as well as an obstacle to public confidence in the licensing and regulatory process. The only means of ascertaining that a nuclear plant has achieved a quantitative safety goal is through the use of probabilistic risk assessment. Under standardization, improved risk assessment becomes possible because increased attention can be given to a few well-defined safety issues rather than many diversified ones.

As we have noted, one major reason that utilities have soured on nuclear power is that it takes up to 13 years to get a nuclear power plant licensed, constructed, and operating. This period can be and should be cut back, but it would take the combined efforts of the nuclear industry, the electric utilities, and the NRC to accomplish this vital task without compromising safety.

A Department of Energy task force has recently proposed a series of nuclear licensing and regulatory reform measures. Based on the task forces' recommendations utilities would have the option of applying to the NRC for a Construction and Operating License (COL) in one proceeding in lieu of the present two-step process under which a construction permit and an operating license must be obtained at different stages of the process. Furthermore, the NRC would be authorized to approve generic designs for entire plants or major subsystems thereof and the utilities would have the option of choosing a plant of preapproved design instead of a custom-designed plant. The task force reckons that this would lead to improvements in safety, and that the associated time and cost savings should be significant.

In connection with the issuance of the nuclear licensing and regulatory reform proposals, Assistant Secretary for Nuclear Energy Shelby Brewer remarked that the adoption of such provisions could shorten by as much as five years the nuclear licensing and construction process. The regulatory reform could result in a possible 20 percent reduction in the cost of electricity from new nuclear power plants.[58]

By strengthening reactor safety *and* reducing the cost of construction, the reform proposals could make nuclear power acceptable once again to the general public.

CONCLUDING OBSERVATIONS

The Nuclear Regulatory Commission staff predicted recently that perhaps as many as 19 nuclear plants currently under construction will be canceled or delayed indefinitely by the utilities that own them. In January 1982, the NRC predicted that 33 new plants would be ready to start up by the end of 1983; however a recent staff study has reduced this number to 23. Beyond these plants there are 19 units presently under construction, due to be completed later in the 1980s, that the NRC staff estimates will likely be canceled. In congressional testimony, former Commissioner Peter Bradford noted, "New orders are not likely without a substantial period of accident-free operation, a general drop in capital costs, a larger rate of growth in electricity demand, viable insurance against the cleanup and perhaps replacement power costs of major accidents, renewed investor confidence and a public willing to have plants sited in some communities."[59]

It is clear that the nuclear power industry today is at a critical juncture; perhaps its very survival is at stake. J. J. Taylor, Vice President and General Manager, Water Reactor Division of the Westinghouse Corporation, offered the following pertinent observations: "Today the nuclear industry stands ready for a dramatic expansion. But continuing the present climate may drastically hamper the capability of our industry to respond in the future. *For no industry can afford to maintain idle capacity for a market that does not exist.*" (Emphasis added.) He went on to note: "Those of us who firmly believe that nuclear energy is essential to America's security and well-being are determined to keep the nuclear option alive as long as possible."[60] Taylor in effect argues that nuclear power has at least some of the characteristics of a "public good" such as national defense, and should be treated accordingly. Under conditions of a national emergency--such as a loss of the entire Persian Gulf oil supply--nuclear power production can be increased rapidly so as to substitute for imported oil in the generation of electric power.

In 1980 the United States generated 11 percent of its electricity from oil, consuming about 1.15 MMb/d of petroleum in the process, slightly less than was imported from Saudi Arabia during the same period. These 1.15 MMb/d could be saved directly and almost immediately saved by substituting nuclear electric power. Furthermore, nuclear power could be also used to generate electric power that can substitute for natural gas, since in the event of a sudden petroleum supply disruption, natural gas would be in great demand for industrial, residential, and commercial use. In 1980 some 3.7 trillion cubic feet of NG was used by utilities for generating electric power. The point is that a significant and quick expansion of nuclear power generation can be attained based entirely on existing capacity and on nuclear projects that are well underway. Without a substantial contribution from nuclear power over the next two decades, it will be more difficult to reduce our dependence on imported oil sufficiently, and thus to reduce the risk of future oil price and supply shocks with all their well-known negative consequences for economic growth and employment. This is even more pertinent for OECD countries other than the United States, in which the 1980 share of oil in electricity generation ranged from over one half in Italy and Ireland to 7 percent in Germany.

Given a national emergency related to the loss of Middle Eastern oil supplies, nuclear power production can provide a margin of safety. Thus the essence of my argument is that the nuclear industry in a very real sense has some of the characteristics of a "public good." Consequently, the provision of nuclear power-generating capacity will be suboptimal from a national point of view, and without some form of government intervention, our collective needs for nuclear power will not be adequately met.

There are no technical reasons why nuclear power in the United States and other OECD countries could not grow more rapidly than at present. However, in addition to slower electricity demand growth, there are a number of other factors that hamper the future prospects of nuclear power. As noted previously, it is essential that the time period required for the design, licensing, construction, and testing of nuclear power plants be shortened *without* compromising safety. The industry believes that with standardized design, a preselected site, and elimination of nonessential regulatory delays, nuclear plants can be placed in operation in a much shorter time period than is currently the case.

I stated earlier that the public distrust of nuclear power, whether "objectively" justified or not, may be the most important uncertainty facing nuclear power today. Public opposition to nuclear power has had an impact on the executive, legislative, and judicial branches of government in many countries, and it also influences utilities in the area of investment policy. This results in longer lead times, higher construction costs, and gradual erosion of competitiveness of nuclear power relative to other energy sources.

A respectable argument can be made that the government should take steps that would lift the clouds of uncertainty that currently hang over the industry. Specifically, the government could undertake to fully insure operators of nuclear plants against liability in the event of a serious accident of the kind that happened at TMI. This means that the federal government's limits on liability in the event of a TMI-like accident be removed. The Price-Anderson Act of 1957 limits liabilities from "off-site" damage and sets up methods for covering claims up to the legal limit. Although both liability and property insurance coverage has grown since 1957, the TMI accident has demonstrated that currently available coverage for on-site damage is clearly inadequate. Some increase in property insurance coverage has taken place since the accident at TMI, but nuclear plants remain woefully underinsured because insurance companies have been reluctant to commit their resources to an industry whose very existence is questioned.

Given such uncertainty as exists today, private firms (utilities) that are risk averse have every incentive to delay investment in new baseload nuclear power-generating capacity. As shown by Arrow and Lind, an appropriate remedy in this case is to transfer part of all of the risk of such an investment decision to the public domain, by providing adequate insurance to current or prospective operators of nuclear power plants.[61]

Two separate bills pending in Congress would provide expanded insurance coverage for the type of damages incurred by the TMI-2 plant owners. House bill 2512 proposes the establishment of a quasi-governmental National Property Insurance Corporation, with mandatory participation by all utilities that own nuclear facilities. Annual premiums paid by the utilities would cover 75 percent of the noninsured costs of TMI-2 cleanup if certain conditions regarding the financial integrity of General Public Utilities Corporation (GPU)--the owners of the TMI plant--are met. Under the cleanup assistance part of the plan, half of the insurance contributions to GPU's cleanup costs would be a grant with the remaining half to be repaid by GPU over some future time period through an increase in premiums.[62]

The Edison Electric Institute board of directors, representing some 200 investor-owned utilities, voted to ask electric utilities nationwide to contribute $192 million in TMI cleanup funds. Also the federal government has increased its contribution from $75 million for R&D expenses projected for three years, by another $48 million to help with water cleanup and core removal.[63]

One previously contentious issue--the question of the management of radioactive waste--has apparently been resolved. Radioactive waste consists of a combination of natural uranium and thorium decay products, fission products, products of neutron activation, and other items with intermediate to very long half-lives. Such radioactive waste materials must be sequestered from the biosphere for as long as the radiation represents a hazard.

Until the late 1970s all plans for waste disposal anticipated that the fuel from LWRs would be reprocessed and that the resulting high-level waste from the reprocessing plants would be solidified and prepared for geological storage, most likely in salt formations. But for political and technical reasons this has never materialized. In the meantime spent fuel from existing nuclear plants was temporarily stored in water basins adjacent to reactors.

It is important though to note that waste management does not present hazards of large consequence. The risk, if there is one, is of slow leakage due to unforeseen contact with water and subsequent possible exposure of people to low levels of radiation. While adequate technical solutions to radioactive waste disposal are at hand (for example, geological disposal) the implementation of such a program will require overcoming some formidable political and institutional roadblocks.

For one there is misunderstanding by the general public of the nature of the problem of waste disposal. This is manifested by hostility in many communities to further investigation of potential disposal sites; it appears that people are under the misapprehension that waste management poses local, high-intensity risk, rather than at worst, widespread low-intensity risk.[64] Solving the political, social, and institutional problems associated with nuclear waste management would constitute an important step forward for the nuclear industry. The chief stumbling block seems to be in devising a reasonable method of balancing national and local interest in such a way that people's concerns are adequately addressed.

Thus it is significant that after a long stalemate the Congress finally passed and the president signed into law a bill that would establish a permanent geological repository for radioactive waste by the mid-1990s.[65] This compromise legislation calls for the Department of Energy to conduct environmental reviews of five potential burial sites and recommend three of them to the president for more detailed study. The president would then recommend to Congress by March 31, 1987, the site to be designated as the first repository, with a second permanent site being chosen by March 31, 1991. The legislation calls for these facilities to be paid for by a one mill per KWh surcharge on power produced by nuclear plants. This user's fee, which the government likely will start collecting by mid-1983, would raise about $400 million in its first year. One can only hope that this legislation will play a positive role in alleviating public apprehension with respect to the issue of radioactive waste disposal.

In conclusion there is some movement, albeit agonizingly slow, in the direction of resolving several of the outstanding problems and uncertainties associated with nuclear power. Delays and uncertainties have diminished the luster that nuclear power once held for firms involved in the development of power stations and those involved in other parts of the nuclear fuel cycle, such as spent-fuel reprocessing. It is well to remember that the extent of the nuclear contribution will directly affect the overall availability of energy and thus prospects for economic growth and employment in the United States and other countries, in the coming decades. Furthermore, a greater contribution from nuclear power can lead to reduced pressure on other energy sources, including petroleum and natural gas.

NOTES

1. From an interview with Shelby Brewer, Assistant Secretary for Nuclear Energy, in *Nuclear News,* December 1981, p. 67.
2. Patrick O'Donnell, "Energy Crisis: Fate of Nuclear Power in U.S. Could Depend on Troubled Project," *Wall Street Journal,* January 8, 1981, p. 1.
3. Jay Mathews, "Pacific Northwest May Face a Long Rainy Day if "Whoops Busts," *Washington Post,* December 29, 1982, p. A2.
4. Edward E. Carlson, John Elorriaga, and George H. Weyerhauser, "A Report on the Economic Impacts of the Alternatives Facing the Region on Washington Public Power Supply System Units 4 and 5," September 1981 (mimeo), p. I-3.
5. Much of the background information is taken from the following sources: Washington State Energy and Utilities Committee, *Causes of Cost Overruns and Schedule Delays on the Five WPPSS Nuclear Power Plants,* vol. I, January 12, 1981, p. 8; Carlson, Elorriaga, and Weyerhauser, "Report on Economic Alternatives."
6. WPPSS has overall responsibility for these nuclear projects, yet the design and actual construction of the five plants lies in the hands of engineering firms and private contractors hired by WPPSS.

Plant	Architect-Engineer	Reactor Supplier	Construction Manager (since 1980)
WNP-2	Burns and Roe	General Electric	WPPSS
WNP-1/WNP-4	United Engineers & Constructors	Babcock & Wilcox	Bechtel
WNP-3/WNP-5	EBASCO	Combustion Engineering	EBASCO

7. In reality recent financing costs have turned out to be higher than those used in the above estimates. See Carlson, Elorriaga, and Weyerhauser, "Report on Economic Alternatives," p. II-4.
8. These projections reflect all elements of costs (including inflation), in addition to the cost increases resulting directly from WPPSS.
9. See Carlson, Elorriaga, and Weyerhauser, "Report on Economic Alternatives," p. 14.
10. The direct service industries are a group of 17 industrial customers, mainly aluminum companies, that have contracts with BPA for direct service. In fiscal 1980, the

DSIs received about 35 percent of BPA's power.

11.   The legislation's official title is "The Pacific Northwest Electric Power Planning and Conservation Act of 1980" (P.L. 96-501, December 1980).

12.   The Federal Base System includes federal hydropower, some of the power of the Hanford reactor, and 30 percent of the Trojan Nuclear plant output. WPPSS nuclear units 1 and 2 plus 70 percent of unit 3 are also part of the system, as are Goodnoe Hills Wind Turbines 1, 2, and 3.

13.   Carlson, Elorriaga, and Weyerhauser, *Report on Economic Impacts,* p. I-5. The quote above appears almost prophetic in view of ensuing developments. As was noted above, WNP-4 and 5 were canceled as of January 1982. Three months later WPPSS suspended work on WNP-1, which is 63 percent completed, effective possibly for five years. Finally the president of WPPSS executive board said recently that the system's board will have to decide in February whether to slow down construction on WNP-3 plant. This 1,250 MWe plant that cost almost $5 billion so far, will apparently require an additional $1 billion to complete. There are lingering doubts whether financing for the completion of this plant can be obtained under present circumstances. The fifth plant, WNP-2, is 94 percent and is scheduled to be loaded with fuel in September 1983. "Washington Public Power May Delay Completion of a Fourth Nuclear Reactor," *Wall Street Journal,* January 12, 1983, p. 7.

14.   These types of contractual arrangements are referred to (in the vernacular) as "Take or Pay" or "Hell or High Water" clauses.

15.   Office of Applied Energy Studies, Washington Energy Research Center, *Independent Review of Washington Public Power Supply System Nuclear Plants 4 and 5, Final Report to the Washington State Legislature,* pp. 53-54.

16.   Washington State Energy and Utilities Committee, *Causes of Cost Overruns and Schedule Delays on the Five WPPSS Nuclear Power Plants,* p. 40.

17.   The following example dramatically illustrates the extent of the management control problem faced by WPPSS. The original contract for concrete placement on WNP-3 and 5 awarded to the Morrison-Knudsen Co. was for $40 million requiring 1.5 million man-hours to complete the project. Based on M-K's estimate (as of 12/80) it will take almost five times as many man-hours to complete the contract at a total contract cost of $214 million, a 435 percent cost overrun. Ibid., p. 33.

18.   Patrick O'Donnell, "Energy Crisis: Fate of Nuclear Power in the U.S. Could Depend on Troubled

Project," *Wall Street Journal*, January 8, 1981, p. 1.

19. Washington State Energy and Utilities Committee, *Causes of Cost Overruns*, p. 5. A 1979 study done for BPA by a private consulting firm criticized WPPSS for inefficient contract auditing procedures and most significantly for a management system unable to control project progress and quality. *Independent Review of Washington Public Power Supply System Nuclear Plants 4 and 5*, p. 38.

20. The Nuclear Regulatory Commission staff predicts that as many as 19 nuclear plants presently under construction will be canceled or delayed indefinitely by the utilities that own them. For example Duke Power Company has canceled the building of two units of its Cherokee nuclear station in South Carolina. See Arlen J. Large, "NRC Sees Utilities Cancelling or Delaying 19 Nuclear Plants Currently Being Built," *Wall Street Journal*, March 15, 1982, p. 20.

21. Using the supply system's budget estimates of $4.7 billion for construction in FY 1982, the *Independent Review* estimated that the capitalization of interest adds $4.2 billion to the total debt issued and increases interest costs by $10.2 billion. *Independent Review of Washington Public Power Supply System Nuclear Plants 4 and 5*, p. 53.

22. Only lawyers are likely to benefit from WPPSS's financial woes. There are reports that various parties in the growing number of lawsuits are trying to settle responsibility for the $2.25 billion debt out of court before the case goes to trial. Once begun, a trial could drag on for so long that the supply system would run out of money. Trial to resolve the issue was postponed at least till March 1983 by a State Supreme Court decision to review pretrial rulings. "Pacific Northwest May Face Rainy Day if Whoops Busts," *Washington Post*, December 29, 1982, p. A-2.

23. It is indicative of the state of the industry that the Department of Energy highlights the fact that no nuclear plants were canceled in the second quarter of 1982 as compared to seven cancellations during the first quarter of 1982. Department of Energy, Energy Information Administration, *Monthly Energy Review*, September 1982, p. 75.

24. U.S. Department of Energy, *Energy Projections to the Year 2000 July 1982 Update*, August 1982, p. 7-3.

25. International Energy Agency, OECD, *World Energy Outlook* (Paris, 1982), pp. 333-35.

26. International Energy Agency, OECD, *World Energy Outlook*, p. 352.

27. From 1977 to 1981, average consumption per res

idential customer has fallen from 15,592 KWh to 14,097 KWh, a decline of 9.5 percent. See TVA, *Review of the TVA Load Growth/Plant Construction Situation,* January 1982.

28. By way of comparison, demand for electricity in the Pacific Northwest is projected to grow between 1 and 2 percent per year in the 1980-2000 period. The growth of electrical consumption is expected to be relatively slow until the mid-1980s and somewhat more rapid thereafter. See Washington Energy Research Center, *Independent Review of WPPSS Nuclear Plants 4 and 5; Final Report to the Washington State Legislature,* March 1982, p. 9.

29. This background narrative relies heavily on Robert Perry et al., *Development and Commercialization of the Light Water Reactor, 1946-1976* (Santa Monica: Rand Corporation [R-2180-NSF], June 1977).

30. For a brief technical explanation of the working of the light-water reactor refer to Samuel McCracken, *The War Against the Atom* (New York: Basic Books, 1982), ch. 1.

31. Robert Perry et al., *Development and Commercialization of the Light Water Reactor,* p. XVI.

32. W. E. Mooz, "Cost Analysis for LWR Power Plants," *Energy,* VI, 3 (March 1981), pp. 197-225.

33. W. E. Mooz, *A Second Analysis of Light Water Reactor Power Plants,* Rand Corporation (R-2504-RC), December 1979, p. 32.

34. Mooz, "Cost Analysis for LWR Power Plants," p. 223.

35. Capacity factor is the ratio of the kilowatt-hours of electricity generated during a given time period to the rated generating capacity of the plant multiplied by the number of hours in the period.

36. Charles Komanoff and Nancy A. Boxer, *Nuclear Plant Performance/Update: Data Through December 31, 1976,* Council on Economic Priorities, 1977, p. 10.

37. Reprinted in Ford Foundation, *Nuclear Power Issues and Choices* (Cambridge, Mass: Ballinger, 1977), p. 120.

38. U.S. Department of Energy, *A Review of the Economics of Coal and Nuclear Power,* September 1981, p. III-24.

39. U.S. Department of Energy, Energy Information Administration, Office of Coal, Nuclear, Electric and Alternate Fuels, *Projected Costs of Electricity from Nuclear and Coal-fired Power Plants,* vol. I, August 1982.

40. The "bus-bar" costs represent the cost per kilowatt-hour of producing electricity at the power plant, and it includes the cost of debt service on capital invested

in the plant, plus the cost of operating, maintaining, and fueling the plant on a daily basis. The "levelized bus-bar costs" are obtained by converting the present value of the power plant's cost into a fixed annual charge over its economic life, and then dividing the annual charge by the number of kilowatt-hours of energy the plant is expected to produce. The result is the levelized bus-bar costs, measured in mills per kilowatt-hour. For further details consult ibid., ch. 2.

41. Ibid., p. 14.

42. Ibid., p. 47.

43. John H. Crowley and Jerry D. Griffith, "U.S. Construction Cost Rise Threatens Nuclear Option," *Nuclear Engineering International,* June 1982, p. 28.

44. Among most prominent reports are *The Report of the President's Commission on the Accident at Three Mile Island, the Need for Change: The Legacy of TMI,* Washington, D.C., 1979; NRC Special Inquiry Group, Mitchel Rogovin, Director, *Three Mile Island, A Report to the Commissioners and the Public,* January 24, 1980; *Report to the Governor's Commission on Three Mile Island,* State of Pennsylvania, February 26, 1980; for a review of those or other studies see U.S. General Accounting Office, *Three Mile Island: The Most Studied Nuclear Accident in History,* September 9, 1980.

45. Initial camera inspection was performed inside the TMI-2 vessels during July and August 1982. Based on what the camera revealed, GPU Nuclear, the plants owner, reached several preliminary conclusions:

--A significant portion of the Unit 2 fuel assemblies was severely damaged during the accident.

--An approximately five feet deep void exists in the upper portion of the core.

--No evidence of melted fuel pellets has been observed, thus far; thus it is not known at this time whether any of the fuel pellets within the core had melted.

--The plenum, a major reactor component just above the core, appeared to be substantially undamaged.

R. L. Freemerman and R. L. Rider, "Taking a Look Inside TMI-2," *Nuclear Engineering, International,* October, 1982, p. 30.

46. For a more general discussion of the health effects of radioactive releases from nuclear reactors see Samuel McCracken, *The War Against the Atom* (New York: Basic Books, 1982), pp. 11-20.

47. For example, this may involve the installation of "controlled filtered venting" systems that would prevent the

containment building from overpressurizing during an accident.

48. Nevertheless, much more needs to be done. Out of the 31 operators at TMI who took a recent federal licensing test, 12 have failed. Nine of those who passed the test incorrectly answered questions about turning off the emergency cooling pumps. See "Many Nuclear-Plant Perils Remain Three Years After Three Mile Island," *Wall Street Journal,* February 26, 1982, p. 29.

49. Criticisms of the government's regulation of nuclear power are not new. An earlier study that evaluated the regulatory performance of the Atomic Energy Commission (AEC) concluded: "The AEC contributed to its own regulatory problems by ignoring changes in public values, by refusing to address some safety questions in a timely fashion, by failing to equip itself with a strong safety R&D capability that responded to regulatory need, and by failing to pace the development and commercialization process at a speed it could handle." Elizabeth Rolph, *Regulation of Nuclear Power: The Case of the Light Water Reactor* (Santa Monica: Rand, June 1977), p. VII. A much more extreme criticism of the AEC is contained in a recent book by Daniel Ford, *The Cult of the Atom* (New York: Simon and Schuster, 1982).

50. Kemeny Commission, *Report of the President's Commission on the Accident at Three Mile Island, the Need for Change: The Legacy of TMI* (Washington, D.C., October 1979), p. 20.

51. A recent study of public perceptions and attitudes toward electric utilities, nuclear energy, and other energy issues noted: "Nuclear energy continues to divide Americans. There is significant national concern that utilities have not been honest with the public about nuclear waste or safety and that the quality of construction of new nuclear plants is less than good." The study goes on to emphasize, "it is significant that the two *key nuclear issues continue to be safety and costs, with each issue sharply dividing Americans.*" (Emphasis added.) U.S. Department of Energy, Office of Policy, Planning and Analysis, *Public Perceptions of Future Electric Supply, Utility Financial Conditions and Related Issues,* November 1982, p. IV and p. 60. Such attitudes toward nuclear power have taken on more ominous and threatening forms in the Pacific Northwest, to wit: ". . . an open rebellion against sky-rocketing electric rates is gathering momentum in Washington, Oregon, and Idaho communities large and small. Jolted by doubling and tripling of electric bills and faced with the prospect of similar stiff hikes this year, customers

are organizing, marching, packing legislature hearings and withholding payment of rate increases." Victor F. Zonana, "Rebellion Breaks Out in the Northwest Over Skyrocketing Electricity Rates," *Wall Street Journal,* March 19, 1982, p. 27.

52. Taken from "Many Nuclear-Plant Perils Remain Three Years After Three Mile Island," *Wall Street Journal,* February 26, 1982, p. 29.

53. U.S. General Accounting Office, *Greater Commitment Needed to Solve Continuing Problems at Three Mile Island,* August 26, 1981, pp. 42-44.

54. Samuel McCracken, *The War Against the Atom,* p. 32.

55. Nigel Evans, "Hidden Costs of the Accident at Three Mile Island," *Energy,* VII, 9 (September 1982): 723-30.

56. After TMI the NRC held up any new licenses for about a year. Later on, moving very deliberately, it approved five licenses for operation (as of mid-1981) of new reactors in Virginia, Tennessee, Alabama, New Jersey, and North Carolina. Except for the North Carolina case there was no local challenge to the licensing of the nuclear plants. Arlen J. Large, "Atomic Snarl: Nuclear Power Industry, and Agency Seek to Speed Procedures for Licensing Plants," *Wall Street Journal,* July 8, 1981, p. 46.

57. Aside from the two major types of light water reactors (BWR and PWR) there are many possible variations in design that could range from minor changes in piping layouts to different numbers of steam generators. Some of the differences stem from the varied designs provided by the four vendors that supply LWR. Other variations in design result from site-specific factors, for example, reactors built in areas subject to earthquakes must be designed for higher reaction loadings for such features as the containment building and mechanical and electrical equipment. For further details consult Congress of the United States, Office of Technology Assessment, *Nuclear Power Plant Standardization Light Water Reactors,* April 1981, Ch. 3.

58. From U.S. Department of Energy, Office of Public Affairs, "Energy Department Considers New Licensing Reform Proposals for Nuclear Power Plant Construction," October 15, 1982.

59. Statement of Peter A. Bradford, Commissioner, U.S. Nuclear Regulatory Commission, in U.S. House of Representatives, *Nuclear Safety--Three Years After Three Mile Island,* March 12, 1982, p. 7. The information on nuclear plant cancellation is contained in ibid., pp. 18-21.

60. J. J. Taylor, "The Potential Contribution from Nuclear Power in an Energy Emergency," Westinghouse Electric Corporation, June 17, 1980 (mimeo), pp. 5-1 and 5-3.

61. Arrow and Lind demonstrated that if the government undertakes a risky investment and spreads it over a large number of people the effect is to reduce substantially the cost of such a risky undertaking, even though the risk would not be optimally allocated among individuals as it would be in an economy with complete markets for claims contingent upon states of the world. For details of the argument see Kenneth J. Arrow and Robert C. Lind, "Uncertainty and the Evaluation of Public Investment Decisions," *American Economic Review,* June 1970, pp. 364-78.

62. The Senate version of the bill (S.1226) would provide all insurance proceeds on a grant basis to GPU-- with no repayment required. Both the House and Senate bills died in the 97th Congress; their fate in the 98th Congress is uncertain.

63. Arlen J. Large, "Fallout: Battle Opens on Paying $1 billion Cleanup Bill for Three Mile Island," *Wall Street Journal,* October 21, 1981.

64. A recent opinion survey conducted by the Battele Memorial Institute showed that people rank nuclear-waste disposal sites along with toxic-chemical waste dumps as a hazard ahead of nuclear plants themselves. Arlen J. Large, "Consensus for Nuclear-Waste Burial Grows, but a Sharp Debate Over Methods Persists," *Wall Street Journal,* June 6, 1982, p. 29.

65. Milton R. Benjamin and Howard Kurtz, "Congress Passes Nuclear Waste Measure," *Washington Post,* December 21, 1982, p. A-5.

Conservation

— 5 —

The Missing Piece of the Energy Puzzle

Few energy experts nowadays would question the value of energy conservation as a major policy option. Conservation now receives recognition as an "energy resource" with regional, national, and global energy policy implications. The successful exploitation of this "new" resource, like the development of any other energy resource, will depend on skillful management from both the private and public sector. Because of limited experience with conservation at the policy level, there is a need to clarify the most advantageous roles the private sector and government can play in order to enhance economic efficiency and societal well-being.

The following sections provide an overview of several energy conservation efforts in the United States, with reference to international examples whenever appropriate. These conservation efforts illustrate two important points: first, the technical details of energy conservation vary greatly; and second, specific conservation programs tend to reflect existing or potential conflicts between economic efficiency and institutional constraints. These two points can be observed in the implementation of regulatory, programmatic, and price-induced conservation measures. These two factors further underscore the need for private sector and public decision makers to identify areas where their combined endeavors will produce the most effective results.

133

ENERGY CONSERVATION
IN THE
PACIFIC NORTHWEST*

On November 12, 1970, Governor Daniel Evans of Washington State delivered an unconventional message to electric
utility representatives attending the Northwest Public Power
Association's first "nuclear symposium." Governor Evans
did not focus his remarks on nuclear power, but instead,
he cautioned that a reassessment of the Pacific Northwest's
energy future was needed--an assessment that included a
careful review of the role of electric power conservation:
"Conservation of energy is not only highly desirable--it is
absolutely necessary. . . . We had better get at the job of
doing something about wasted energy. I suggest research
into how to do things with less electricity, not more."[1]
Governor Evans's words were prophetic, for ten years
later, he became chairman of the Pacific Northwest's first
"independent" electric power planning body, the Pacific
Northwest Electric Power and Conservation Planning Council. One of the Regional Power Council's primary respon-
sibilities is to develop a cost-effective electric power conservation plan.

The Regional Power Council's authority is derived from
the Pacific Northwest Electric Power Planning and Conservation Act of 1980 (Regional Power Act).[2] The Regional
Power Act represents the Northwest congressional delega-
tion's response to the convergence of conflicts over environmental quality, equitable distribution of federal
hydropower, the economic quagmire of thermal power plant
financing, and the uncertainty of electric power demand
forecasts, all of which collectively "deadlocked regional
power planning" in the late 1970s.[3] The act addresses
economic, environmental, social, and political issues, and at
present, it constitutes the most comprehensive and intricate
federal energy legislation in effect.

The Regional Power Act mandates that electric power
conservation receive "resource" status, and Bonneville
Power Administration (BPA) must acquire cost-effective
conservation in the same manner as it would acquire conventional electric power generation resources. Conservation
receives the highest priority for future planning, with a
ten percent cost advantage over the acquisition of other

---

*"Energy Conservation in the Pacific Northwest," was
authored by Darryll Olsen, Office of Applied Energy
Studies, Washington State University.

resources. Renewable resources receive second priority, followed closely by industrial cogeneration measures. Conventional electric power generating resources such as thermal electric plants receive the lowest priority. To ensure uniform energy planning, the Regional Power Council is sanctioned as the Pacific Northwest's dominant electric power planning body and must prepare a comprehensive fish and wildlife enhancement and protection program, a set of model conservation standards, a twenty-year power demand forecast, and a regional power plan by April 1983. The council consists of two representatives from each participating state (Washington, Oregon, Idaho, and Montana) along with a planning staff.

A review of the Regional Power Act's major conservation provisions attests to the congressional attempt to grapple with both economic efficiency and institutional considerations (see Table 5-1). The act's economic and institutional parameters assume major importance given that the region possesses the highest per capita electric power consumption rate in the nation, and hosts 129 public and investor-owned utilities and the Bonneville Power Administration--a federal, wholesale electric power distribution agency. From an economic efficiency perspective, the act offers the region's utilities a "carrot and stick" policy toward adopting conservation measures. The "carrot," in this case, is billing credits and BPA's financial and technical assistance programs. Basically, billing credits are a form of rate rebate. Electrical utilities may have their power bills from BPA reduced by actively adopting conservation measures which exceed BPA requirements. Billing credits will be based on the cost of conservation measures employed and the actual amount of power saved. In addition to billing credits, BPA provides technical and financial assistance programs. These programs include access to technical information and instruction, financial support for local communities to hire energy planners, and financial assistance to utilities to purchase conservation savings. On the other hand, the "stick" is represented by the possible implementation of electric power surcharges to the utilities. Utilities that fail to achieve electric power savings equivalent to the savings achievable via the Regional Power Council's model conservation standards may find a surcharge attached to their wholesale power sales from BPA.[4]

The Regional Power Council represents a new institutional body, which must assess its own actions and success within the constraints posed by the region's public power systems, the investor-owned utilities, and the Bonneville Power Administration. These power actors possess a wide

TABLE 5-1. Major Conservation Provisions of Pacific Northwest Electric
Power Planning and Conservation Act

- In future power planning, the Regional Power Council must give first priority to conservation measures, with a ten percent advantage over other resources.

- Two years after the Regional Power Council is established, it must prepare and transmit to the BPA administrator a regional conservation and electric power plan (the plan may be amended and reviewed not less frequently than once ever five years). The administrator's actions shall be consistent with the plan under most circumstances.

- The Regional Power Council must prepare studies of conservation measures that are reasonably available to the region and consistent with sound business practices.

- Model conservation standards shall be included in the plan that are cost-effective for the region and economically feasible.

- The BPA administrator shall acquire conservation resources consistent with the regional power plan through loans and grants to customers for weatherization, increased system efficiency, cogeneration measures, and energy planning; financial and technical assistance to customers in implementing model conservation standards; and conducting demonstration projects.

- The Regional Power Council may recommend to the BPA administrator a surcharge, and the administrator may impose such a surcharge on BPA customers that fail to achieve energy saving possible through implementing the model conservation standards.

- The BPA administrator shall grant billing credits to customers for independent conservation activities.

- The Regional Power Council shall prepare a report and make recommendations on retail rate designs that will encourage conservation and efficient use of electric power.

- Upon request, the BPA administrator may provide technical assistance to customers in analyzing and developing retail rate structures that will encourage cost-effective conservation.

- The regional power plan, in addition to outlining conservation and other resources, must give due consideration to environmental quality, compatibility with the existing regional power system and fish and wildlife.

Source: Pacific Northwest Electric Power Planning and Conservation Act, 16 U.S.C. 837-839 (1980) [P.L. 96-50].

range of autonomous powers and goals that do not necessarily conform to the mission of the Regional Power Council.
The Regional Power Council's success will depend, to a
large degree, on the perceived ease with which BPA and
the utilities can comply with the council's plans. The
Regional Power Council faces several thorny issues trans-
gressing across public/investor-owned utility service areas
and state and federal jurisdictions.

Until recently, low-cost hydroelectric power dominated
the Pacific Northwest electric power picture, providing little
incentive to consumers or utilities to pursue conservation
measures. But this picture is changing, due to the addition of thermal electric plants to the regional power grid;
and while hydroelectric power still dominates total generation, this new thermal plant addition requires an upward
adjustment of both Bonneville Power Administration wholesale rates and utility retail rates. Consequently, the
theoretical limit for conservation achieved through consumer
price response and programmatic conservation measures is
substantial. Conservation reflects a largely unexploited
resource of approximately 2,800 megawatts or the generation
capacity equivalent to four nuclear power plants the size
now under construction by the Washington Public Power
Supply System (see Table 5-2). This electric power savings is based on regional power demand forecasted to grow
at 1.5 percent average annual rate of growth per year to
the year 2,000.[5]

Electric power savings are expected to occur in response to rate increases resulting from Bonneville Power
Administration wholesale rate increases--to retire the debt
service of WNP-1,2, and 3--and the electrical utilities debt
service and termination costs of WNP-4/5.[6] The conservation programs listed in Table 5-2 are related strictly to
price response and are exclusive of possible programmatic
conservation savings. Conservation savings provided by
price response are generally in the 2 to 35 mills per kilowatt hour range (1980 dollars), with a potential savings of
7,520 million kilowatt hours (800 average megawatts) by the
year 2000.[7]

Programmatic conservation savings listed in Table 5-2
represent savings beyond price induced measures. Programmatic savings would result from incentive programs
designed to limit electric power consumption to a level equal
to the savings possible if retail rates were based on regional marginal costs rather than average embedded costs.
Programmatic conservation could result in an additional
17,340 million kilowatt hours saved by the year 2000.[8]

Table 5-2. Potential Electric Power Conservation Savings in Pacific Northwest

Conservation from Price Response	Average Cost Mills/KWh (1980 $)	Electricity Savings by 2000 (Million KWh)
Energy Hotline	18	320
Weatherization Clinics	14	230
Class "A" Audits	48	180
Appliance Labeling	2	610
Weatherization Loans	20	550
Weatherization Grants	17	280
Shower Flow Restrictors	1	310
Hot Water Tank Wraps	6	130
Tank Wraps for New Homes	3	450
Commercial Building Grants	15	2,010
Institutional Building Grants	2	1,510
Industrial Conservation	15-38	950
Total		7,520
TOTAL: Price Response and Programmatic Conservation		24,860

Collectively, the potential electricity savings acquired through price response and programmatic conservation measures have a significant and perhaps unpredictable influence on existing and future regional power planning. The load forecast/resource balance summary provided in Table 5-3 indicates that, despite the actual rate of load/growth in the region, moderate conservation measures (programmatic conservation) would delay the need for new electric power generation plants. In the case of moderate power demand, the delay could be four years or more. The high cost of thermal power plants and the long lead times necessary to build them require precise planning. Failure to accurately gauge the impact of future conservation programs could result in a formidable economic penalty to the Pacific Northwest.

Existing and Future Conservation Programs

The region's initial experience with conservation has demonstrated that moderate conservation measures are cost-effective, produce jobs locally, and provide decision makers

Programmatic Conservation	Average Cost Mills/KWh (1980 $)	Electricity Savings by 2000
Appliance Rebates[a]	16	2,490
Conversion Fee[b]	0	2,780
New Residential Building Incentives	12	3,910
Conversion Standards	15	470
Commercial Lighting Rebate	7	1,990
New Commercial Building Incentives	25	2,280
Industrial Conservation Measures[c]	15-39	1,670
Transmission and Distribution Loss Reduction	16	1,750
		17,340

(Million KWh) or 2,844 Average Megawatts

[a]Based on moderate electric power demand (1.59% average annual rates of growth).

[b]Conversion fee would apply to dwellings converted to electricity heating system.

[c]Includes utility purchase of energy savings (buy-back programs), PURPA rates, revised rate structures and/or utility rebates for the purchase of energy efficient equipment.

Source: Office of Applied Energy Studies, Washington Energy Research Center, Independent Review of Washington Public Power Supply System Nuclear Plants 4 and 5 (Pullman, Wash.: OAES, March, 1982).

with a "time buffer" to formulate carefully long-term energy policies and programs. Conservation programs already underway have displayed significant electric power savings available from various end use sectors. For example, residential weatherization programs have yielded savings from 30-40 percent on applicable homes--including rental and multi-family housing. In the commercial and public building sector, electric power savings ranging from 20-35 percent have been achieved through energy efficient operation and maintenance practices. Conservation programs in the irrigation sector, while still experimental, have achieved electric power savings from 10-20 percent. And in the industrial sector, energy efficient operation and maintenance practices, combined with cogeneration opportunities, have brought about additional electric power savings.

TABLE 5-3. WSU Electric Power Demand Forecast Assumptions and Options

	Year When Additional
High Demand (2.0% AARG)	Resources Are Needed
Conventional supply[a]	1990
Moderate conservation[b]	1992
All options[c]	1996
Moderate Demand (1.5% AARG)	
Conventional supply[a]	1991
Moderate conservation[b]	1995
All options[c]	2000+
Low Demand (1.2% AARG)	
Conventional supply[a]	1996
Moderate conservation[b]	2000+
All options[c]	2000+

[a]Conventional supply: Electrical power plants planned and under construction, conservation as a result of scheduled electric power rate increases.

[b]Moderate conservation: Includes Conventional Supply, with programmatic conservation savings.

[c]All options: Includes Conventional Supply and Moderate Conservation, with development of moderate levels of additional renewable resources (mostly small-scale hydro).

Source: Office of Applied Energy Studies/Washington Energy Research Center, Independent Review of Washington Public Power Supply System Nuclear Plants 4 and 5. OAES: Washington State University, March 1982.

Bonneville Power Administration holds the key to successful implementation of a systematic, regional electric power conservation program. Given the actual rate of load growth in the region, moderate conservation measures (programmatic conservation) would delay the need for new electric power generation plants. In the case of moderate power demand, the delay could be four years or more. The high cost of thermal power plants and the long lead times necessary to build them require precise planning. Failure to accurately gauge the impact of future conservation programs could have a serious impact on the economy of the Pacific Northwest.

CONSERVATION AT THE TENNESSEE VALLEY AUTHORITY (TVA)

In this section we will examine in detail several of the conservation programs currently offered by TVA and the lessons that the nation as a whole can draw from their experience. The TVA is a corporate agency of the federal government created by a 1933 Act of Congress, with the primary mission of developing the Tennessee river system and other resources of the Tennessee Valley and the adjoining areas. TVA provides electricity to about 2.8 million consumers by selling power wholesale to some 160 municipal and cooperative distributors of electricity in the Tennessee Valley. It also serves directly the needs of 62 very large industrial customers and federal installations.

The goal of efficient use of energy has become an integral part of TVA's operating philosophy. In response to rising energy costs the TVA has started several conservation and load management programs that could save as much as $7.8 billion in operating and building costs by 1990.[9] These programs represent a demand reduction of about 3,950 MW or roughly equal to about four large nuclear plants. The conservation programs, few of which will be reviewed forthwith, are designed to save money for the power system and for electricity users by reducing short run demand for high-cost peak load power, and over the longer haul by reducing or even perhaps eliminating the need to build new and expensive central generating stations. The program will also provide means of rapidly reducing electrical consumption in the event of emergencies such as power plant failures. A brief description of selected TVA conservation programs follows:

The Home Insulation Program

For the twelve-month period ending December 31, 1981, the average residential energy use of TVA customers was 14,030 kwh per year, almost twice the national average. A good deal of this electrical consumption is due to the extensive use of electrical heat in the home, 41 percent of TVA's customers have such heat, compared to only 13 percent nationally. Consumers with electrical space heating used on the average 17,580 KWh during the same period, with an approximate cost of $885 per year to them.

TVA's home insulation program that started in August 1977 has been expanded several times since then. The program provides onsite free inspection of residential dwellings and interest-free loans to finance weatherization schemes. The goal is to weatherize 680,000 homes by 1990; as of March 1982 about a quarter million customers have received weatherization loans of about $200 million. The program is expected to save TVA some 1,110 MW of *peak demand* by 1990, with an attendant benefit to consumers of $115 million saved based on *current* electric rates.

The Heat Pump Program

The electric heat pump is a heating and cooling device that functions like an air conditioning unit, but takes only about half of the electricity required to heat a home as compared to central electric resistance heating. Compared to conventional electric heating and cooling, a heat pump can save a TVA area homeowner an average of $148 per year, once again based on current rates. Low-interest loans for the purchase and installation of a heat pump are available to qualified TVA customers. As of March 1982 about 16,000 heat pumps have been installed and about $52 million of loans have been dispensed under the program. This is a relatively modest program with an expected savings of only 300 million KWh per year by 1990.

Energy Conservation Programs Directed to the Poor

Of the 2.5 million households in the area served by TVA about one-third are officially classified as poverty stricken. They fall below the $8,000 annual income level for a family of four. TVA has targeted several special programs toward this group, with the aim of reducing their energy expenditures and their use of electricity. There is an effort underway to weatherize all the electrically heated public housing units in the TVA service region. As of March 1982, 43,000 units have been surveyed and almost 9,000 insulated under this plan. Another project underway is the so-called warm room project, which allows customers to finance the weatherization of one or more rooms of their home. An effort is also being made to expand the level of participation of landlords in weatherization retrofit measures. Finally, neighborhood weatherization demonstration projects are undertaken in low-income areas at no cost to the participants. TVA is now investigating the possibility of weatherizing entire blocks of low-income housing, without charge to the occupants.

Energy Saver Home Program

The Energy Saver Home program is a voluntary program that "encourages the design and construction of energy efficient new homes." Since 1975 the TVA has had in place something called the Super Saver Home Program, which exhorts consumers to build homes to TVA recommended standards. Homes built to TVA specifications can lower their space heating costs by up to 70 percent and cooling costs by up to 33 percent. This could result in an annual savings of 5,300 kwh to the average user of electricity. Solar and other energy-saving measures could make a further 1,000 KWh reduction possible thereby saving the fortunate consumer another $46 a year. The only fly in this ointment is the fact that to date very few customers have availed themselves of this particular program.

Commercial and Industrial Conservation
and Energy Management Program

TVA offers energy management surveys and low-interest loans to assist commercial and industrial customers--who buy more than half of the power generated by TVA--to implement feasible energy conservation measures. An energy management survey is available to all TVA commercial and industrial customers at no cost to them. For implementation of energy-saving measures the TVA will lend amounts ranging from $1,000 to $100,000 at below market rates. The program is estimated to cost $110 million through 1990, and it is expected to reduce peak demand for electricity by 474 MW.

Beyond these five conservation programs TVA offers alternative energy possibilities, including a Residential Solar Heating Program, a Wood Heater Program, Solar Homes for the Valley Project, Commercial and Industrial Solar Water Heating, and many, many more.[10] The solar homes project is of particular interest. The program involves the design, construction, and monitoring of several *passive* solar homes. The homes are designed to take full advantage of the sun without using mechanical devices for the collection and storage of solar energy. This program is essentially a demonstration project where the performance of some 35 passive solar homes is carefully monitored and recorded. The owner of the house receives a one-time payment of $2,500 for allowing TVA to install monitoring equipment and use his/her home for demonstration purposes. The homes are moderately priced from $33,000 to $73,000. Each home is expected to save from 2,400 KWh to 7,300 KWh of electricity per year as compared to conventional homes.

Homes that incorporate passive solar techniques take advantage of such factors as the angle of the sun at various times of the year, the siting of the house, the shape of the house, and the construction materials. Features such as greenhouses, thermal storage walls, and water storage containers are used first to absorb and then to distribute the sun's heat throughout the house after sundown. Ralph Johnson, president of the National Association of Home Builders' Research Foundation, is certainly nothing if not ebullient about the future of passive solar: "We're very bullish on passive solar technology. We've already seen it take off very rapidly, and if the government provides passive-solar tax credits we could be building a half a million passive homes a year within five years."[11] There are other signs of an emerging new "industry": Mayhill Homes Corporation of Gainesville, Georgia, has designed six relatively inexpensive passive-solar *models* since 1978.[12] The "bottom line" for homeowners is the attainment of considerable savings in heating and air-conditioning expenses. In terms of potential for energy savings, passive solar's added savings on heating amounts to 20 percent or more of the heating requirements of a normal building. Good conservation practices in general can reduce the amount of energy used for heating in conventional homes by perhaps as much as 50 percent. It is estimated that passive solar designs can increase the conservation potential of a house up to 80 percent in the Northwest and up to 90 percent in certain areas of the Southwest and West.[13] The cost of this added increment of energy savings varies based on climate and the site-specific nature of passive solar systems. A rough estimate of the added cost is approximately $4 per square foot of building space, or about 7-10 percent of the purchase price of a new house. The Electric Power Research Institute (EPRI) has a program to assess the effectiveness of passive solar systems and their impact on electric utilities. The study's interim conclusion is that "our results clearly indicate that in some locations of the country, passive design should be a preferred option."[14] Thus it appears that this particular form of energy conservation is here to stay, and it appears to be economically viable with or without government tax credits or other tax subsidies.

In a speech to the Energy and Utilities Committee of the Washington State Senate, the following observation was made by a TVA official: "Certainly, conventional generating plants are still being built, but power producers increasingly are turning to conservation and Alternative Energy sources as a means of meeting some of the public's future energy needs at the lowest possible cost."[15] Conservation is viewed by the TVA as a capital investment in energy efficiency, and as such it is expected to yield the consumer immediate savings in the form of reduced utility bills while maintaining an adequate degree of comfort as judged by the homeowner. As a pioneer in this area, TVA has had the chance to learn important lessons on how conservation programs can be most effectively planned and managed and they are now in a position to share their experience with other utilities. TVA candidly notes, ". . . not all conservation and decentralized energy programs will cost as little or displace as much energy as initially projected."[16] One lesson learned by the TVA was that to run conservation programs effectively requires that a utility "devote some of its best talent to the effort, simply expanding the traditional customer relations department won't get the job done."[17]

Beginning in 1978, there has been a steady *decrease* in the average residential use of electricity in the TVA service area. Once again the bottom line is not conservation per se, but rather conservation that results in substantial savings to the power system in the long run, because *conservation costs the TVA less* than an equal amount of generating capacity in the form of a new nuclear plant. By 1990 TVA plans to eliminate the need for some 3,600 MW of added capacity through a variety of conservation programs at a cost to TVA of about $600 million. (See Figure 5-1.) By comparison, had they had to construct nuclear plants to produce this much power, it would have cost them $8 billion. One can only recommend that utility managers and planners all across the country study the TVA conservation experience carefully so as not to repeat some of the mistakes that a pioneering organization inevitably will make.

ENERGY CONSERVATION: THE ROAD TRAVELED
SO FAR AND HOW FAR DO WE HAVE TO GO?

In its National Energy Policy Plan, the Reagan administration has correctly stated that the American people and

FIGURE 5-1. TVA Load Forecasts, 1982-2000

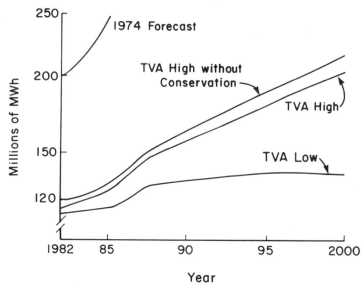

Source: Statement by Robert F. Hemphill, Jr. Deputy Manager of Power, TVA, For subcommittee on Energy Development and Application, House Science and Technology Committee, June 23, 1981.

indeed people everywhere are "responding to market conditions" in terms of their level and pattern of energy consumption.[18] In this section we will examine the record with regard to energy consumption and conservation in the post-embargo period in the U.S. and in other advanced industrial nations.[19] Since the oil embargo of 1973, but especially in the last few years, there has been a marked change in the world oil and energy situation. Largely in response to the sharp run-up of petroleum prices there has been a significant reduction in the use of energy per unit of output in the United States and other affluent countries, and also a marked substitution of non-oil energy resources for oil.[20] As pointed out by the IMF's *World Economic Outlook,* ". . . available evidence indicates strongly that the major factors behind the recent large improvement in energy efficiency and the fall in oil consumption have been the effects of the substantial increases in overall energy prices and the even sharper rise in oil prices in promoting energy conservation and encouraging the substitution of alternative energy sources for oil."[21] Most industrial countries have adopted energy policies that are likely to enhance effectiveness in the use of energy and that also contribute to a reduction in the share of oil in overall energy consumption. But it must be recognized that there are long time lags before the demand (or supply for that matter) for energy *fully* reflects the *changes* in *behavior* that are brought about by higher energy prices. This is so because of the time needed to replace the existing stock of capital with more energy-efficient capital equipment that reflects the higher relative prices of energy. It also takes a long time to develop the capacity for the production of new energy sources to replace petroleum. However, the present trend toward increased efficiency in energy use and interfuel substitution is likely to continue well into the 1980s, even without any *further* increases in the real price of oil and other energy resources.

What has happened to the price of oil and the price of other fuels in seven of the largest OECD countries is clearly and dramatically illustrated in Table 5-4.[22] The price of imported crude oil in real terms has increased at an average annual rate of almost 25 percent during 1973-80, after falling at an average rate of 1 percent a year in the 1960-73 period. Table 5-4 also indicates that there has been a substantial increase in the real prices of non-oil energy resources since 1973. Because of the low short-run elasticities of demand and supply for alternative energy sources, increases in the price of petroleum and petroleum products tend to be matched quite closely by "sympathetic" increases in prices of nonpetroleum products.[23]

Calculations, performed by the International Energy Agency indicate that in the seven largest OECD countries, increases in oil prices in the industrial sector have been followed by an increase in the price of natural gas on an almost one-to-one basis and also by significant increases in coal and electricity prices as well.[24] Thus a given increase in the price of crude oil will cause oil product prices (such as gasoline or heating oil) to rise, which then will be followed by a sympathetic increase in other energy prices.

Energy Consumption by Primary Economic Sectors[25]

For the advanced industrial--or perhaps post-industrial-- countries, energy demand in the industrial sector constitutes the biggest component of total final energy use. For the seven largest OECD economies as a whole energy consumption by industry grew at an annual rate of about 5 percent during the years from 1960 to 1973. However, since the sharp 1973-74 rise in energy prices, there has

TABLE 5-4. Fuel and Energy Price Trends to Final Users for Seven OECD Countries*

	1960	1973	1980	Annual Average Growth Rage (in percent) 1960-73	1973-60
Nominal price of imported crude oil in US$ per barrel CIF	2.53	3.81	32.84	3.2	36.0
Real price of imported crude oil in 1973 US$ per barrel	4.37	3.81	17.66	-1.0	24.5
Industry indices (1973=100)					
Real price of oil	111.40	100.00	268.40	-0.8	15.1
Real price of non-oil fuels	95.40	100.00	199.50	0.4	10.4
Transportation indices (1973=100)					
Real price of gasoline	121.60	100.00	150.90	-1.5	6.1
Residential/Commercial indices (1973=100)					
Real price of oil	110.60	100.00	257.80	-0.8	14.5
Real price of non-oil fuels	109.20	100.00	145.30	-0.7	5.5

*Weighted average after-tax prices for the following countries: United States, Japan, Germany, France, United Kingdom, Italy, and Canada.

Note: The fuel prices presented in this table (as well as in most other tables or graphs in this study) have been collected from both IEA and national data banks. In particular, the new IEA quarterly fuel price survey forms the basis of fuel prices from 1978 onwards. For past years individual country sources and various international studies (such as those undertaken by the EEC on the historical prices for oil, gas, coal, and electricity) have been used in order to create a price data bank, which covers the complete 1960-80 period for the largest OECD countries.

Source: International Energy Agency, World Energy Outlook (Paris: OECD, 1982), p. 80.

been essentially *no growth* in the consumption of energy by industry in this group of seven countries. In fact, the intensity of energy use per unit of output in industry has shown a steady tendency to decline during that period. Between 1970 and 1980 the Energy to Industrial Output ratio has declined by about 3 percent per year, after rising steadily throughout the 1960s. The changes in the energy intensity quotient partly reflects conservation efforts by industry brought about by the sharp rise in real energy prices during the 1970s. But it also reflects changes in the composition of industrial output (for example, a switch from heavy to light or technologically more sophisticated industries), as well as greater efficiency in the use of energy by industry.[26]

The energy intensity quotient of industry has declined most perceptibly in the United States, Japan, and the United Kingdom, although it also fell in other large OECD countries. However, as the IEA's *World Energy Outlook* noted: ". . . insofar as the energy/output ratio indicates gains in energy efficiency, the general trend in all countries is toward improved efficiency since 1970, becoming more pronounced after the oil price rise in 1973 and reinforced (except in Canada) by further price rises in 1979."[27] For the United States, Department of Energy projections indicate that the use of energy per unit of industrial output is expected to decline by 2.2 percent per annum to the year 2000, reflecting the prospects for substantial energy savings made possible by both past and future (expected) increases in the price of energy.[28]

It is possible to cite many cases of successful energy conservation programs in industry and commerce. One good example that is close to (my) home is that of the Boeing Company, whose headquarters and major production facilities are located in the Puget Sound area of Washington State.[29] Boeing, the world's largest manufacturer of commercial jet airliners has designed and is geared to produce a new generation of jets (the 757 and 767), which will use 35 to 45 percent less fuel than the airplanes that they are scheduled to replace. The company has also been engaged in the development and testing of solar wind power systems, and other energy efficient products and processes.

Boeing has had an active conservation program since 1973, and according to the company it has resulted in a 40 percent energy efficiency improvement between 1972 and 1981.[30] Some of the energy-saving steps taken simply involve more energy-thrifty habits on the part of workers and management. Others include weatherization and the upgrading of heating and air conditioning systems. Heat pumps have been designed and installed to convert and recapture wasted heat from computer operations and use it to heat building at the Kent Space Center, thereby replacing oil or natural gas.

One of the newest developments involves the construction of a boiler system at Boeing's Everett (Washington) plant, designed to burn the plant's own refuse and
thereby provide steam and process heat to the company's
assembly plant where the 747 and the new 767 are being
built. This project was undertaken in response to both
energy-saving and cost-cutting needs (garbage is replacing
purchased fuel), as well as the need for alternatives to
traditional refuse disposal sites.

Yet another energy conservation project involves a
cogeneration unit at Boeing's fabrication facility in Auburn.
This facility will be capable of generating 9 megawatts of
electricity for the local utility when completed while providing steam for the factory at the same time. The Department of Energy fully expects the trend toward greater
efficiency in energy use by industry--as exhibited by the
example of Boeing to continue--albeit at a somewhat slower
rate to the turn of the century.

In the residential/commercial sector energy consumption
is dominated by household demand for space heating (or
cooling) and for domestic appliance use. Consumption in
this sector is strongly influenced by the number of dwellings and by the saturation levels reached in domestic
appliance use. Throughout the 1960s and up until 1973,
the energy consumption in the residential/commercial sector
grew at 5 percent per year--in the seven major industrial
countries. During the more recent 1974-80 period this rate
was slightly below 1 percent a year, and in fact in the
United States it even fell by a small amount (by 0.2 percent
a year).

In order to analyze conservation trends in this sector,
we chose to examine the ratio of final energy consumption
to total private consumption expenditure. The amount of
energy used in conjunction with each unit of private consumption was stable from 1960 to 1973, but since 1973 there
has been a continuous and marked decline in this ratio. I
would also add parenthetically that conservation trends in
the household sector take longer to materialize than in other
sectors of the economy, because saturation levels for appliances are reached only slowly and people's behavior, as
reflected in the amount and types of energy they use, also
changes only gradually. Undoubtedly, in the longer run,
higher energy costs do affect changes in people's lifestyles
such as moving closer to work, or moving from single
housing to an apartment, or changing one's vacation habits,
or perhaps bringing about even more fundamental changes
in the patterns of our socialization. But these indeed are
long-term changes, and it may be well into the twenty-first

century before they are fully formed and shaped.

In the residential/commercial sector, higher energy prices tend to foster the design and construction of new and at times innovative structures with much-improved thermal efficiency, and they also lead to the insulation and retrofitting of existing structures. Several examples of such programs were discussed in the previous sections that dealt with the conservation effort in the PNW and at the TVA.[31] Figure 5-2 shows an earth-sheltered house recently built in Eastern Washington (State).

Next, we turn to energy consumption in the transportation sector where almost all of the energy used consists of oil. Within this sector, gasoline accounts for about 85 percent of total energy consumed. One of the significant factors in the transportation sector is that large-scale interfuel substitution in the short run is virtually impossible. However, this does not preclude the possibility of substitution between different modes of transportation. For example, as gasoline prices rise, people can drive less, they can use carpools or public transport more extensively and substitute more fuel-efficient cars for gas guzzlers, and other similar gasoline saving steps.

Gasoline consumption in the seven largest OECD countries has generally followed the growth path of the passenger car fleet. In those countries where car sales have been brisk (such as Japan, Italy, Germany, and France) the rate of growth of gasoline consumption has been also high. In countries where the stock of cars grew relatively slowly (the United States, Canada, and the United Kingdom) so did gasoline consumption. Gasoline consumption is determined to a large extent by the interaction of the following economic, technical, and social factors: fleet size (number of vehicles); fleet efficiency (miles per gallon); and people's driving habits (vehicle-miles traveled per year, per vehicle). Each one of these factors is in turn linked to other variables--for example, fleet size largely depends on economic growth and interest rates; fleet efficiency is tied to technical advances in new cars and to economic considerations as they relate to purchases of new cars; while driving patterns are tied to behavioral and sociological factors such as the use of the automobile to commute to work or for family vacations.

In the seven OECD countries average gasoline consumption per car declined ever so slightly between 1960 and 1973. In the United States on the other hand, during the same period gasoline consumption per car actually increased, by about 3 percent. (See Figure 5-3.) In Japan, the rapid expansion of the automobile industry in the 1960s

FIGURE 5-2. Earth-sheltered house, Wawawai Canyon, Washington State

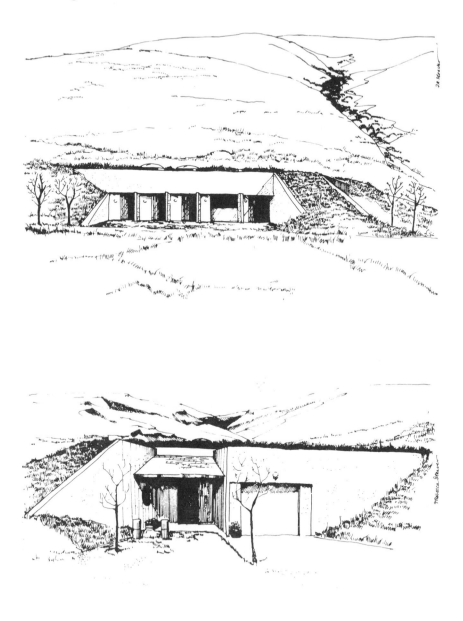

Artist: F. Rebecca Steever.

has led to a large increase in the stock of cars. Most of the new cars, however, are smaller and much more fuel-efficient than the cars they replaced, resulting in a large reduction of the average amount of gasoline used per car.

FIGURE 5-3. U.S. Average Annual Motor Vehicle Mileage and Fuel Consumption

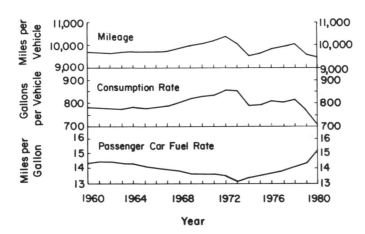

Source: Department of Energy, Energy Information Administration, *1981 Annual Report to Congress,* vol. II, May 1982, p. 190.

Since 1973 all OECD countries have seemed to be moving in the direction of a more efficient car fleet and less intensive use of the automobile in general. Gasoline consumption per car declined by almost 3 percent annually for this group of countries in the 1973-80 period, with the most pronounced changes taking place in the United States (a decline of 3.5 percent a year) and Italy (a fall of 3.8 percent per year). With rising gasoline prices fuel economies have been achieved by consumers opting for smaller cars and for vehicles with more efficient engines.

In the 1974-80 period, with real prices of gasoline rising by 5 percent a year, one finds that the automotive fuel efficiency of U.S. cars rose by 2 percent per year to reach an average of 15.5 miles traveled per gallon, by 1980. Department of Energy projections show that miles traveled per gallon are expected to continue to rise at a rate of about 5 percent between 1980 and 1990, but only by 1.8 percent per year from 1990 to the year 2000. Evidently marginal car efficiency gains will become harder and harder to attain during the 1990s.[32] Due to the lead time that is required for new--more fuel-efficient cars to replace the older gas guzzlers, gasoline prices cannot greatly affect the overall efficiency of the total fleet, in the short run. The higher price of gasoline, though, is an important determinant of new car purchases, and since new car registrations constitute anywhere from 10 to 15 percent of the total car fleet, changes in the *average* fleet efficiency will be only gradual. Nevertheless, for the United States the Department of Energy projects that the fleet average miles traveled per gallon will rise to 19.3 in 1985 and then to 31.7 by 1990, from the 15.5 registered in 1980.

In any event, the second oil price shock (1979-80) increased public awareness of energy issues in general and the question of higher prices of petroleum products in particular. Thus, it is likely that as a result of higher gasoline prices, a new generation of even more fuel-efficient cars will be developed and sold in the United States and other advanced countries in the coming decades. In the United States of course there are *laws* and *regulations* that require automobile manufacturers to attain specific efficiency standards by 1985. As a result of the recent round of oil and gasoline price increases, the industry fully expects that its automobiles will meet and perhaps even exceed government mandated efficiency standards.

However, as has been pointed out by Lester B. Lave, federal regulations regarding fuel economy could well be in conflict with two other avowed objectives of government regulation of the automobile--emission controls and automobile safety.[33] For one, it is well known that increases in vehicle size and weight do add to automotive safety. Larger vehicles are safer in a crash, since they have more space to absorb the crash impact and thereby protect their occupants. By the same token the increased size and weight of the vehicle will increase fuel consumption. A change in vehicle weight is estimated to change fuel consumption in the range of 8.4 to 16.8 gallons per 100 pounds of added weight for each 10,000 miles traveled, with the median estimate being about 11 gallons. Note that the addition of safety features to automobiles increased their weight by about 200 pounds on the average, with airbags adding another 60 pounds, and passive seat belts about 13 pounds. Finally, emission control equipment has added about 50 pounds on the average to each car. As noted, for every 100 pounds of extra weight, gasoline consumption per car goes up on the average by about 11 gallons a year. Therefore, the extra safety features and emission controls equipment just mentioned add about 325 pounds to the weight of the "average" car. For a fleet of 117 million cars, the increase in annual fuel consumption is estimated to be in the range of 3.38 to 4.0 billion gallons.[34]

We can look at this question from yet another angle: The weight reduction required in order to achieve greater fuel economy will have a significant impact on safety. A reduction in the average weight of automobiles from 4,500 to 3,000 pounds (a one-third reduction) is estimated to increase by 4 to 6 percent the probability of a driver being seriously injured or killed in a car accident.[35] The main point of this discussion, leaving aside the gruesome statistics of highway carnage, is that regulations can be, and often are, in conflict with each other. This example simply illustrates the existence of such a conflict among the desirable goals of safety, emission standards, and fuel economy. The fuel economy standards case dramatically shows the interdependence and tradeoffs that exist between fuel economy and safety standards, that in general you can have more of one at the cost of having less of the other. As pointed out by Lave in his conclusion: "Analysis can clarify the implications of each regulation and tradeoffs among goods, but only Congress can clarify the goals."[36]

The large energy price increases that have taken place between 1973 and 1980 have created strong incentives to change energy consumption habits and to realize potential efficiency gains. The effect of these price incentives, though, could be dampened over time.[37] The increased level of conservation and energy efficiency will be maintained, but it will become progressively more difficult (that is more costly) to attain added gains in energy savings. Conservation and energy efficiency gains will tend to slow down in the absence of greater incentives in the form of higher price, strengthened government conservation policies, or new and better energy-saving technologies.

In this section the post-oil embargo record in the area of energy conservation has been briefly presented and evaluated. In the following section we will directly examine the meaning of energy conservation and then proceed to analyze United States policies in this area.

AN ECONOMIST'S VIEW
OF ENERGY CONSERVATION

The term "energy conservation" is often used in two quite different ways. At times it encompasses restrictions or curtailments in the quality or volume of economic activities or services, such as reduced consumption, lowered thermostats, or reduced driving. The second view of conservation refers to those energy-saving investments, operating decisions, and changes in goods and services we use that save money over the life of the energy-consuming product or service. This type of conservation does not depend on sacrifice or on doing without but rather on improved efficiency in the use of energy--which need not reduce the amount or the quality of goods and services available--and in fact may even enlarge it. In principle, if energy resources were priced correctly--that is, at a price that equals their long-run marginal cost plus factors such as the cost of depletion, environmental degradation, and national security--there would be no need for energy policies that promote conservation. In general, the operation of market forces would make sure that each energy user would purchase just enough energy to satisfy needs that could not be met at lower cost in any other way. Thus, the most effective mechanism for achieving the "correct" amount of conservation is to make sure that market signals, especially price signals, are passed on to the end user with the minimum of delay and with the maximum of clarity and haste.

A useful way of looking at energy conservation is to consider the cost of saving a "unit" of energy. One needs to carry conservation activities only up to the point where the added costs in terms of new capital equipment, or for completing the task in some other way, are just equal (on the margin) to the cost of saving that unit of energy. Engaging in more conservation than that would be economically inefficient, in that the value of the scarce resources used to save a unit of energy would exceed the value of the unit conserved to the user. The kind of energy conservation I have in mind is consistent with the view expressed in the following quote: "We believe that a system in which energy conservation depends on whether it makes economic good sense is much more adequately validated by the behavior of large numbers of people than any system that starts with an a priori judgement of the kind of lifestyle that others should adopt."[38] The single most important action that we as a nation can take to encourage economically efficient conservation measures is to decontrol all energy prices--foremost among them being natural gas. If all energy prices were based on marginal cost (or marginal cost plus a surcharge whenever appropriate), a large amount of economically justifiable conservation could be achieved simply through more efficient use of our existing energy resources.

There exists considerable evidence that the energy conservation potential of the U.S. economy is both relatively large and in good part yet untapped. Certain studies have suggested that we could use 30 to 50 percent less energy than we use presently while maintaining the same standard of living.[39] Comparative International Studies of the pattern of energy use suggest that there exists substantial flexibility in energy use per unit of output among countries. One case often cited is Sweden, which uses on the average 25 percent less energy per dollar of GDP than the United States. The implication drawn by some from these studies is that the United States has the potential to lower its overall energy intensity by at least as much as 15 percent through efficiency improvement alone.[40]

One important explanation of the cause of energy demand differences among countries lies in the relative energy prices faced by consumers in different countries. In countries where the price of gasoline and other petroleum products are low, such as the United States and Canada, there exists very little incentive to conserve, but in countries where the price is high (for example, Japan, France, or Italy) users of gasoline find ways of adjusting to this reality by using more fuel-efficient cars, or switching to public transportation. In general it has been noted that ". . . this selective inquiry into examples of the flexibility of energy use in a few specific applications suggests that the demand for energy can often be reduced without substantially impairing productivity in diverse processes that use energy as one among many inputs."[41]

Some tentative conclusions can be arrived at from the perusal of studies on energy demand. First, there has been a significant reduction in the net-energy per unit of GDP ratio in the United States. Second, certain studies suggest that there exists a substantial *potential* for further reduction in the intensity of energy use, and that at this time we are in the midst of a period of adjustment to a regime of higher energy prices.[42] This bears restating the perhaps obvious refrain that the *central* element of a rational energy conservation policy is to set and maintain appropriate and consistent price signals to energy users. Subsidies and other intervention policies that lead to excessive energy consumption should be avoided like the plague. One example of such behavior is the practice on the part of some regulated public utilities of offering declining block rates for their large industrial and commercial customers. Such a rate structure enables large users of electricity (or gas) to pay less than smaller users, for the "last" unit of energy used. Even a conservation-minded organization like the TVA has replaced its declining block rate structure with flat rates only as late as April 1981. The practice of declining block rates simply encourages inefficient and excessive use of energy and should be discarded forthwith.

Finally, there remains the question as to what role if any can government policy play in the area of energy conservation, other than the obvious one of not taking steps, and engaging in policies, that lead to wasteful use of energy. President Reagan's stand on energy conservation is clearly enunciated in the following quote: "Motivated by rising energy prices, individuals, business, and other institutions are undertaking serious efforts to use energy more efficiently, generally substituting capital, labor and known and new technology to modify energy-use patterns of the recent past."[43] Now, there is no question in my mind that without proper price signals a sound and effective energy policy cannot be designed. It is therefore important that energy prices reflect the full incremental costs of energy replacement. Only when energy is priced based on its marginal costs will consumers have the correct signal to guide them in determining how much to invest in conservation if they are to husband their resources efficiently. But, one can legitimately question whether this is all that is required in designing a reasonably effective energy policy in the area of conservation.

There are reasons to believe that the "market" may not generate an adequate amount of conservation because of a number of imperfections and what economists broadly refer to as externalities. The highly respected National Academy of Sciences study on Nuclear and Alternative Energy Systems has stated, "For the most part, conservation is the least risky energy strategy from the standpoint of direct effects on the environment and public health."[44] All energy systems inevitably result in some risk to and degradation of the environment and risks to the health and well-being of people.[45] Energy production technologies, such as nuclear plants or coal-burning facilities, have different levels of risk of accidents and injuries associated with them. Furthermore, in the process of burning fossil fuels a great variety of pollutants, such as sulfur, nitrogen oxides, carbon monoxide, particulates, and others, are released into the air affecting human health as well as plant and animal life. Often there are other adverse ecological consequences associated with energy production, such as loss of arable land, detrimental impact on water resources and wilderness areas, and the habitat of wild populations and species.

Another area of concern relates to the climatic effects

of increasing the CO_2 content of the atmosphere as a result of the worldwide combustion of fossil fuels. I am referring of course to the so-called greenhouse effect that comes about due to the accelerated consumption of our fossil fuel resources. The above is merely an indicative rather than an exhaustive list of the risks and problems associated with most, if not all, currently available energy production systems. On the basis of the environmental and public health aspects conservation compares well with currently available energy supply system. The Academy of Sciences study concludes: "The maximum conservation achievable *without adverse socioeconomic effects* will likely have health and environmental benefits and therefore should have the highest priorities in policies to reduce the risks of energy systems."[46] (Emphasis added.) Thus by substituting energy conservation for a certain amount of conventional energy production, the risk of damage to the environment and to the well-being of people is reduced.[47] In somewhat more technical terms, we could say that the marginal social benefits of energy conservation exceed the private marginal benefits thereof and consequently the market is not likely to provide the socially optimal amount of energy conservation.

There is yet another argument regarding energy conservation that has been advanced recently, based on the fact that future energy prices are known only with uncertainty.[48] If one assumes that future energy prices are characterized by a certain probability distribution, then it is possible to calculate the optimal conservation investment strategy given uncertainty as regards energy prices. The introduction of uncertainty leads to the conclusion that a larger investment in energy conservation would be more desirable than would be attained under complete certainty. This conclusion is based on the notion that the upside risk to energy consumers associated with unexpectedly high energy prices is *greater* than the downside gains that would be forthcoming due to an unexpected decline in energy prices. Given such conditions it is worthwhile both for the individual and the nation as a whole to "overinvest" in conservation. In other words in order to protect itself from the risk of *higher and uncertain energy prices* the nation should invest more in conservation than would be the case if future energy prices were known with certainty.[49]

Equally important is the fact that in most countries (including the United States) there exist institutional barriers to the effective transmission of price signals that can lead to inefficient energy use. Furthermore, even where the market signals (that is, higher energy price) reach their intended destination the reaction to higher energy prices for a variety of reasons could be exceedingly slow.[50] I will illustrate the existence of a major market impediment by reference to the case of space heating and cooling in the residential sector where investments in energy saving of fuel-switching measures are often hampered by low capital availability and high interest rates.

      1. As regards new structures, often the person building the structure is not the one who will pay the energy bills and thus is somewhat less than totally committed to energy-saving features.

      2. There exist more serious problems with regard to rentals. The building's owner who is responsible for efficiency-enhancing investments is generally not the person who pays the fuel bills, and therefore has only limited incentive to make extensive improvements. This situation can be further aggravated whenever there are rent controls, which prevent the landlord from passing the cost of the investment to the tenant. Also in many rentals, potential tenants find it difficult if not impossible to obtain adequate information on the energy-efficiency features of a certain unit.

      3. Although the useful life of many buildings is 40 to 80 years, many dwellers live in a building for a much shorter time than this and are thus willing to consider only those improvements that return their cost during the period of stay. The technical potential for energy savings in buildings has been estimated to be as much as 30 to 50 percent in existing structures and 60 to 70 percent in new ones. Of course much of this energy conservation potential may only be realized in the longer run, if at all, and it will depend on developments with respect to future energy prices, interest rates, consumer spending power, and the removal of institutional barriers at various levels of government and society at large.[51]

In short, in cases such as those listed above there is room for government action to make sure that the correct market signals are transmitted to those who can act on them, and that institutional and regulatory barriers to the efficient use of energy, in the home, the car, the factory, or the office, are promptly eliminated.

GOVERNMENT CONSERVATION PROGRAMS:
AN EVALUATION[52]

This section will describe and evaluate the Reagan administration's attitudes and actions in the area of energy conservation. Inevitably certain comparisons will be drawn with
the record of the Carter administration in this respect. Let
me emphatically state at the outset that such comparisons
are not intended to be a political or a partisan statement,
or endorsement of either point of view.

The philosophy that guides the Reagan administration in
the area of energy conservation is succinctly stated in
OMB's budget documents for FY 1983, to wit: "Realistic
energy prices have eliminated the need for much government spending on conservation. The budget authority
request for energy conservation is reduced from $.2 billion
enacted in 1982 to $27 million in 1983."[53] By contrast the
attitude of the Carter administration, as exhibited in the
appropriate budget documents, is as follows:

Oil and natural gas prices that reflect market
realities and accurate public information are
essential to promote conservation in the public
and private sectors. Conservation is also
achieved through tax incentives and sound
regulatory policies such as efficiency standards
for automobiles, buildings, and appliances.
Direct Federal spending programs for conservation
include technology development; state and local
conservation grants; financial and technical
assistance to public agencies, industries, and
individuals; and energy efficiency improvements
in Federal Buildings. Outlays for conservation
program in the Energy function are estimated at
$1.013 million for 1982, up 38% from $733 million
in 1981.[54]

The contrast between the attitudes of the Carter and
Reagan administrations toward the government's role in
energy conservation is clearly reflected in these two
statements.

The Federal Government's Role in
Energy Conservation R&D

Table 5-5 provides a detailed breakdown of DOE's budget
request for FY 1983 in the area of energy conservation and

TABLE 5-5. Department of Energy Detailed Budget Comparison of the Energy Conservation, Solar Energy, and Other Renewable Energy Programs (budget authority in millions)

Program	FY81[a]	FY82[b]	FY83[c]
Energy Conservation R&D			
Buildings	91.3	47.7	0
Industrial	69.6	28.8	0
Transportation	105.0	58.9	0
Multisector	9.4	8.6	17.5
Subtotals	275.3	144.0	17.5
Percentage of grand totals	21%	21%	17%
Energy Conservation Grants			
Weatherization	175.0	144.0	0
Schools and hospitals	150.0	48.0	0
State planning (EPCA)	47.8	24.0	0
Energy extension service	20.0	9.6	0
Inventions	5.8	5.2	0
Appropriate technology	12.0	2.9	0
Impact assistance	10.0	0	0
Program direction	9.5	6.3	4.3
Subtotals	430.1	240.0	4.3
Percentage of grand totals	32%	34%	4%
Total percentage for conservation	53%	55%	21%
Solar R&D			
Active	38.4	11.5	0
Passive	30.2	10.6	0
Photovoltaics	133.2	74.0	27.0
Thermal	112.0	53.0	18.0
Biomass	27.2	20.5	6.6
Wind	54.2	34.4	5.5
Ocean	34.6	18.8	0
Other Solar	23.9	24.1	12.1
Subtotals	453.7	246.9	69.2
Percentage of grand totals	34%	35%	67%
Other Renewables R&D			
Alcohol fuels	18.0	10.0	2.9
Geothermal	156.0	53.6	9.8
Hydropower	3.2	3.0	0
Subtotals	177.2	66.6	12.7
Percentage of grand totals	13%	10%	12%
Total percentage for renewables	47%	45%	79%
GRAND TOTALS	$1,336.3	697.5	103.7

[a] Includes Reagan administration FY81 rescissions.
[b] Includes FY81 deferrals.
[c] Represents administration request for FY83.
Source: United States Senate, Committee on Energy and Natural Resources, Department of Energy Fiscal Year 1983 Authorization (Conservation Programs), Washington, D.C., March 30, 1982.

solar energy and other renewable energy programs. The contrast with previous years is stark and amounts essentially to the elimination of the federal government's active involvement in the energy conservation area. The Reagan administration proposes to support only "long term generic and technology base research (e.g., materials and catalysis research and instrumentation) and environmental research. . . ."[55] The reason behind this change in direction is based on the belief that with the decontrol of oil prices and given the administration's new tax provisions, ". . . the pace of development of new technologies by the private sector should accelerate."[56]

It is the stated belief of the Reagan administration that the government's role with respect to nonnuclear R&D programs, including energy conservation research, should be merely *supportive* of private-sector R&D efforts. Consequently, the budget authority requested for nonnuclear energy R&D for FY 1983 is reduced to $376 million from $2.2 billion actually spent in FY 1981 and from $1.75 in FY 1982.[57]

To provide more specific illustrations of the likely effects of the proposed changes in nonnuclear technology R&D, I will examine in somewhat greater detail two cases--those of solar energy research and energy storage R&D. The General Accounting Office has noted that the Reagan administration's FY 1983 request, should it be enacted by Congress, amounts to a 72 percent reduction in solar energy R&D.[58] The GAO noted that the elimination of federal government support for certain solar technologies--such as active and passive solar space heating, and solar hot water systems--is entirely appropriate, since such systems appear to be cost competitive in certain regions of the country without government support. On the other hand, there are novel and promising technologies whose development without further government support will be retarded or perhaps even abandoned. One such emerging technology that is likely to be affected by the budget cuts is that of solar photovoltaics. GAO studies indicate that "industry is reluctant to make additional investments due to the high uncertainties and risks associated with making this technology economical."[59] Other solar technologies, such as ocean thermal energy conversion systems, call for costly, large-scale development to test their potential, which once again is not likely to be undertaken by private industry without sizable federal involvement.

Another case in point is the Energy Storage Systems program, which the administration proposes to phase out in

FY 1983. This program attempts to develop and demon-
strate reliable, low-cost, environmentally acceptable energy
storage systems, such as batteries for buildings, industry,
transportation, and utilities. The FY 1983 budget document
cryptically notes that "generic research related to those
activities will be funded through other programs." However, as the GAO report noted, in order for electric vehicles to becomes viable transportation alternative, long-term
advanced batteries (such as aluminum-air, lithium metal-
sulfide, or sodium sulfide) will likely be needed. In FY
1983, support for such R&D efforts is being phased out and
because work on these advanced storage batteries is inherently long-term and high-risk in nature, the private sector
will most likely stay away from such high-risk endeavors.
The GAO report concludes that ". . . Federal R&D on
long-term advanced battery candidates should continue while
the proposed funding of near-term batteries does not
appear appropriate."[60]

Deputy Assistant Secretary Maxine Savitz in an earlier
interview in fact viewed efforts such as those cited above
as an excellent opportunity for government to help close the
gap in existing conservation programs through the development of a good technology base.[61] Now, it seems to me
that all the talk about focusing government R&D efforts on
"generic" or basic research appears to be no more than an
excuse for essentially eliminating any significant role for
government in supporting the development of new and
promising nonnuclear energy technologies, including basic
conservation technologies. This attitude, although misguided in my view, could be understood in terms of the
philosophical stance taken by the Reagan administration as
regard the appropriate roles of the government and private
sectors with respect to nonnuclear energy R&D. What is
unacceptable is the disparity between the administration's
rhetoric and its actions: "The government can perform an
important role in support of private sector technology
development by focusing Federal funding on technology base
research. . . ."[62] But then observe the insignificant
amount of resources ($17.5 million for conservation R&D)
actually committed to such "generic" energy-related R&D
activities. I am sure that the Reagan administration personnel responsible for these statements know full well that
*basic, long-term energy R&D will not be undertaken by the
private sector without substantial and sustained federal
government support.* Despite veiled references to the
possible impact of lower interest rates and more favorable
tax treatment (including the 25 percent tax credit for

certain incremental R&D investments) on *private* energy R&D effort, it is clear to me that a statement such as "The FY 1983 budget reductions will not have a significant effect on the overall national energy R&D effort,"[63] is no more than wishful and I believe highly misleading thinking. The Department of Energy's own analysis appears to contradict such far-fetched statements: "The existence or lack thereof, of Federal programs aimed at accelerating investment [in energy conservation] can have a measurable effect. Their need however, must be determined on the basis of demonstrated market failure."[64]

I believe that even the most ardent supporters of a free and competitive market system will acknowledge that in general the "market" will underinvest in socially desirable and profitable *basic* research. Basic research has some of the characteristics of a "public good" that can be defined as a good that once it has been provided to anyone can be provided to everyone else at no extra cost; in other words a public good can be used concurrently by many economic agents.[65] The traditional examples cited in the literature of a *pure* public good is a lighthouse or national defense; *basic* research while perhaps not a pure public good has certain properties associated with public goods. Once the results of *basic* research (for example, materials and catalysis research or research in photobiology) has been made available, any individual can avail himself of this knowledge without reducing its availability to anyone else. The marginal cost of providing this information to additional users is essentially zero. Under these circumstances it can be easily shown that public goods or near-public goods will tend to be inadequately supplied by private firms.[66] Thus a reasonable and valid case can be made for government support of basic energy (including energy conservation) research on the basis of its public good or near-public good characteristics.

Finally, the Energy Research Advisory Board in its report to the DOE made the following pertinent observation: "Relative to their potential contributions to the solution of the near-and-medium term energy problems, there is an imbalance in the allocation of R&D funds between the conservation programs and those directed at supply. *The budget needs reordering of priorities to reflect better the opportunities that exist for efficiency improvements and the unique Federal role in conservation R&D.*"[67] (Emphasis added.) In view of the fact that only 8 percent of the total FY 1982 Energy R&D budget was allocated to conservation technologies, all I can add to the above quote is *Amen!*

Energy Conservation Programs at DOE: An Evaluation

A Department of Energy position paper notes that higher energy prices do bring forth added investment in energy conservation. But it also points out that certain DOE programs intended to stimulate private investment have been "much more effective" than tax credits in inducing the private sector into further conservation investments. Now, this is not to say that all DOE programs in the area of energy conservation are equally effective or worthy of support even at a reduced level. In a detailed review of Conservation and Solar Energy (C&SE) programs at the Department of Energy, undertaken by the Congressional Office of Technology Assessment (OTA), numbers of serious deficiencies and shortcomings have been detected. The OTA study reached the following conclusions: ". . . *C&SE lacks a clear vision of where it is going and how it will get there.* Some of the programs are doing as well as might be expected, but no coherent theme permeates the entire office and guides the directions and paces of the various programs."[68] Another major problem that has been detected is the lack of adequate program evaluation. As certain DOE-supported conservation or solar energy technologies reach advanced stages of development, evaluation becomes crucial in determining whether a certain program should be abandoned or expanded further until it becomes cost-competitive with respect to other alternatives.

Let me briefly illustrate some of the issues involved with regard to one program that has been thoroughly examined by OTA. OTA's analysis indicates that *cost-effective investments* in conservation technologies could decrease residential energy use by the year 2000 (compared to 1977) *with no loss of comfort* and despite a substantial amount of new construction.[69] Table 5-6 indicates the possible impact of implementing an aggressive program of retrofitting the U.S. housing stock and setting strict standards for new construction. It shows that about two thirds of the potential savings result from retrofitting of existing structures. Additional energy conservation can be obtained by incorporating solar energy systems into the retrofit programs. More and better information, though, is needed to clarify what combinations of conservation measures *and* solar energy systems can be most cost effective. The OTA study emphasizes that the fact that many cost effective retrofit products and processes are not being used may suggest that a case of "market failure" may be at hand. For example, financing is more difficult to obtain where retrofitting is involved as compared to new con-

TABLE 5-6. Potential Energy Savings by 1990 From Housing Retrofits and Strict Building Standards (millions of bbl/d oil equivalent)

	Oil and gas	Other	Total
Retrofit savings	1.9	0.4	2.3
Strict building standards	0.7	0.9	1.6
Total savings	2.6	1.3	3.9

Assumptions:

--Baseline case continues present construction practices to 1990 and includes no further retrofits.

--Retrofit savings are based on 50% heating savings and 20% hot water savings in all existing housing still used in 1990.

--Strict building standards incorporate BEPS and 35% hot water savings in new buildings.

Source: Congress of the United States, Office of Technology Assessment, Conservation and Solar Energy Programs of the Department of Energy: A Critique. Washington, D.C., June 1980, p. 66.

struction. Consumers are often in the dark as to what changes can be implemented and at what cost and which conservation programs would result in the greatest monetary savings to them.[70]

Having mentioned some of the problem areas involved in the residential conservation effort I do not want to leave the reader with the impression that a government program or a government solution is necessarily the preferred course of action in this area. Often the preferred solution would be the elimination of impediments in the area of finance and information acquisition, so that individuals acting in their own self-interest could make an informed and rational decision regarding this aspect of energy conservation be able to carry it out as quickly as possible.

In any case the record of DOE with respect to conservation programs is spotty at best. The DOE has numerous programs directed at encouraging energy conservation in buildings, among them the Weatherization and State Energy Management program, the Energy Extension Service, Low Income Weatherization program, Building Energy Performance Standards program, and the Schools and Hospitals Grant program. No systematic evidence is available to date to indicate whether these programs have made a notable difference in terms of energy conservation--in other words, whether they really work.[71] A recent GAO review of selected DOE Conservation and Renewable Energy Programs offered the following observation: ". . . some Federal Conservation programs have made contributions to reducing national energy use; others have shown the potential to do so. Many could be improved and made more effective."[72] I will now examine a few cases of government energy conservation programs and consider their effectiveness.

Building Energy Performance Standards (BEPS)

The Energy Conservation and Production Act (August 14, 1976), as amended, directs DOE to develop and promulgate energy performance standards for new buildings. These standards were supposed to achieve the "maximum practical" level of energy savings through energy-efficient building designs. Some people at DOE expressed the belief that these new standards could lower energy consumption in buildings by 25 percent compared to what otherwise would have been the case.[73] As originally conceived, BEPS would *require* that new buildings be designed so that they are consistent with an energy "budget" expressed in BTU per square foot per year. However, the Omnibus Budget Reconciliation Act of 1981 made BEPS voluntary except for federal buildings, and changed the effective date to April 1, 1984. A GAO review of this program concluded that "while a mandatory standard may not be justified, establishing a voluntary standard could facilitate market forces by identifying the optimal level of energy conservation that could be effectively achieved."[74] In my view neither mandatory nor voluntary BEPS are called for. What could be useful in this area is some additional information provided by government on the energy performance and lifetime costs of buildings designed to incorporate new energy saving construction techniques and energy conservation standards. Such information should be widely disseminated to builders, utilities, and the public at large.

The Residential Conservation Service
and The Energy Extension Service

The National Energy Extension Service Act established the Energy Extension Service (EES) and directed it to develop and implement a comprehensive program for the identification, development, and practical demonstration of energy conservation practices and measures. The idea behind the

EES was to establish an energy "outreach" program directed at small businesses and individuals so as to stimulate and support their energy conservation efforts. Following an initial pilot program involving ten states, EES was expanded nationwide in FY 1980. The Reagan administration requested no funds for the program in its FY 1983 budget request. A review of this program by the GAO was generally unfavorable: "GAO found that the lack of effective management of their programs at the Federal level had severely diminished their potential impact."[75] Thus there appears to be a good reason for the elimination of this program; its performance is faulty and it is unlikely to improve under DOE stewardship.

Federal Energy Management Program

The federal government is the nation's largest single energy user. It spent over $12 billion for energy in FY 1981, about 2 percent of total national energy use. In FY 1981 energy use by the federal government increased by 3.4 percent above the FY 1980 level. In its FY 1982 budget request the Reagan administration stated that its internal energy conservation program would be retained; however in the FY 1983 submission no funds were requested, because the program is slated for termination. This means that the federal government's effort to set its own energy "house" in order through better data collection, federal buildings conservation efforts, and overall coordination and leadership in energy conservation matters is being terminated. The GAO in a number of its reports concluded that the federal government ought to have an aggressive internal energy conservation program. Presently the government's in-house conservation effort is inadequate because of "insufficient commitment in the areas of organizational visibility, staffing, and management support."[76] Identifying cost-effective conservation opportunities within the federal government and acting upon them could result in both energy and budgetary savings. For example, a one percent decrease in energy consumption could save the government over $100 million. This is one program that I believe is worth maintaining if for no other reason than for its symbolic and educational value. It seems incongruous that an administration that considers conservation to be an essential part of its overall energy strategy would not take the necessary steps to make sure that energy is used effectively within the federal government's own bailiwick.

The DOE's own analysis indicates that certain so-called "outreach" or informational programs may have had greater impact than I have given them credit. One analyst noted that $5 of *private* investment may in fact have resulted from each $1 spent by the federal government on one such outreach program, with perhaps additional $2 of private spending planned for the future.[77] Even if one accepts this particular energy conservation "multiplier," I do not think it is correct to conclude that most or all federal government's information or outreach programs have been as effective in inducing private spending on conservation as the one mentioned above.

SOME CONCLUDING COMMENTS

In this chapter we have reviewed the record of energy conservation in the United States and other advanced countries with special emphasis on the achievements of the post-1973 period. It is clear from the examination of the evidence that as a result of higher energy prices a good deal of conservation has in fact taken place in the United States and other countries. Higher energy prices led to greater efficiency in energy use, giving individuals and businesses the incentive to economize on the use of a more expensive resource (energy) and substitute whenever possible cheaper resources and services, such as one's own labor, for it. Furthermore, higher energy prices provided the necessary impetus for economic agents to invest in technologies and industrial processes that are more energy efficient. This process is relatively slow, and in fact the United States economy is now in the midst of a far-reaching change in its stock of productive capital and its stock of durable goods (such as automobiles and refrigerators). However, this transition to a more energy-efficient capital stock will take many years to complete.

According to Clifton C. Garvin, Jr., chairman of the Board of Exxon Corporation, at least two thirds of the recent drop in demand for petroleum products was due to conservation, and since the economic recovery projected for the United States and other OECD countries will be anemic, he predicts that world oil demand will be roughly flat in 1983.[78] Throughout this book I have emphasized that the best way of dealing with the so-called energy problem is to unleash the creative powers and ingenuity of millions of individuals and businesses acting through the market mechanism in the pursuit of their own goals, wishes, and dreams. Therefore large scale governmental solutions or remedies to our energy problems are in general unnecessary and in some cases may be downright harmful (case in point, energy price controls). There are two areas, though, where government programs may be helpful. First, government support of *basic* conservation R&D is essential, as I have argued earlier in this chapter. Such research, unless financed in large part by government, simply will not be undertaken. Second, the government can play a useful role in the dissemination of relevant energy conservation information, and in making sure that individuals and small and medium-size businesses have an accurate and conveniently available factual basis for making decisions as regards the amounts and types of energy resources that they will use in their various endeavors.

NOTES

1. Harry Dutton, "Symposium Told Significance of Nuclear Era," *Northwest Public Power Bulletin* 24 (December 1970):5.

2. Pacific Northwest Electric Power Planning and Conservation Act, 16 U.S.C. 837-839 (1980) [P.L. 96-501]. Hereinafter cited as PNEPPCA.

3. U.S. Comptroller General, *Region at the Crossroads: The Pacific Northwest Searches for New Sources of Electric Energy* (Washington, D.C.: U.S. General Accounting Office, 1978), i–iii, 7.2.

4. PNEPPAA, Sec. 839d, 839e; Northwest Conservation Act Coalition, "Conservation Alert," Seattle, Washington, January 25, 1981; Bonneville Power Administration, "Staff Evaluation of the Official Record, Proposed Billing Credits Policy [Draft]," Portland, Oregon, August 1982.

5. Office of Applied Energy Studies/Washington Energy Research Center, *Independent Review of Washington Public Power Supply System Nuclear Plants 4 and 5* (Pullman: OAES, Washington State University, March 1982), executive summary, 85-91. Various electric power conservation estimates exist. Estimates depend both on measures employed and implementation costs. For a review of conservation measures and potential savings under review by the Regional Power Council, see Battelle Pacific Northwest Laboratories, *Assessment of Power Conservation and Supply Resources in the Pacific Northwest* [Drafts] 4 vols. (Richland, Wash.: BPNL, 1982).

6. For example, the debt service on WNP-1,2,3 (Washington Public Power Supply System nuclear projects) is approximately 50 percent of Bonneville Power Administration's projected 1982 priority firm rate revenue obligations. Personal Communication, Division of Rates, Bonneville Power Administration, August/November 1982.

7. OAES, *Independent Review*, 85-91.

8. Ibid.

9. The program details have been obtained from: Tennessee Valley Authority, Office of Power, Division of Energy Conservation and Rates, *Program Summary*, April 1982.

10. For details and particulars of these and other programs consult ibid., pp. 114-29.

11. Benton R. Schlender, "Energy Savers: Passive-Solar Homes Are Enjoying a Boom Amid Housing Slump," *Wall Street Journal,* September 1, 1981, p. 1.

12. Those houses are priced in the $43,000 to $78,000 range: ibid., p. 15.

13. "Evaluating Passive's Potential" *EPRI Journal,* July/August 1982, p. 21.

14. Ibid., p. 23.

15. See comments by Thomas W. Swanson, Chief, Planning and Communications Staff, Division of Energy Conservation and Rates, TVA, before the Energy and Utilities Committee of the Washington State Senate, October 15, 1982.

16. Ibid., p. 2.

17. Ibid., p. 3.

18. U.S. Department of Energy, *Securing America's Energy Future: The National Energy Policy Plan,* July 1981, p. 16.

19. This section draws on factual material from the following sources: International Energy Agency, *World Energy Outlook* (Paris: OECD, 1982); International Monetary Fund, *World Economic Outlook,* Occasional Paper no. 9, Washington, D.C., April 1982, pp. 126-29. Department of Energy. *Energy Projections to the Year 2000 July 1982 Update,* Washington, D.C., August 1982.

20. Oil consumption per unit of real GNP in the OECD area has declined at an average annual rate of 7 percent between 1979 and 1982, while during the 1973 through 1979 period it only declined at 2.5 percent a year. U.S. Dept. of Energy, Energy Information Administration, *Short-term Energy Outlook Quarterly Projections,* Washington, D.C., August 1982, p. 7.

21. IMF, *World Economic Outlook,* April 1982, Appendix A, p. 128.

22. The countries included in this sample are United States, Japan, Germany, France, United Kingdom, Italy and Canada. For further details consult *International Energy Agency, World Energy Outlook,* pp. 80-88.

23. For further evidence on this see IMF, *World Economic Outlook,* Occasional Paper no. 4, Washington, D.C.,

June 1981, p. 100.

24. International Energy Agency, *World Energy Out-look*, p. 85.

25. The factual information has been taken from International Energy Agency, *World Energy Outlook*, pp. 88-103 and U.S. Department of Energy, Office of Policy, Planning and Analysis, *Energy Projections to the Year 2000*, Washington, D.C July 1980, ch. 4.

26. For example there has been a decline in the share of final energy used by the iron and steel industry, resulting essentially from the decline of the iron and steel business relative to industry as a whole. International Energy Agency, *World Energy Outlook*, p. 90, Tables 3.6 and 3.7.

27. Ibid., p. 92.

28. Department of Energy, Office of Policy, Planning and Analysis, *Energy Projection to the Year 2000*, pp. 4-16.

29. Information on Boeing's energy conservation programs has been obtained from Boeing's Corporate Office of Energy and Environmental Controls.

30. This includes energy used for manufacturing, heating, and lighting. The measure Boeing uses for energy efficiency comparisons, is Btu's per square foot of building area. In 1981 the company saved nearly $19 million on energy costs alone.

31. An example of an innovative building can be found right here in Southeastern Washington, at a place where the Wawawai Canyon links with the Snake River. It is an earth-sheltered house that blends gracefully into the majestic scenery of the Snake River Canyon. This underground house was designed and its construction was supervised by David M. Scott, Professor of Architecture at Washington State University (see Figure 5-2).

According to Professor Scott, an earth-sheltered house that is properly designed, appropriately detailed, and carefully constructed will be more energy-efficient than a traditional above-grade house. The annual energy savings can be as high as 75-80 percent.

Energy savings, however, are only one of the many reasons why earth sheltering should be considered. It is possible to reduce maintenance, provide protection from external natural and man-made disasters such as fire, rain, hail, wind, and nuclear fallout. It is also possible to minimize damage internally from the spread of fire between dwelling units.

Earth sheltering can provide for multiple uses from the same land; it allows for close but private living, it allows people to *use* all surfaces of the structure to grow food, for recreation, patios, and so on. Earth sheltering permits development while reducing the ecological and visual impact on the landscape.

If there is a limitation to the concept, it is that it requires subtle differences in skill and ability to design and construct such housing units.

32. Department of Energy, Office of Policy, Planning and Analysis, *Energy Projection to the Year 2000,* pp. 4-25.

33. Lester B. Lave "Conflicting Objectives in Regulating the Automobile," *Science,* vol. 212, May 22, 1981, pp. 893-99.

34. Note that this is merely a hypothetical calculation that assumes that the entire fleet had these safety and emission devices installed.

35. A fleet made of small cars could increase the number of fatalities by 11,400 a year compared to a fleet consisting of larger cars. Lave, "Conflicting Objectives," p. 897.

36. Ibid., p. 898.

37. Some energy demand models have shown surprisingly high values for the longer run price elasticity of energy demand. One such model forecasts that the ratio of energy demand and GNP will decline by an extra 34 percent if real energy prices remain at their current (1980) level for the next twenty years. See David B. Reister, "Energy Conservation: The Post-Embargo Record," *Energy* VII, (1982):403-11.

38. The Ford Foundation, *Energy: The Next Twenty Years* (Cambridge Mass., Ballinger, 1979), p. 123.

39. Ibid., pp. 124-26.

40. About 40 percent of the difference between the United States and other countries in energy use per unit of output can be attributed to the differences in the mix of activities in the different countries. The rest--i.e., 60 percent--is principally attributed to differences in the efficiency of energy use. William W. Hogan "Dimensions in Energy Demand" in Hans H. Lansberger (ed.), *Selected Studies on Energy Background Papers for Energy: The Next Twenty Years* (Cambridge, Mass., Ballinger, 1980), pp. 7-12.

41. Ibid., p. 12.

42. For the evidence consult ibid, pp. 20-27.

43. U.S. Department of Energy, *Securing America's Energy Future: The National Energy Policy Plan,* July 1981, p. 15.

44. National Academy of Sciences, Final Report of the Committee on Nuclear and Alternative Energy Systems,

Energy in Transition 1985–2000 (San Francisco: W. H. Freeman, 1980), p. 59.

45. For additional details see ibid., pp. 48–59.

46. Ibid., pp. 59–60.

47. It is possible to postulate the existence of a conventional supply function for energy conservation. Its "output" is units of energy conserved or saved, production of which requires the commitment of resources such as capital, labor, and technology. Subsequently, one can talk about the marginal cost of energy conservation as well as the marginal benefit. The marginal value of energy conservation refers to the incremental returns associated with a unit of increase in energy savings. An individual who has to decide on investing in an energy-saving piece of equipment will have to evaluate the marginal benefits in terms of the discounted present value of future savings and compare it to the cost of capital. For an actual attempt to construct energy conservation supply curves see A. Meier, A. H. Rosenfield, and J. Wright, "Supply Curves of Conserved Energy for California's Residential Sector," *Energy,* vol. 7, no. 4, pp. 347–58.

48. P. P. Craig, M. D. Levine, and J. Mass "Uncertainty: An Argument for More Stringent Energy Conservation," *Energy,* vol. 5, no. 10, pp. 1073–83.

49. Take for example the case of an electrically heated house located in Washington, D.C.; assume that the most likely growth rate of energy prices is 5 percent per year, but there is a normally distributed uncertainty around this price path. Then one should calculate the optimal investment in energy conservation as if the price rise is 6.8 percent a year. Ibid., p. 1073.

50. Nevertheless there is little doubt that in time consumers do respond to changes in energy prices; the Congressional Office of Technology Assessment noted that such changes in consumer behavior are largely motivated by a "basic desire to save money and resist rising prices." The Congressional study added cryptically: ". . . public statements or campaigns that link conservation and sacrifice, such as suggestions that conservation means that residents should be cold in their homes may be ineffective if not counterproductive." Congress of the United States, Office of Technology Assessment, *Residential Energy Conservation,* vol. I, July 1979, p. 7.

51. With respect to energy use in the transportation sector, I have noted previously that in the U.S. government, regulation of the automobile is a bit schizophrenic. For example strict pollution control standards for cars can have a negative impact on fuel consumption, and the same

is true of the extensive safety equipment required in the automobile.

52. The facts referred to in this section were largely obtained from the following sources: Congress of the United States, Office of Technology Assessment, *Conservation and Solar Energy Programs of the Department of Energy: A Critique,* Washington, D.C., June 1980; United States Senate, Committee on Energy and Natural Resources, *Department of Energy Fiscal Year 1983 Authorization (Conservation Programs),* Washington, D.C., March 30, 1982.

53. Executive Office of the President, Office of Management and Budget, *Budget of the United States Government FY 1983,* Washington, D.C., pp. 5-47.

54. Executive office of the President, Office of Management and Budget, *Budget of the United States Government Fiscal Year 1982,* Washington, D.C., p. 143.

55. Executive office of the President, Office of Management and Budget, *Major Themes and Additional Budget Details Fiscal Year 1983,* Washington, D.C., p. 97.

56. Ibid., p. 98.

57. Ibid., p. 97.

58. United States Senate, Committee on Energy and Natural Resources, *Department of Energy Fiscal Year 1983 Authorization (Conservation Programs),* Washington, D.C., March 30, 1982, pp. 8-9.

59. Ibid., p. 8.

60. Ibid., p. 11.

61. See the interview with Dr. Savitz in "Conservation: DOE's High-Priority Program," *EPRI Journal,* May 1980, p. 34.

62. Executive Office of the President, Office of Management and Budget, *Major Themes and Additional Budget Details Fiscal Year 1983,* p. 98.

63. Ibid.

64. Robert C. Marlay "Effects of Investment in Energy Conservation of DOE's Program and of Market Forces," in U.S. Senate, Committee on Energy and Natural Resources, *Department of Energy Fiscal Year 1983 Authorization Conservation Programs),* p. 96.

65. For further analysis see for example: Jack Hirshleifer *Price Theory and Application,* 2nd ed. (Englewood Cliffs, N.J.: Prentice-Hall, 1980), pp. 539-43.

66. Ibid., pp. 541-42.

67. U.S. Senate, Committee on Energy and Natural Resources, *Department of Energy Fiscal Year 1983 Authorization (Conservation Programs),* p. 313.

68. Congress of the United States, Office of Technology Assessment, *Conservation and Solar Energy Programs of the*

Department of Energy: A Critique, Washington, D.C., June 1980, p. 3.

69. Ibid., p. 66.

70. For more detailed examination of these issues see Congress of the United States, Office of Technology Assessment, *Residential Energy Conservation,* vol. 1, Washington, D.C., July 1929, ch. 8.

71. For further details concerning these programs consult ibid., pp. 194-208.

72. U.S. General Accounting Office, "Views on Selected DOE Conservation and Renewable Energy Programs and Their Program Mandates," prepared for Richard L. Ottinger, Chairman, Subcommittee on Energy Conservation and Power, U.S. House of Representatives, June 22, 1982.

73. "Conservation: DOE's High-Priority Program," *EPRI Journal,* May 1980, p. 33.

74. U.S. Senate, Committee on Energy and Natural Resources, *Department of Energy Fiscal Year 1983 Authorization (Conservation Programs),* March 30, 1982, p. 21.

75. Ibid., p. 18.

76. Ibid., p. 22.

77. Robert C. Marlay, "Effects on Investment in Energy Conservation of DOE's Programs and of Market Forces," in U.S. Senate, *Committee on Energy and Natural Resources, Department of Energy Fiscal Year 1983 Authorization (Conservation Programs),* p. 98.

78. "Oil Executives Say Industry's Deep Slump Will Continue Even if Economics Recover," *Wall Street Journal,* November 9, 1982, p. 6.

Energy Policy
— 6 —
An Agenda for the 1980s

The experience of the past ten years has taught us how vulnerable the United States and other advanced industrial nations are to oil price shocks and sudden oil supply interruptions. The two price shocks experienced in the 1970s have contributed significantly to the dismal performance of the world economy during the past decade. The widespread slowdown in real economic growth among industrial countries during the last three years was initially caused by the deflationary impact of the 1979-80 oil price surge, but it was made deeper by a policy-induced slowdown in aggregate demand. The underutilization of economic resources has increased sharply throughout the industrial world in recent years, while at the same time inflationary pressures intensified as individual groups attempted to protect themselves against the negative impact of energy price increases. What had started as an oil price shock eventually turned into a widespread, deep, and costly economic crisis. It is imperative that we put in place policies that will minimize the impact of another energy supply shock, should one materialize. Sound and consistent energy policy can bring about structural changes in the economies of oil-importing countries--resulting in continued decline in the relative share of energy in real output and large-scale substitution of other fuels for oil.

This final chapter looks into the reasons behind our inability to form consistent and effective energy policies in the past, and our lack of success in dealing with energy price uncertainty to date.

THE ZERO-SUM NATURE OF
ENERGY POLICY: A CRITIQUE

The belief that U.S. energy policy is essentially a zero-sum game has been to some extent at the root of our inability to generate energy policies that will deal effectively with our ingrained energy problems.[1] In a chapter titled "Economy That No Longer Performs," Lester C. Thurow argued:

> Throughout our society there are painful, persis-tent problems that are not being solved by our system of political economy. Energy, inflation, unemployment, environmental decay, ever spread-ing waves of regulations, sharp income gaps between minorities and majorities--the list is almost endless. Because of our inability to solve these problems, the lament is often heard that the U.S. economy and political system have lost their ability to get things done."[2]

He goes on to say that our economic problems-- includ-ing our energy problems--may not be insoluble, but rather the required solutions have a substantial zero-sum compo-nent to them, thus imposing large economic losses on some groups in our society, while benefiting other groups.

In Thurow's parlance, a zero-sum game is any "game"--be it football, basketball, or a political "sporting" event--where the losses exactly offset the winnings. In fact, the sports lingo permeates the discussion of zero-sum policies in the energy and the larger economic arena. However, it behooves the reader to remember that the formation of economic policy in general and energy policy in particular only partly resembles a sporting event, one where the "winners" and "losers" sit on opposite sides of the playing field.

To stretch Thurow's sporting analogy a bit, one could compare energy policy to a charity athletic match where the outcome of the "game" is of secondary importance, given the greater social purpose of raising money for the local United Way campaign, the Salvation Army, or some other worthy charity. Once the game is over, it will matter little who the "losers" and the "winners" were, but instead people will take notice of how much money was raised by this event for the local charity. While there may be losers and winners in a narrow sense, in a greater sense, everyone is better off.

Thurow goes on to make the valid point that because of

our unrelenting and understandable quest for economic security, people turn to government for protection whenever they feel that their economic security (that is, their jobs, lifestyles, or real income) is threatened. When the 1973-74 oil price explosion took place, there were demands that government "do something" about high energy and food prices. As a result, the oil and NG industry became a ward of the state (that is, they were regulated) and an embargo was imposed on grain exports. Thurow correctly points out that "at the heart of capitalism and competitive markets lies the doctrine of failure."[3] Namely, those enterprises that do not meet the exacting requirements of a competitive market *must* be allowed to go the way of the dinosaurs. It is also true that bailing out the Chryslers and Lockheeds of the business world creates a demand that additional aid be extended to small businesses, farmers, or the steel industry. Such aid and comfort as there is takes the form of price supports, subsidized credit, "cheap" energy, inexpensive water for irrigation, quotas or tariffs on imports, and the list goes on and on.

It is true that economic growth and the change attendant on it does have its share of losers--new products replacing old ones, more energy-efficient manufacturing processes being used in lieu of older ones, workers with new skills supplanting those whose skills were deemed obsolete, and so on down the line. In fact, what I am describing is the type of change and adaptation that a dynamic society such as ours undertakes continuously, almost without notice. It is generally untrue, and to his credit Thurow does not make this point, that if only we gave up economic progress (that is, economic growth) and the turmoil sometimes associated with it, we would be more secure and therefore in some sense better off.

I believe that very few Americans would be attracted to a way of life where the challenge and opportunity attendant to economic growth and change are nonexistent, or where people's only concern is with maintaining their share of an unchanging, or even shrinking, proverbial economic pie. In fact, several of our social and economic problems in the areas of energy, the environment, or even poverty would be made considerably worse in a stagnant economy, where progress and the *possibility* of change are either absent or very difficult to come by. Thurow is, of course, well aware of this as he notes: "Slowing the entire economy to stop pollution is roughly equivalent to using an atomic bomb to swat a fly. Pollution would go down, but at enormous cost, since nonpolluting activities would be slowed down along with polluting ones."[4]

There are many obvious problems with a "zero economic growth" (ZEG) and a no-economic-change approach to our energy and environmental problems. For one, such a "solution" would lead to rising unemployment, to a more unequal and polarized society, as well as to cut-throat competition for existing jobs. Rather than making the world appear more secure and benign, a ZEG strategy would imply a society where *only zero-sum games would be possible.*

Thurow understands what such a solution entails and he states its implications when he brings up the possibility of limiting every worker's hours of labor. He observes: "As a result there is no doubt that there would be severe enforcement problems. Work probably could be rationed, but there is no doubt that the end result would be a substantial increase in economic controls. *Many individuals would have to be forced to do what they do not want to do.*"[5] (Emphasis added.) I can state the outcome of such a solution much more directly and plainly: What we would need in order to implement it would be a totalitarian or police state. *Remember, 1984 is just around the corner!* Clearly the "solution" in this case is much, much worse than the so-called problem it is intended to alleviate.

Next, Thurow turns his attention to energy policy, which he believes to be an excellent example of his thesis that because of the fundamental zero-sum nature of our energy problems, the country finds itself tied up in knots in trying to form a workable energy policy for the 1980s and beyond. He concedes that a free market in energy would solve our problems, to wit: ". . . there would be no gas lines, no shortages and no Energy Department full of complex and sometimes counterproductive regulations."[6] Yet he finds himself rejecting this simple yet elegant solution, because it would lead to "enormous" changes in our income distribution.

At the outset, I will grant the obvious that the rise in the price of oil or NG to world market levels does have the distributional implications. The real income of those who drive their cars to work and heat their homes with NG will clearly fall. Furthermore, those small or even large businesses that use NG or diesel fuel to produce and distribute their wares will be negatively impacted.

Large enterprises that are especially heavy users of energy, such as steel, aluminum, or petrochemicals, will see their costs rise sharply and profits deteriorate. Of course, this is the "invisible hand's" way of nudging them toward energy conservation and toward substituting other factors, such as capital or human ingenuity for energy, for the long-term viability of their enterprises. Most large and small businesses will heed these signals and in time adopt more energy efficient processes and technologies, while others may turn to government for security and protection, and some may do a little of both.

Now, the primary reason Thurow and others cannot accept the "free market" solution to the energy question is rooted in a belief that poor people would be hurt disproportionately by higher energy prices. Thurow cites government statistics to the effect that the real income effect of higher energy prices on the poor is "almost seven times as large as they are among the rich."[7] However, other studies have not found such extreme disparity in the burden of higher energy prices across income classes. For example, Kenneth J. Arrow and Joseph P. Kalt concluded in their study that "the burden of energy price increases falls somewhat but not a great deal more heavily on poor consumers than on rich consumers."[8]

The Arrow and Kalt conclusion is supported by two detailed studies of total energy requirements of consumers based on 1960-61 and 1972-73 consumer expenditure survey data.[9] In an earlier study, Herendeen and Tanaka concluded that the average energy intensity (Btu per dollar) does decrease with the level of expenditure (income). On the average, energy intensity decreases by about 30 percent from the poorest to the richest income class. The 1972-73 data show that the overall energy intensity at all levels of expenditure has increased; however, the *relative* energy intensities across income classes have not changed much, if at all. A more recent study found that while the burden of higher energy prices does fall more heavily on low-income families, significant variations exist within the low-income group itself. Energy expenditures among poor people differ widely depending on climate, the type of energy used for heating, and the thermal integrity of their housing.[10] Therefore, the assertion made by Thurow that "a free market for energy would have resulted in a *sharp* shift toward inequality in the distribution of income" is based on tenuous and incomplete evidence at best.[11]

This is important, because the supposed extreme distributional inequities associated with a market-oriented energy policy are often cited as the primary, perhaps the only, objection to its immediate adoption. However, it would be callous and factually incorrect to claim that the poor would not be harmed by higher energy prices, and I am obviously not making such a claim.

The problems of defining "equity" are manifold, and consequently the claim that greater inequities exist today, when high energy costs prevail, as compared to the 1960s, is difficult to evaluate properly. Fortunately, for our purposes we need not address that difficult and value-laden question. The problems of poverty and inequality ought to be addressed and dealt with on their own merit and separated as much as possible from the question of energy pricing and energy markets. As a society we have a moral obligation to address the question of poverty directly, and it only acts to confuse the debate over proper energy policies when energy issues are interspersed with social and economic equity issues.

Of course, Thurow is aware of the serious pitfalls and distortions that are associated with government regulation of energy prices and energy markets. After noting that the regulation of petroleum prices led to shortages and in general created inconveniences for petroleum products users, he goes on to state very eloquently the "fatal flaw" of the regulatory solution to the energy problem: "Government regulations can control prices and to a lesser extent production, *but in our system they cannot control new investment.* No one can be forced to invest. Eventually new investments are necessary, and they will not be made unless they are as profitable as investments made in countries that do not control energy prices."[12] (Emphasis added.)

Thurow goes on to point out that under-investment in energy production sooner or later leads to "severe shortages," and then almost casually he offers the following observation: "Eventually we are forced to decide whether we want free market pricing (with its large income losses and gains) or a nationalized energy industry where government makes the necessary new investments."[13]

This is indeed a dramatic and stark choice that he puts before us, one that really brings the energy debate into sharp focus. Thurow laments that the current energy system (that is, one that is convoluted and badly distorted by regulations) does not work, but he argues that because of unfavorable consequences of market pricing on income distribution, it is not possible to shift to a system that we know to work reasonably efficiently without imposing unacceptable income losses on some people and unconscionable gains on others.

To my mind, the issue of income distribution raised by Thurow simply tends to obfuscate the discussion; the issue *really* is whether we desire a semblance of rationality with regard to energy policy and energy pricing, or if we want to gravitate toward a nationalized energy industry. While the answer is obvious to me, clearly some individuals would not agree with the proposition that energy problems are best solved through free, impersonal, and workably competitive markets.

It is my belief, to be more fully articulated in the following sections, that somehow we have managed to have the worst of both worlds. We have not allowed the "invisible hand" to guide the allocation of energy resources, yet government intervention and regulation have had on the whole a counterproductive and disruptive effect in the energy area.

THE GOVERNMENT AND ENERGY MARKETS:
LET'S GIVE FREE MARKETS A CHANCE

We really do not know how effective free energy markets could be in dealing with current and prospective energy "problems," because we have not yet given them a chance to function unfettered. President Reagan's philosophy as regards the overall thrust of U.S. energy policy is clearly articulated in his *National Energy Policy Plan* of July 1981. It can be summarized in the following quote: "Increased reliance on market decisions offers a continuing national referendum which is a far better means of charting the nation's energy path than stubborn reliance on government dictates or on a combination of subsidies and regulations."[14]

The President's Energy Manifesto goes on to state that an interventionist U.S. energy policy has attempted to "protect" U.S. consumers from higher world energy prices. In fact, domestic price controls and government regulation of energy markets had disastrous effects--they discouraged efficient energy use, inhibited domestic production and investment in developing local energy resources, and in general led to uncertainties and unnecessary inconvenience to energy users in industry, commerce, and everyday life.

Since this book does not offer a historical discourse or political analysis, it cannot provide an in-depth explanation as to how we got into the present energy morass in which we are so deeply embedded. In the preceding section, zero-sum approach to energy policy making has been highlighted because I believe it to be responsible in part for the very poor choice of energy strategies deployed by the United States in the last quarter century.

In the following sections of this chapter, I will discuss some of my ideas regarding the formation of an appropriate energy policy for the 1980s and beyond.

THE CARTER ADMINISTRATION'S
ENERGY POLICIES: A CRITIQUE

This section discusses briefly the Carter administration's approach to energy policy and contrasts it with the Reagan administration's approach to energy issues. Inevitably the comparison will be selective and incomplete and thus not fully balanced.[15] One of the earliest opportunities for President Carter to comment on energy policy came during his January 30, 1976 trip to Pittsburgh, an area that at the time was suffering from a very cold winter and intermittent fuel shortages.

On February 2, 1977, the president, clad in a cardigan sweater, presented his first televised "fireside chat" to the nation, regarding the natural gas shortage and the need for national sacrifice, which would be a recurring theme in the coming years. In his address, President Carter said in part: "Oil and natural gas companies must be honest with all of us about their reserves and profits. We will find out the difference between real shortages and artificial ones. We will ask private companies to sacrifice, just as private citizens must do . . . [S]imply by keeping our thermostats . . . at 65 degrees in the daytime and 55 degrees at night we could save half the current shortage of natural gas . . . ."[16] The themes of sacrifice, lack of honesty on part of the energy industry, and the need for a "fair" distribution of the energy burden would be recurrent throughout the Carter presidency.

Further on in writing about the energy crisis, Carter stated: "Following the fireside chat, I began a series of public forums within the White House and around the country to emphasize the importance of the [energy] legislation. It was like pulling teeth to convince the people of America that we had a serious problem in the face of apparently plentiful supplies, or that they should be willing to make some sacrifices or change their habits to meet a challenge which, for the moment, was not evident."[17]

At this time, James R. Schlesinger, Carter's "Energy Czar," entered the picture.[18] According to the account given by J. L. Cochrane: "Schlesinger's views on national economic policy were closer to French indicative planning than to the invisible hand of Adam Smith, Alfred Marshall, or Milton Friedman."[19] Be that as it may, Schlesinger assembled a small group of "planners" and set out to develop a master plan for energy, a plan that was to emphasize conservation by attempting to change consumers' energy use patterns and habits. According to the account given by Cochrane: "Although Schlesinger's team met with people from industry and government agencies, they essentially operated in isolation."[20] In fact, they were so isolated that they did not even coordinate their efforts with other major policy makers in their own administration!

Finally, after generating considerable suspense, Carter unveiled his eagerly awaited National Energy Plan to a joint session of Congress on April 20, 1977. The Carter energy plan considered the 1980s to be a period of transition from rapidly depleting domestic or foreign sources of oil and natural gas and toward renewable sources of energy. However, the most immediate concern of Schlesinger's team was with the 1977-85 period and with the issue of "dependence" on foreign oil. The plan therefore focused on reducing U.S. dependence on imported petroleum and its success would be largely judged in those terms.

The Energy Plan for the period beyond 1985 was only stated in general terms, and it would involve some unspecified solutions based on "solar," geothermal, and fusion technologies. [21]

On the other hand, the 1985 energy targets were specified in the most excruciating detail:

1. Reduce the annual growth of total energy demand to below 2 percent.
2. Reduce gasoline consumption 10 percent below its current level.
3. Reduce oil imports from a potential level of 16 million barrels per day to 6 million, roughly one eighth of total energy consumption.
4. Establish a Strategic Petroleum Reserve of 1 billion barrels.
5. Increase coal production by two thirds, to more than 1 billion tons per year.
6. Bring 90 percent of existing American homes and all new buildings up to minimum energy efficiency standards.
7. Use solar energy in more than 2.5 million homes. [22]

The Carter energy plan expected oil imports to reach 11.5 MMb/d by 1985 *if* no action was taken, and 7 MMb/d projected petroleum imports if the Carter plan was implemented, with imports declining perhaps another 1 MMb/d with certain other conservation programs in place. [23] The bulk of those so-called savings was supposed to come from the industrial sector; by comparison, the reduction in petroleum use that was expected from the transportation sector was quite modest.

The Carter National Energy Plan of April 1977 included about *one hundred* different initiatives, consisting of pricing policies, the creation of a regulatory apparatus, and a variety of administrative actions. Space will not permit a full review of all of Carter's energy programs; however, to savor their flavor, a few will be highlighted. As regards pricing of energy resources, the Carter plan had to deal with some thorny issues. In the first place, Carter insisted that the energy pricing system must be "fair." That came to mean that the U.S. Treasury should capture the bulk of the *rents* associated with higher prices of domestic petroleum and natural gas that otherwise would accrue to oil producers. On the other hand, energy prices were to reflect more closely marginal replacement costs of energy *and* provide sufficient incentives for oil or gas exploration and development.

The first objective of the pricing scheme--"fairness"-- reflected both Mr. Carter's populist sentiments and the influence of the type of ideology that I have described in the previous section. Perhaps the president actually believed that such a thing as a "fair" price for NG or petroleum could be devised by an all-wise government "planner."

THE PRICING OF ENERGY RESOURCES: A KEY TO AN EFFECTIVE ENERGY POLICY

An outline of a reasonably effective and lucid energy policy is contained in an important book by the staff of Resources for the Future. The RFF staff perceives energy prices primarily as an allocative mechanism and not as a tool for the distribution of income. Let me quote them directly: "Effective energy policy is best served by a pricing system that tells each consumer accurately and directly what it costs our economy to use more energy, as well as each producer or importer how much these additional supplies will contribute. In such a system, energy prices reflect the full marginal costs of the energy supplied."[24]

The authors tackle the issue of "fairness" directly by noting that energy price ceilings benefit both rich and poor, providing on balance little, if any, assistance to the poor. Further, they emphasize that using energy pricing policy as a distributive tool is not the best way of dealing with either energy or equity issues. They underscore this point by noting, "Instead of trying to use energy policy itself to achieve equity, we would increase our chances of assuring an *efficient and equitable outcome by concentrating on general instruments which affect the distribution of income.*"[25] (Emphasis added.)

A specific example of these principles was provided by the Carter administration's proposals with respect to oil and natural gas prices and energy taxes. The oil-pricing scheme suggested by the plan was intended to ease the transition to a higher world price of oil. But the higher domestic prices of petroleum would provide substantial amounts of revenue to oil producers and to the owners of oil leases; and since one of the principles underlying the Carter plan was that our energy problems must be solved in an "equitable" manner, a crude oil equalization tax was devised to address the fairness question. Thus, the cornerstone of Carter's energy plan was a proposal to raise energy prices through a crude oil equalization tax, much of which would then be rebated to the public.

Carter's proposal would have resulted in prices of petroleum products that more closely reflect their replacement cost, but it would not have yielded total efficiency gains that could be attained from having domestic petroleum production based on world prices. The early pricing and tax proposals of the Carter administration were intended to spread the surplus accruing to petroleum producers from rising world oil prices among the major participants in the U.S. oil markets. This underscores the point that to gain a better understanding of post-embargo oil policy, it is most appropriate to view it primarily as an exercise in income redistribution.

In general, the present energy pricing system fails to meet the criteria for rational energy decision making, because in many instances prices fail to reflect the marginal cost of producing energy. Under competitive market conditions, the amount of goods and services the economy can provide is maximized when the price of each good or service is equal to the marginal cost of supplying it. For example, when the alternative to domestic oil is foreign oil purchased at the world price, efficient use of our resources calls for producing domestic oil, up to the point when its cost is equal to the price of imported oil. If the marginal cost of domestically produced oil is above the price of imported oil, it is possible to economize on the use of our scarce resources by reducing domestically produced oil and replacing it with cheaper imports.

The RFF study notes that present energy pricing practices are inferior to marginal cost pricing because they lead to inefficient patterns of energy production and use, both in terms of the type of energy resources used and in terms of their location.[26] In addition to the allocational benefits of a free market system in energy resources, it would also reduce the scope and complexity of the policy issues that federal and state regulatory agencies must decide on in the coming years, because individual choices would for the most part replace bureaucratic and political decision-making processes.[27]

The Natural Gas Policy Act (NGPA) was part of the energy legislation signed into law by Carter on November 9, 1978. The act provided for a series of price ceilings for various categories of NG, while eliminating the former distinction between interstate and intrastate markets. The new NG pricing arrangements consist of a complex maze of over 17 different categories of NG, based on such distinctions as those between onshore and offshore gas, or whether the NG was committed to interstate markets before or after December 1, 1978. As I have argued at some length in Chapter 3, the pricing provisions of the NGPA violate many of the criteria required for a rational energy policy. The NGPA was in good part responsible for a paradoxical situation where NG prices subject to controls rose sharply in 1982 while at the same time a large excess supply of gas was known to exist.[28] Prices of *decontrolled* gas at the wellhead have fallen as much as 50 percent, while at the same time pipelines are renegotiating supply contracts downward. As old low-cost reserves have been depleted and replaced by new higher-cost gas, the purchasing costs of pipelines have kept edging up. Furthermore, some pipelines are locked into buying high-cost gas as a result of long-term contracts they signed during the shortages of the 1970s, although cheaper gas has become available to them since then.

It is instructive to contrast the recent behavior of NG prices under controls (or under partial decontrol) with the free market prices of two alternative fuels--No. 2 residential heating oil and No. 6 residual fuel--that compete with gas. In 1980 residential users of NG consumed roughly one fourth of gas used in the United States, while industrial customers and electric utilities consumed about 60 percent of the total. While prices of NG at the wellhead as well as prices paid by residential customers of gas were moving upward, just the opposite was the case for the market prices of the two competing fuels mentioned above.

The average price of No. 6 residual fuel oil sold to utilities, industry, and other ultimate users during the June-August 1982 period was 7.6 percent below that of the same period in 1981. The price of heating oil sold to residential customers during the June–August 1982 period was 3.6 percent lower than that sold in the same period in 1981.[29]

Price decontrol would also simplify certain other aspects of energy policy--it would eliminate the need for the maze of regulations, subsidies, and taxes that have been put in place to deal with distortions created by past and present energy policies.

A major objection to the immediate decontrol of natural gas prices has to do with the effect of this action on the price of gas paid by residential users and the supposed adverse macroeconomic effects of such a drastic step. As one observer noted: "Decontrol decisions entail huge political and economic risks because gas provides more than 25 percent of all U.S. energy needs and heats more than 45 million homes."[30] A recent study by the Congressional Budget Office (CBO) contains estimates of the macroeconomic effects of alternative natural gas policies, including a full decontrol of NG prices. Table 6-1 presents a summary of the CBO's report, specifically comparing two policy options: one of complete decontrol of NG prices at the wellhead as of January 1, 1984, and the other of merely advancing to January 1984 the date of *partial* decontrol envisioned in the NGPA of 1978.[31]

According to the CBO study, full decontrol would increase NG prices by 32 percent, raise inflation by 1.1 percent, while lowering gross domestic product by 0.3 percent during 1984. As a byproduct of decontrol, the projected increase in the federal government's revenues and royalties would amount to $7 billion in FY 1984, leading to a reduced budgetary deficit. Further note that in 1985 and beyond, decontrol would have practically no macroeconomic effects--that is, all the negative macroeconomic effects, such as they are, would be confined to 1984. Admittedly, the CBO analysis presents the worst-case scenario while ignoring the longer-term efficiency gains to be attained as a free market in NG permits producers and consumers to use energy more efficiently.

The decontrol of natural gas would eliminate the large exchange inefficiencies that exist under the NGPA. Currently, different classes of users of NG pay different prices for the same commodity, and these prices diverge substantially from those of competing fuels. In addition, industrial users and electric utilities are constrained in their ability to purchase and use NG. As a result, they are forced to use fuels such as oil or coal that are more costly at the margin.

TABLE 6-1. A Comparison of Macroeconomic and Budgetary Effects of Three
Natural Gas Policy Options: Changes from NGPA Base Case
(by calendar year)

Variable	1983	1984	1985	1986	1987
Real Gross Domestic Product (GDP)(percent change)					
Complete decontrol	0.00	-0.30	0.01	0.04	0.03
Partial decontrol	0.00	-0.10	0.05	0.03	0.00
Administrative decontrol	-0.05	-0.03	0.03	0.02	0.00
GDP Deflator (rate of change)					
Complete decontrol	0.00	1.10	-0.40	0.00	0.00
Partial decontrol	0.00	0.40	-0.30	0.00	0.00
Administrative decontrol	0.20	0.00	-0.20	0.00	0.00
Net Budgetary Effect (by fiscal year, in billions of dollars)*					
Complete decontrol	0.00	3.60	0.70	0.20	0.50
Partial decontrol	0.00	1.10	-0.50	-0.50	-0.30
Administrative decontrol	0.40	0.30	-0.50	-0.40	-0.20
Nominal Wellhead Natural Gas Prices (percent change)					
Complete decontrol	0.00	31.80	14.40	14.40	14.40
Partial decontrol	0.00	10.30	0.00	0.00	0.00
Administrative decontrol	4.40	4.20	0.00	0.00	0.00

*Positive numbers indicate a reduction in the deficit; negative numbers indicate an increase.

The three gas-pricing options considered are as follows:

1. Complete decontrol of wellhead NG prices on January 1, 1984.

2. Advancing the date of partial decontrol under NGPA to January 1, 1984.

3. Administrative decontrol where prices of some older categories of gas would be raised to the higher levels allowed for new gas on January 1, 1983.

The macroeconomic effects are based on the assumption that oil prices will rise to $39 per barrel in 1985.

Source: Congress of the United States, Congressional Budget Office, Natural Gas Pricing Policies: Implications for the Federal Budget, January 1983, p. XV.

Decontrol would result in improved efficiency and further real output gains simply by directing existing supplies of NG from lower to higher valued uses. [32]

Presently, certain potential residential users of gas are not allowed free access to it. Consequently, they are forced to rely on higher-cost substitutes in lieu of NG. Higher gas prices under decontrol would lead some existing users of gas to switch to alternative sources of fuel, while at the same time allowing other consumers to switch to NG, which heretofore was unavailable to them. Thus, even without any changes in NG production, decontrol would result in substantial efficiency gains and ultimately in lower gas prices.

Furthermore, decontrol of NG prices would tend to increase the responsiveness of U.S. gas and energy supplies to changes in the world price of oil and thus limit the pricing options available to OPEC. Should the price ceilings on NG be lifted, the price responsiveness of the demand for OPEC oil will increase, and further downward pressure will be exerted on oil prices. The additional NG produced in the United States tends to replace an equivalent amount of imported oil, leading to a decline in the cartel's market share, raising the elasticity of demand for OPEC oil, and thus further reducing their optimal price structure. [33]

Another study that examined the effects of NG decontrol on the economy of the industrial Northeast found it on the whole to be beneficent to that region's economy. The study reached the following overall conclusion:

> . . . both in terms of income flows and industrial competitiveness the Northeast will benefit from policies which allow natural gas prices to move toward parity with competitive fuels. Our analysis yields this conclusion despite the fact that we chose not to consider several unambiguous positive aspects of decontrol including improved efficiency of the national economy, reduced vulnerability to an oil supply disruption, and possible reductions in the level and prices of oil imports. [34]

Based on a detailed analysis, the Harvard Energy and Environmental Center group concluded that, following a relatively short adjustment period, NG prices "are likely to remain stable or even decline into the next decade."

As a result of energy price reform, the patterns of energy production and consumption will shift. Certain individuals will benefit while others may be harmed (although they could be compensated through the use of general socio-economic policy instruments); some firms will expand and profit while others will see their fortunes wane; and some regions of the country may prosper more than others.[35] Energy price reform inevitably will lead to changes in the structure of the U.S. economy that will be resisted by those who believe themselves to be unfairly dealt with under the new circumstances. Relative wage rates will change, as certain skills become more valuable to society. Certain capital assets (such as NG reserves or leases) will become more valuable while others will be worth less. Certain regions will become relatively less expensive and thus more attractive to work and live in, while others may experience decline due to higher cost of living. This is part and parcel of the adjustment process to a regime of market-determined energy prices, one that in the long run yields greater efficiency, larger output of goods and services, and a more harmonious social fabric.

If a policy of deregulation and the elimination of subsidies for energy use is adopted, it will result in some people becoming worse off, at least temporarily, as a result of this change. I have emphasized that regardless of what measures of poverty one chooses to use, higher energy prices affect the real incomes of poor people proportionately more than those who are better off.

A rough estimate, provided by Thomas Schelling, is that the poor--defined as those below 125 percent of the official poverty level, which includes the poorest one sixth of the U.S. population--were made poorer as a result of fuel price increases that took place over the last decade, by about $5 billion per year (in 1981 dollars). The 1979-80 increase in the world price of oil added more than $50 billion to the fuel bills that Americans had to pay to foreign suppliers, and another $7 billion was due to the higher cost of domestic oil released from controls; much of that, though, has been captured by the government through windfall profit and other taxes. Partial decontrol of natural gas prices brought the overall increase in our annual fuel expense, due to the 1979-80 price hikes, to almost $200 billion. Thus, the $5 billion--which was the real income loss of the poor--is small compared to the impact of energy price increases on the U.S. population as a whole.

This is not to belittle the extent of the hardships faced by the poorest in our society, but rather to suggest that, given its size, the question of the impact of higher energy prices on the poor can be readily addressed within the framework of existing general income maintenance programs.

In general, I sympathize with Thomas Schelling's view that people who are rendered poor because of energy price hikes are neither more nor less deserving of help than people who are impoverished due to other factors that are beyond their control.[36]   The best way to protect the poor from the adverse impact of higher energy cost is to leave prices to be determined by free markets, and make the requisite increase in income maintenance programs that assist the needy.

Some will argue that existing income transfer programs (such as Social Security programs, Supplemental Security Income, Aid to Families with Dependent Children, and others) simply do not provide adequate relief to the poor from the rising burden of higher energy costs.[37]   Therefore, they would propose that the problem be addressed through a separate fuel bill assistance program and/or large-scale weatherization cum conservation program.

What it implies is that in the current political climate, the chances of getting something done in a way of specific energy assistance programs for the needy are better than obtaining overall relief for the poor through existing income maintenance schemes.   Be that as it may, one can still be sympathetic to the idea that energy is like any other commodity or category of the consumer's budget and that fuel assistance and/or weatherization schemes are ineffective vehicles for transferring income to the poor.

ENERGY MARKETS: THE REAGAN ADMINISTRATION'S RECORD

As I previously noted, for a variety of reasons, genuinely free markets for energy resources have not been allowed to function in the United States.   The great advantage of free markets is that they permit energy prices and the allocation of resources to be decided by a complex of impersonal forces, rather than through government fiat.   The alternative to the operation of free markets in energy is the existence of some type of an energy "plan."   The problems with this concept are numerous, not the least of which is the presumption that in a pluralistic society it is possible to identify a common national goal, translate it into operational objectives, and then find the economic-political instruments necessary for its implementation.

The formulation of a comprehensive energy plan requires detailed understanding and reliable projections of future energy demand patterns, estimates of the costs of a variety of energy sources, and of whether they will be supplied domestically or through imports. It also calls for a reliable forecast of future progress of energy technologies, some of them still in their infancy. The difficulties involved in formulating a national energy plan are succinctly stated by Crawford D. Goodwin: "Energy planning as a substitute for the free market had two dimensions. The long run brought serious uncertainties and difficulties of implementation. As presidents discovered in the 1970s, however, the short run could yield near-chaos."[38]

Despite the often repeated rhetoric extolling the virtues of competitive capitalism, much has been done in the last three decades to discredit and impede the functioning of free markets in almost all major energy resources. With regard to petroleum, a complex structure of legislation and control mechanisms enabled the oil industry, in cooperation with government, to restrict output so as to match demand at above market prices. During that early era, government involvement in the petroleum markets took an increasingly anti-competitive and pro-industry direction. This was accomplished by limiting domestic oil production through so-called conservation or pro-rationing regulations and through special tax treatment of crude oil production.

In the mid-1950s, when abundant foreign supplies of petroleum threatened to undermine the domestic price structure, the government sought to implement a voluntary crude oil import control program. After unsuccessful attempts to obtain compliance with this program, it was replaced in April 1959 by a mandatory oil import program. The oil import restrictions in effect until early 1973 generated substantial rents for domestic producers, while at the same time imposing losses on the U.S. economy as a whole. During the early 1970s, not only were oil import restrictions dismantled, but the oil depletion allowance was first reduced and then eliminated, while comprehensive price controls and subsidies to crude oil users were put into effect.

The effect of the postembargo U.S. petroleum policy has been to capture, for domestic refiners and final users of petroleum products, substantial parts of the large increases in income that would have otherwise accrued to U.S. crude oil producers. As noted by Joseph P. Kalt, it is entirely appropriate to view the system of federal price controls on crude oil and the associated entitlement program as part of a large income redistribution scheme--transferring wealth from crude oil producers to refiners and consumers of petroleum products.[39] In the United States, the entitlement subsidy and crude oil price regulation have resulted in excessive levels of petroleum consumption and below optimal levels of domestic production, with the further undesirable outcome of increased dependence on imported crude oil. Over the long run, the increased uncertainty investors faced, due to the arbitrary nature of the regulatory mechanism, imposed even greater costs, by discouraging domestic oil exploration and development efforts.

On January 22, 1981, in one of the first acts of the new administration, President Reagan issued an executive order decontrolling the prices of petroleum and petroleum products. This was in line with Reagan policies that sought "to let market forces, rather than government fiat, direct the pricing and sale of petroleum products, as well as investment within the exploration, production, and refining segments of the industry."[40] The negative effects of crude oil price controls would have been eliminated at that point if it were not for the Windfall Profits Tax (WPT). The WPT that went into effect on March 1, 1980, together with existing taxes, will garner about 70 cents of every dollar of crude oil price increases over the 1980s. The WPT will have the effect of perpetuating multitier price regulation, and also of discouraging production from new exploration and development efforts. Kalt estimates the output-reducing impact of a fully implemented WPT to be somewhere around 1 million barrels of petroleum per day.[41] Thus the general belief that petroleum markets have been freed from the burden of price controls is not entirely correct, given that a differential excise tax structure has replaced the previous price controls regime. The previous effects of federal regulation of petroleum prices--underproduction of domestic oil and the subsequent overconsumption of imported oil--have not been fully remedied.

With regard to NG, not much needs to be added to what has been already written concerning the necessity of cutting the "Gordian Knot" of price regulation. Perhaps bowing to current political realities, the Reagan administration is still "assessing options for future natural gas policy." As we have noted, the NG industry is regulated at various levels--wellhead prices of gas are regulated by the FERC, which also sets the allowable rates charged by pipelines to local distribution companies; finally, the rates charged by local utilities to individual customers are generally set at the state level.

Typically, the local utility is charged a price that reflects the average cost of the gas supplied by its pipelines. The costs of transportation and distribution are also allocated, though usually on the basis of embedded rather than marginal costs. Consequently, the distribution companies and their customers do not pay rates that reflect the marginal costs experienced by the pipelines themselves. As a result, at the level of the local gas distribution company, little has been done to bring the full cost of gas to the attention of its ultimate users. Instead, the government has adopted policies that result in direct allocation of gas, refusal of new hookups to potential users, and other devices, in lieu of the allocative mechanism of a free market.

Although, to date, the market for electricity has not been disrupted by curtailments and allocations, price distortions at the level of the final user are also present.[42] Thus, for example, certain electric utilities, while charging industrial users on the average only 2 cents per kilowatt-hour, are adding new generating capacity that could result in prices of 4 to 5 cents per kilowatt-hour. The low average prices of electricity led to rapidly growing consumption throughout the 1960s that could be met by utilities only through much higher replacement costs. The utilities' customers, though, were discouraged from investing in energy conservation or in substitute fuels that cost less to produce than the new supplies the utility was adding. Furthermore, presently costly new sources of energy can be added to the system without a full market test. This is because the new sources are "rolled in" with cheaper sources of energy and, as a result, consumers are not faced with a rate structure that truly reflects the costs of these added supplies of energy.

Thus, an urgent case can be made for adopting policy measures that would correct such distortions and lead users of electricity or NG to behave, as much as possible, as if they were facing the full incremental costs that the entire system is experiencing. It is easy enough to state the principles that would lead to a situation that is more desirable from the standpoint of economic efficiency: Consumers should pay the full marginal cost of the electricity and NG that they use. But, though simple to state, this principle is not easy to implement in practice. In the first place, there are serious problems in defining marginal costs and of metering consumer use on a continuous basis.[43] In addition, changing to marginal cost pricing would inevitably result in a sharp increase in the net revenues of utilities, as income would be transferred from rate payers to the utility's shareholders. That could be objected to on the grounds of equity. To meet this objection it would be possible to tax this excess revenue and use such funds to pay for general social welfare programs. Ironically, current regulatory practices, requiring utilities to serve all the demand that exists at rates that have been set so as to provide a "fair" rate of return on their original investment, may lead to much higher rates and less dependable service in the future. As pointed out by Peter Navarro, "if electricity consumers paid higher rates now (5% to 10% more) so that utilities had the capital to undertake economic investments, the rate on the amount that consumers would save in most cases would greatly exceed that on any other investment in a typical portfolio. . . ."[44] In sum, pricing reform with respect to electricity and NG must assure that consumers are faced with rates that reflect as closely as possible the marginal costs associated with their greater use of energy. The alternative to this reform is continued distortion in this important segment of the market and failure to bring about efficient use of these energy resources. The present regulatory structure also makes it difficult for utilities to raise adequate revenues to finance new capacity. The high interest rates that prevailed in recent years have made it even more difficult for utilities to undertake such highly capital-intensive investments with long lead times. And finally we should realize that the policy of keeping prices of conventional energy sources below their replacement costs discriminates against new and unconventional energy sources and thus retards their rate of introduction.

ENERGY POLICY: THE UNFINISHED AGENDA

The 1970s and early 1980s have seen some important adjustments in the way the U.S. economy uses energy. Implementation of market-oriented energy policies, however tentative, together with the higher prices of oil, have already generated gains in both energy efficiency and in the substitution of other fuels for oil. Evidence of the cumulative effect of energy price hikes may be seen in the declining share of both total energy, and especially oil, in real output. In 1981, real GNP in the United States was 20 percent above its 1973 level, but overall energy consumption was slightly below the 1973 level, and oil use was down by almost 8 percent.[45] Petroleum imports, which at first rose much faster than total petroleum consumption, peaked in 1977 and have been declining steadily since then.

U.S. dependence on petroleum imports, which reached 46 percent in 1977, was below 30 percent for the first two quarters of 1982. The share of the Arab members of OPEC in the total supply of petroleum products in the United

States fell even more sharply. In the second and third quarters of 1982, it was 70 percent below its 1977 level.[46] The declining oil imports, and especially the falling share of such imports coming from the vulnerable Persian Gulf area, makes the United States somewhat less susceptible to sudden oil import disruption than it was in 1977.

The balance of forces in the world market for petroleum now favors the oil-importing nations, a fact that should bring special relief to the poorest among the non-OPEC developing countries. While the world economic downturn has certainly been an important factor behind the soft petroleum market, one should not overlook the impressive energy savings attained by the OECD countries as a group during the 1970s. Governments in major oil-consuming countries took active steps to promote conservation by raising taxes on oil consumption and by removing price controls.

The downward pressure on petroleum prices resulted from a combination of short-term factors--the world recession and the rundown of crude oil stocks, and some permanent factors--increased conservation and the larger oil output of non-OPEC producers. Early in 1982, the slump in oil production and sales worsened and large price discounts were offered in the spot market. Faced with an oil market glut, OPEC oil ministers met in March 1982 and agreed on an overall production limit of 17.5 MMb/d. However, by June-July 1982, OPEC production was in fact around 18.5 MMb/d, well above the previously agreed-upon ceiling; and with the demand for oil still being weak, prices kept on sliding. Thus by August-September 1982, U.S. refiners' acquisitions costs of imported oil fell by about $6 per barrel from the lofty heights they achieved in the first few months of 1981.[47] Given the recent failed effort by OPEC oil ministers to hammer out a binding production quota and a new pricing structure, the prospects are for further erosion in oil prices in the near term.[48]

Further actions on the part of OECD governments to pass higher petroleum costs on to motorist and other users of petroleum products, plus financial and tax incentives to promote conservation in cases where price signals do not work adequately, would act to restrain world oil prices in the early stages of the much awaited economic recovery. Over the short haul, supply conditions also favor the oil-importing nations. At present, the large excess capacity among OPEC producers is sufficient to absorb the increased demand when the world economy recovers from the depth of the current recession.[49] Furthermore, given the worsening payments position of several oil exporters both inside and outside OPEC, we are likely to see efforts by countries such as Mexico, Nigeria, Venezuela, and Indonesia to expand their exports, which can only be done under prevailing market conditions, by significantly lowering prices.

However, one should not be lulled into complacency by these short-term developments that appear to favor oil-importing nations. A warning of the possible longer-term danger resulting from a sharp drop in petroleum prices has been sounded by the IEA in the recent *World Energy Outlook*: ". . . growing OECD oil demand, confronted with both constrained world oil production and increasing requirements in other areas of the world, could again set the stage for significant oil price increases and major market disruptions."[50] The IEA added a cautionary note: The fine balance between oil supply and demand, forecast by the OECD for the second half of the 1980s, could be suddenly upset by political events in the Middle East.

The central question we are faced with is whether continuing gains in efficiency and substitutions of other fuels for oil can be accomplished through more effective implementation of consistent energy policies, or whether it will be brought about by periodic sharp increases in the real price of petroleum that would result in large income losses. Structural adjustments to changed energy prices have been underway in all sectors of the economy since 1973, and they should be reinforced and not allowed to wither away. In fact, there are some early signs that conservation gains that were especially pronounced in the 1978-81 period have slowed down recently in the United States, Germany, and the United Kingdom.[51]

As long as policies are in place that will continue the process of reducing oil consumption per unit of real output and of substituting cheaper alternative fuels for petroleum, the chances of avoiding future oil price shocks will be enhanced. As noted by Hall and Pindyck, the real output of Western economies is particularly susceptible to energy price shocks.[52] Following the oil price shocks of 1974 and 1979, because of the failure of real wages to decline, employers proceeded to lay off workers, which brought on a drop in real output and rising unemployment. The recession induced by the energy shocks was also made worse by the close interaction between the United States and other Western economies. The IEA analysis underscored the point that the slowdown in economic activity in 1980-81 can be attributed to the effects of the 1979 oil price shock. The total loss of real income in the OECD, resulting largely from the second oil price shock, has been estimated to be in excess of *one trillion dollars* by 1981. This underscores the urgency of designing economic energy policies that will minimize the impact of future oil price shocks on output and employment.

The Reagan administration's energy policy did not fully live up to the goal of providing "a healthy economy and policy environment that enables citizens, businesses, and state and local governments to make rational energy production and consumption decisions. . . ."[53] In the United States (and in other advanced countries), various forms of government intervention and numerous barriers still discourage energy conservation, domestic production of certain energy sources, and mutually beneficial international trade in energy. Examples include price controls, leasing policies, licensing and permitting procedures, regulatory regimes, export restrictions, and others. One such constraint that is now receiving some attention in the United States involves the need to streamline utility regulating procedures--particularly for nuclear power plants. As I have argued in some detail elsewhere in this book, the increasing uncertainty that surrounds the planning process for new investments in nuclear, coal, and other energy sources acts as an effective barrier to their expansion at this time. Institutional barriers to the effective transmission of price signals that lead to inefficient energy use should be avoided at all costs and would be an appropriate object of further government action.

The experiences of the 1970s remind us that the only effective way of avoiding fuel shortages and wasteful use of energy is through free market pricing and allocation. The pricing mechanism should be the basis for consistent and effective energy policies intended to reduce the dependence on oil and to enable the United States and other free world economies to adjust with the least possible disruption to any unforeseen adverse changes in energy prices and energy supplies.

NOTES

1. Lester C. Thurow, *The Zero-Sum Society* (New York: Basic Books, 1980); also see Robert Stobaugh and Daniel Yergin (eds.), *Energy Future* (New York: Random House, 1979), especially chs. 1, 3, and 8.
2. Ibid., p. 9.
3. Ibid., p. 21.
4. Ibid., p. 109.
5. Ibid., p. 120.

6. Ibid., pp. 28-29.

7. Thurow defines the "poor" as the poorest one tenth of the population in terms of income. Ibid., p. 29.

8. Kenneth J. Arrow and Joseph P. Kalt, *Petroleum Price Regulation: Should We Decontrol?* (Washington, D.C.: American Enterprise Institute for Public Policy Research, 1979), p. 29.

9. Robert Herendeen and Jerry Tanaka, "Energy Cost of Living," *Energy,* vol. 1, no. 2, pp. 165-78, and Robert A. Herendeen, Charlotte Ford and Bruce Hannon, "Energy Cost of Living, 1972-73," *Energy,* VI, 12 (December 1981): 1433-50.

10. For further details consult Harold Beebout, Gerald Peabody, and Pat Doyle, "The Distribution of Household Energy Expenditures and the Impact of High Prices," in Hans H. Landsberger's *High Energy Cost: Assessing the Burden* (Washington, D.C.: Resources for the Future, 1982).

11. Thurow, *Zero-Sum Society,* p. 31.

12. Ibid., pp. 33-36.

13. Ibid., p. 34.

14. U.S. Department of Energy, *Securing America's Energy Future: The National Energy Policy Plan,* Washington, D.C., July 1981, p. 1.

15. Much of the factual account of the Carter administration's energy policy is taken from James L. Cochrane, "Carter Energy Policy and the Ninety-fifth Congress," in Crawford D. Goodwin (ed.), *Energy Policy in Perspective: Today's Problems, Yesterday's Solutions* (Washington, D.C.: Brookings Institution, 1981).

16. Jimmy Carter, *Keeping Faith: Memoirs of a President* (New York: Bantam Books, 1982), p. 94.

17. Ibid., p. 97.

18. From the recently published Carter memoirs it is obvious that he has the highest regard for James Schlesinger's intellect and political acumen. In referring to Schlesinger he writes: "I already had working with me as a senior White House Assistant the best-qualified man we could find to develop this new program and help me sell it to Congress." Carter goes on to say: "He was a shrewd analyst of the International scene, and would have been qualified to serve as Secretary of State or to return to his former position as Secretary of Defense." Ibid., p. 96.

19. Cochrane, "Carter Energy Policy and the Ninety-fifth Congress," p. 553.

20. Ibid., p. 555.

21. For further details refer to the plan itself, Executive Office of the President, Office of Energy Policy and

Planning, *The National Energy Plan,* Executive Office of the President, April 29, 1977.

22. Cochrane, "Carter Energy Policy and the Ninety-fifth Congress," p. 561.

23. Ibid., pp. 561-64.

24. Sam H. Schurr et al., *Energy in America's Future: The Choices Before Us* (Baltimore: Johns Hopkins University Press, 1979), p. 46.

25. Ibid., p. 50.

26. Ibid., pp. 439-52.

27. The following examples illustrate the type of complicated decisions and politically charged issues that the Federal Energy Regulatory Commission (FERC) is tackling:

1. The FERC has approved new rules that allow pipelines to charge customers for certain production-related costs. Currently residential customers cannot be billed for most of the costs of gathering, compressing, and cleaning NG before it is shipped by interest rate pipelines. This decision added at least $1.8 billion in consumer gas bills nationwide. "Natural Gas Prices Expected to Rise 25% in 1983 Due to New U.S. Regulatory Rules," *Wall Street Journal,* January 14, 1983, p. 3.

2. The Commission, under the leadership of Chairman Charles Butler, last winter nearly doubled the price of NG produced from deep offshore wells. Butler also would like to raise the price ceiling on gas produced from certain onshore wells. Furthermore, he would like to loosen controls on even larger volumes of so-called old gas, which is being sold through low-cost and long-term contracts. Andy Pasztor, "Agency Speeds Gas Decontrol Stirring Fight," *Wall Street Journal,* February 9, 1982, p. 27.

3. The FERC ordered an investigation into possible irregularities at hundreds of gas processing plants located on pipelines around the country. If a pattern of processing irregularities, found in the case of one company, is repeated with other pipeline companies, overcharges could be in the "hundreds of millions of dollars," according to commission investigators. "Gas Processor Studied by U.S. for Overcharges," *Wall Street Journal,* October 8, 1982, p. 4.

28. One report states that some 2 TCF of natural gas is being kept off the market. This amounts to about 10 percent of the average annual NG consumption in 1980-81. Another report estimates that in the fourth quarter of 1982, consumption of NG was down 15 to 20 percent from the year earlier period. At the same time average residential NG

prices have risen by one dollar per thousand cubic feet between June-July of 1981 and 1982. Maria Shao, "Despite Glut of Heating Oil and Natural Gas Prices Aren't Expected to Drop This Winter," *Wall Street Journal,* October 6, 1982, p. 31; and Steve Mufson, "Oil Firms' Fourth-Quarter Profits to Be Down; Slump Seen Running Through Early '83," *Wall Street Journal,* January 17, 1983, p. 3. For full information on NG prices consult U.S. Department of Energy, *Monthly Energy Review,* November 1982, p. 82.

29. U.S. Department of Energy, *Monthly Energy Review,* November 1982, pp. 84-86.

30. Andy Pasztor, "Reagan Advisers Divided Over Pace of Gas Decontrol, Link with Taxes," *Wall Street Journal,* December 7, 1981, p. 29.

31. In addition the CBO report assumes "moderate" increases in the price of crude oil between 1982 and 1985 and an accommodative fiscal and monetary policy. Should the price of oil continue to fall in 1983 and 1984, the CBO estimate of the macroeconomic costs may turn out to be excessive.

32. In addition to the gains that will accrue from improved allocation of NG among users, supply side gains will likely result from more efficient production of NG. One simulation study found that decontrol of NG is likely to improve industrial energy efficiency. Over the 1982-90 period such efficiency gains could amount to $7.1 billion (in constant 1972 dollars). John C. Felmy, Natural Gas Decontrol: Efficiency Gains vs. Macroshocks, presented at the IAEE meeting, November 1982.

33. While precise estimates of such effects are unavailable, Matt Ott and John Tatom provide some ballpark estimates of possible effects of NG decontrol on world oil prices. Matt Ott and John A. Tatom, "Are There Adverse Inflation Effects Associated with Natural Gas Decontrol?" *Contemporary Policy Issues,* no. 1, October 1982.

34. Joseph P. Kalt, Henry Lee and Robert Leone, *Natural Gas Decontrol: A Northeast Perspective* (Cambridge, Mass.: Energy and Environmental Policy Center, John F. Kennedy School of Government, Harvard University, October 1982), p. 6.

35. It is important to realize that often the conventional analysis of the effects of price reform is misleading and incomplete. Take the case of the effects of NG price deregulation on the Northeast regional economy. The first impression is that NG price decontrol would harm this nine-state region since an increase in gas bills represents a drain on regional income, but on the other hand the Northeast would get a boost of its income due to its ability to

export more goods to gas-producing states, whose income will rise with higher NG prices. Furthermore, Northeast residents who are stockholders in gas-producing companies would stand to receive higher incomes due to the policy of NG decontrol. Ibid., chs. 3, 4, and 7.

36. Thomas C. Schelling, "Energy and Poverty," in, Hans H. Landsberg (ed.), *High Energy Costs: Assessing the Burden* (Washington, D.C.: Resources for the Future, 1982).

37. See for example, Alan L. Cohen and Kevin Kollenbeck, "Energy Assistance Schemes: Review, Evaluation, and Recommendation," in ibid., pp. 60-120.

38. Crawford D. Goodwin, "The Lessons of History," in C. D. Goodwin (ed.), *Energy Policy in Perspective* (Washington, D.C.: Brookings Institution, 1981), p. 673.

39. Joseph P. Kalt, *The Economics and Politics of Oil Price Regulation* (Cambridge, Mass.: MIT Press, 1981).

40. U.S. Department of Energy, *Securing America's Energy Future: The National Energy Policy Plan,* July 1981, p. 5.

41. Joseph P. Kalt, *The Economics and Politics of Oil Price Regulation,* p. 288.

42. Despite much higher construction and operating costs for new generating capacity, whether nuclear or coal-fired, the price of electricity to residential customers in 1980-81 was below the one that prevailed in the mid-1960s (prices are expressed in constant 1972 dollars). U.S. Department of Energy, Energy Information Administration, *1981 Annual Report to Congress,* vol. 2, May 1982, p. 165.

43. For example, marginal cost pricing for both gas and electricity implies that the rates should vary according to the condition of the system. Thus, during peak-hours, when more costly generating units are used, the price per unit should be higher, while during off-peak hours the price should fall. For a more technical discussion of utility pricing reform see Philip J. Mause, "Price Regulation and Energy Policy," in *Selected Studies on Energy: Background Studies for Energy: The Next Twenty Years* (Cambridge, Mass.: Ballinger, 1980), pp. 145-60.

44. Peter Navarro, "Utility Bills: The Real Price of Electricity," *Wall Street Journal,* January 13, 1983.

45. The ratio of energy consumption to the aggregate measure of goods and services produced (thousands Btu per 1972 dollar) has declined from 59.5 in 1973 to 49.2 in 1981, a decline of 17.3 percent. U.S. Department of Energy, *Monthly Energy Review,* December 1982, p. 14.

46. Arab members of OPEC are Algeria, Iraq, Kuwait,

Libya, Qatar, Saudia Arabia, and United Arab Emirates. Data are from ibid., p. 15.

47. Ibid., p. 80.

48. In the aftermath of the January 1983 OPEC meeting, prices of non-OPEC crude fell from $1.50 to $2 per barrel on the spot market. "OPEC Meeting Fails to Agree on Oil Price, Output, Clearing Way for Possible Round of Lower Quotes," *Wall Street Journal,* January 25, 1983, p. 3.

49. The "maximum sustainable capacity" of OPEC's crude oil production through the year 1985 is thought to be between 31.6 and 33 MMb/d. With actual production in July–August 1982 averaging about 18.2 MMb/d, excess capacity ranges from 13.4 to 14.8 MMb/d. International Energy Agency, *World Energy Outlook* (Paris: OECD, 1982), p. 246.

50. Ibid., p. 13.

51. A number of indicators point to the declining role of oil in the OECD economies in the 1978–81 period. Overall oil consumption per unit of GDP has declined by 6.8 percent, while gasoline consumption per automobile fell 6.5 percent per year. See ibid., p. 72. For more recent developments see Edward J. Frydl and William A. Dellaljar, "The Shifting Balance in the World Oil Market," *Federal Reserve Bank of New York Quarterly Review,* VII, 3 (Autumn 1982): 45.

52. Robert E. Hall and Robert S. Pindyck, "What to Do When Energy Prices Rise Again," *The Public Interest,* no. 65, Fall 1981, pp. 5970.

53. U.S. Department of Energy, *Securing America's Energy Future: The National Energy Policy Plan,* July 1981, p. 1.

BIBLIOGRAPHY

BOOKS AND CHAPTERS IN BOOKS

Adelman, M. A. 1982. "OPEC as a Cartel," in *OPEC Behavior and World Oil Prices, edited by James M. Griffin and David J. Teece, pp. 37–63.*

Arrow, Kenneth and Joseph P. Kalt. 1979. *Petroleum Price Regulation: Should We Decontrol?* Washington, D.C.: American Enterprise Institute for Public Policy Research.

Barber, William J. 1981. "The Eisenhower Energy Policy: Reluctant Intervention." In *Energy Policy in Perspective,* edited by Crawford D. Goodwin, pp. 229-61. Washington, D.C.: Brookings Institution.

Beebort, Harold, Gerald Peabody, and Pat Doyle. 1982. "The Distribution of Household Energy Expenditures and the Impact of High Prices." In *High Energy Costs: Assessing the Burden,* edited by Hans H. Landsberger, pp. 1-35. Washington, D.C.: Resources for the Future.

Bohi, Douglas and Milton Russell. 1978. *Limiting Oil Imports: An Economic History and Analysis.* Baltimore: Johns Hopkins University Press.

Bohi, Douglas. 1981. *Analyzing Demand Behavior: A Study of Energy Elasticities.* Baltimore: Johns Hopkins University Press.

Brown, Keith C. (ed.). 1972. *Regulation of The Natural Gas Producing Industry.* Washington, D.C.: Resources for the Future.

Bupp, I. C. and Frank Schuller. 1979. "Natural Gas: How to Slice a Shrinking Pie." In *Energy Future,* edited by Robert Stobaugh and Daniel Yergin, pp. 56-78. New York: Random House.

Camm, Frank A. 1978. *Average Cost Pricing of Natural Gas: A Problem and Three Policy Options.* Santa Monica: Rand.

Carter, Jimmy. 1982. *Keeping Faith: Memoirs of a President.* New York: Bantam Books.

Cochrane, James L. 1981. "Carter Energy Policy and the Ninety-Fifth Congress." In *Energy Policy in Perspec-*

tive: Today's Problems, Yesterday's Solutions, edited by Crawford D. Goodwin, pp. 547-600, Washington, D.C.: Brookings Institution.

Ford, Daniel. 1982. *The Cult of the Atom.* New York: Simon and Schuster.

Gisser, Micha. 1981. *Intermediate Price Theory,* New York: McGraw-Hill.

Goodwin, Crawford, D. 1981. "The Lessons of History." In *Energy Policy in Perspective,* edited by Crawford D. Goodwin, pp. 665-84, Washington, D.C.: Brookings Institution.

Helms, Robert B. 1974. *Natural Gas Regulation: An Evaluation of FPC Price Controls.* Washington, D.C.: American Enterprise for Public Policy Research, July.

Hirshleifer, Jack. 1980. *Price Theory and Application,* 2nd edition. Englewood-Cliffs: Prentice Hall.

Hogan, William, H. 1980. "Dimensions of Energy Demand." In *Selected Studies on Energy, Background Papers for Energy: The Next Twenty Years,* edited by Hans H. Landsberger, pp. 1-92. Cambridge, Mass: Ballinger.

Kalt, Joseph P. 1981. *The Economics and Politics of Oil Price Regulation.* Cambridge, Mass.: MIT Press.

Landsberg, Hans H., et al. 1979. *Energy: The Next Twenty Years,* Cambridge, Mass.: Ballinger.

MacAvoy, P. W., and R. S. Pindyck. 1975. *The Economics of The Natural Gas Shortage (1960-1980).* Amsterdam: North-Holland.

------. 1975. *Price Controls and The Natural Gas Shortage.* American Enterprise for Public Policy Research. Washington, D.C.

Mause, Philip J. 1980. "Price Regulation and Energy Policy: In *Selected Studies on Energy: Background Papers for Energy: The Next Twenty Years,* edited by Hans H. Landsberger, pp. 145-66. Cambridge, Mass.: Ballinger.

McCracken, Samuel. 1982. *The War Against the Atom,* New York: Basic Books.

Mooz, W. E. 1979. *A Second Analysis of Light Water Reactor Power Plants.* Santa Monica: Rand.

National Academy of Sciences, National Research Council. 1980. *Energy in Transition 1985-2010.* San Francisco: W. H. Freeman.

Nuclear Energy Policy Study Group. 1979. *Nuclear Power Issues and Choices.* Cambridge, Mass.: Ballinger.

Perry, Robert et al. 1977. *Development and Commercialization of the Light Water Reactor, 1946-1976.* Santa Monica: Rand.

Rolph, Elizabeth. 1977. *Regulation of Nuclear Power: The*

Case of the Light Water Reactor. Santa Monica: Rand.
Schelling, Thomas C. 1982, "Energy and Poverty." In
    High Energy Costs: Assessing the Burden, edited by
    Hans H. Landsberger; pp. 386-94. Washington, D.C.:
    Resources for the Future.
Schurr, Sam H. et al. 1979. *Energy in America's Future.*
    Washington, D.C.: Johns Hopkins University Press.
Stobaugh, Robert. 1979. "After the Peak: The Threat of
    Imported Oil." In *Energy Future,* edited by R.
    Stobaugh and D. Yergin, pp. 16-65. New York:
    Random House.
Thurow, Lester C. 1980. *The Zero-Sum Game Society.*
    New York: Basic Books.
Yager, Joseph A. 1981. "The Energy Battles of 1979."
    In *Energy Policy in Perspective,* edited by Crawford D.
    Goodwin, pp. 601-36. Washington, D.C.: Brookings
    Institution.

JOURNALS AND REPORTS

Adelman, M. A. 1978. "Constraints on the World Oil
    Monopoly Price." *Resources and Energy,* vol. 1, pp.
    2-4.
American Gas Association Gas Supply Committee. 1980.
    The Gas Energy Supply Outlook: 1980-2000. Arlington,
    Va.
American Gas Association, Department of Statistics. 1981.
    Gas Facts 1980 Data. Arlington, Va.
American Petroleum Institute. 1982. *Basic Petroleum Data
    Book,* Vol. II, Number 1.
Arrow, Kenneth J. and Robert C. Lind. 1970.
    "Uncertainty and the Evaluation of Public Investment
    Decisions." *American Economic Review,* June, pp.
    364-78.
Bennett, Paul, Harold Cole, and Steven Dym. 1980. "Oil
    Price Decontrol and Beyond." *Federal Reserve Bank of
    New York Quarterly Review,* Winter, pp. 36-42.
Bennett, Paul and Deborah Kuenstner. 1981-82. "Natural
    Gas Controls and Decontrols." *Federal Reserve Bank of
    New York Quarterly Review,* Winter, pp. 50-60.
Capra, James R. and David C. Beek. 1981-82. "Combining
    Decontrol of Natural Gas with a New Tax on Producer
    Revenues." *Federal Reserve Bank of New York Quar-
    terly Review,* Winter, pp. 61-66.
Craig, P. P., M. D. Levine, and J. Mass. 1980.
    "Uncertainty: An Argument for More Stringent Energy
    Conservation." *Energy,* October, pp. 1073-83.

Crowley, John H. and Jerry D. Griffith. 1982. "U.S. Construction Cost Rise Threatens Nuclear Option." *Nuclear Engineering International.* June, pp. 25-28.

Dutton, Harry. 1970. "Symposium Told Significance of Nuclear Era." *Northwest Public Power Bulletin,* December.

Evans, Nigel. 1982. "Hidden Costs of the Accident at Three Mile Island." *Energy,* September, pp. 723-30.

Felmy, John C. 1982. "Natural Gas Decontrol: Efficiency Gains vs. Macro-Shocks." Presented at IAEE meeting, November, 1982.

Freemerman, R. L. and R. L. Rider. 1982. "Taking a Look Inside TMI-2." *Nuclear Engineering International,* October, pp. 27-32.

Frydl, Edward J. and William A. Dellalfar. 1982. "The Shifting Balance in the World Oil Market." *Federal Reserve Bank of New York Quarterly Review,* Autumn, pp. 41-43.

Greer, Boyce I. and Jeremy L. Russell. 1982. "European Reliance on Soviet Gas Exports: The Yamburg-Urengui Natural Gas Project. *Energy Journal,* July, pp. 15-37.

Hall, Robert E. and Robert S. Pindyck. 1981. "What to Do When Energy Prices Rise Again." *Public Interest,* Fall, pp. 59-70.

Hemphill, Robert F. 1981. *Statement before Subcommittee of Energy Development and Application House Science and Technology Committee.* June 23.

Herendeen, Robert and Jerry Tanaka. 1976. "Energy Cost of Living." *Energy,* vol. 1, no. 2, pp. 165-78.

Herendeen, Robert, Charlotte Ford and Bruce Hannon. 1981. "Energy Cost of Living 1972-73." *Energy,* December, pp. 1433-50.

Hewett, Edward A. 1982. "The Pipeline Connection: Issues for the Alliance." *The Brookings Review,* Fall, p. 19.

International Monetary Fund. 1981. *World Economic Outlook,* Washington, D.C., June.

International Monetary Fund. 1982. *World Economic Outlook,* Washington, D.C., April.

International Energy Agency. Organization for Economic Cooperation and Development. 1982. *Natural Gas Prospects to 2000.* Paris.

International Energy Agency, OECD. 1982. *World Energy Outlook.* Paris.

Jacoby, Henry D. and Arthur M. Wright. 1982. "The Gordian Knot of Natural Gas Prices." *The Energy Journal,* October, pp. 1-25.

Kalt, Joseph P., Henry Lee and Robert Leone. 1982.

Natural Gas Decontrol: A Northeast Perspective.
Energy and Environmental Policy Center, John F.
Kennedy School of Management, Harvard University,
October.

Levy, Walter, J. 1981. "Oil: An Agenda for the 1980s."
Foreign Affairs, Summer, pp. 1079-101.

Levy, Yvonne. 1981. "Crude Oil Price Controls and the
Windfall Profit Tax: Deterrents to Production?" *Feder-
al Reserve Bank of San Francisco Economic Review.*
Spring, pp. 6-28.

Lowinger, Thomas C. 1980. "U.S. Energy Policy: A
Critical Assessment." *MSU Business Topics,* Winter,
pp. 15-22.

McDonald, Stephen L. 1981. "The Incidence and Effects of
the Crude Oil Windfall Tax." *Natural Resources Journal,* April, 331-39.

McKie, James W. 1978. "Oil Imports: Is Any Policy
Possible?" *Natural Resources Journal,* October,
pp. 731-745.

Mooz, W. E. 1981. "Cost Analysis for LWR Power Plants."
Energy, March, pp. 197-225.

Morgan Guaranty Trust. 1981. *World Financial Markets,*
August.

National Petroleum Council. 1980. *Unconventional Gas
Sources* (Executive Summary). December.

Nesbit, William. 1982. "Evaluating Passive's Potential,"
EPRI Journal, July/August, pp. 18-23.

NRC Special Inquiry Group. Michael Rogovin, Director.
1980. *Three Mile Island, A report to the Commissioners
and the Public,* January.

Office of Applied Energy Studies, Washington Energy
Research Center. Washington State University. 1982.
*Independent Review of Washington Public Power Supply
System Nuclear Plants 4 and 5.* Final Report to the
Washington State Legislature. March.

Ott, Matt and John A. Tatom. 1982. "Are There Adverse
Inflation Effects Associated with Natural Gas Decontrol?"
Contemporary Policy Issues, October, pp. 27-46.

Radetzki, Marian. 1981. "Falling Oil Prices in the 80s."
Scandinaviska Enskilda Banken Quarterly Review, no.
1-2, pp. 20-28.

Reister, David B. 1982. "Energy Conservation: The
Post-Embargo Record." *Energy,* May pp. 403-11.

Report of the President's Commission. 1979. *The Accident
at Three Mile Island: The Need for Change: The
Legacy of TMI.* Washington, D.C., October.

Stockman, David. 1980. "Needed: A Duel Resurrection."
Journal of Energy and Development, Spring, pp.

171-81.
Swanson, Thomas P. 1982. Comments before the Energy
    and Utilities Committee of the Washington State Senate.
    October 15.
------. 1981. "U.S. Activity Is Unprecedented." *World
    Oil,* August, 15, pp. 62-72.
------. 1981. "Six New Fields Make List of U.S. Oil
    Giants." *Oil and Gas Journal,* January 26, p. 153.
------. 1981. Interview with Shelby Brewer, Assistant
    Secretary for Nuclear Engery. *Nuclear News,* Decem-
    ber, p. 67.

PUBLIC DOCUMENTS

Bradford, Peter A. 1982. Commissioner U.S. Nuclear
    Regulatory Commission. Statement in U.S. House of
    Representatives. *Nuclear Safety: Three Years After
    Three Mile Island.*
Executive Office of the President, Office of Management and
    Budget. *Budget of the United States Government Fiscal
    Year 1982,* Washington, D.C.: Government Printing
    Office.
Executive Office of the President, Office of Management and
    Budget. *Budget of the United States Government Fiscal
    Year 1983,* Washington, D.C.: Government Printing
    Office.
Executive Office of the President, Office of Management and
    Budget. *Major Themes and Additional Budget Details,
    Fiscal Year 1983,* pp. 97-98.
Murphy, F. H., R. P. O'Neill and M. Rodekohr. 1981.
    "An Overview of the Natural Gas Markets," U.S. De-
    partment of Energy, *Monthly Energy Review,* December,
    pp. I-VIII.
O'Neill, R. P. 1982. "The Interstate and Intrastate
    Natural Gas Markets," U.S. Department of Energy,
    Monthly Energy Review, January, pp. I-VIII.
Tennessee Valley Authority, Office of Power, Division of
    Energy Conservation and Rates. 1982. Program Sum-
    mary, April.
U.S. Cabinet Task Force on Oil Import Control. 1970.
    The Oil Import Question. Washington, D.C., Govern-
    ment Printing Office, pp. 259-63.
U.S. Congressional Office of Technology Assessment. 1980.
    *Conservation and Solar Energy Programs of the Depart-
    ment of Energy: A Critique.* Washington, D.C., June.
U.S. Congressional Office of Technology Assessment. 1979.
    Residential Energy Conservation, Vol. 1, July.

U.S. Congressional Office of Technology Assessment. 1980. *World Petroleum Availability, 1980-2000.*

U.S. Congressional Office of Technology Assessment. 1981. *Nuclear Power Plant Standardization Light Water Reactors.*

U.S. Congress, Senate. 1982. Committee on Energy and National Resources, *Department of Energy Fiscal Year 1983 Authorization* (Conservation Programs). Washington, D.C., March 30, 1982.

U.S. Congress, Congressional Budget Office. 1983. *Natural Gas Pricing Policies: Implications for the Federal Budget.*

U.S. Department of Energy. 1982. *1981 Annual Report to Congress,* Vol. II, May. Washington, D.C.: Government Printing Office.

U.S. Department of Energy. 1980. *Monthly Energy Review,* January. Washington, D.C.: Government Printing Office.

U.S. Department of Energy. 1980. *Monthly Energy Review,* July. Washington, D.C.: Government Printing Office.

U.S. Department of Energy. 1981. *Monthly Energy Review,* January. Washington, D.C.: Government Printing Office.

U.S. Department of Energy. 1982. *Monthly Energy Review,* December. Washington, D.C.: Government Printing Office.

U.S. Department of Energy. 1981. "A Review of the Economics of Coal and Nuclear Power." *Monthly Energy Review,* September. Washington, D.C.: Government Printing Office.

U.S. Department of Energy, Office of Policy, Planning and Analysis. 1981. *Energy Projection to the Year 2000.* February. Washington, D.C.: Government Printing Office.

U.S. Department of Energy. 1981. *Intrastate and Interstate Supply Markets Under the Natural Gas Policy Act,* October. Washington, D.C.: Government Printing Office.

U.S. Department of Energy. 1981. *Securing America's Energy Future: The National Energy Policy Plan.* July. Washington, D.C.: Government Printing Office.

U.S. Department of Energy, Energy Information Administration. 1981. *The Current State of the Natural Gas Market.* December. Washington, D.C.: Government Printing Office.

U.S. Department of Energy, Energy Information Administration. 1981. *Weekly Petroleum Status Report.*

October 9. Washington, D.C.: Government Printing
Office.

U.S. Department of Energy, Office of Public Affairs. 1982.
"Energy Department Considers New Licensing Reform
Proposals for Nuclear Power Plant Construction."
Washington, D.C.

U.S. Department of Energy. 1982. *Energy Projections to
the Year 2000 July 1982 Update.* August. Washington,
D.C.: Government Printing Office.

U.S. Department of Energy, Energy Information Administration. 1982. *Natural Gas Annual 1980.* February.
Washington, D.C.: Government Printing Office.

U.S. Department of Energy, Assistant Secretary for Nuclear
Energy, Office of Converter Reactor Development.
1982. *Nuclear Power Program Information and Data
July–September 1982.* November. Washington, D.C.:
Government Printing Office.

U.S. Department of Energy, Office of Coal, Nuclear,
Electric and Alternative Fuels. 1982. *Projected Costs
of Electricity from Nuclear and Coal Fired Plants.* Vol.
1, August. Washington, D.C.: Government Printing
Office.

U.S. Department of Energy, Office of Policy, Planning and
Analysis. 1982. *Public Perceptions of Future Electric
Supply, Utility Financial Conditions and Related Issues.*
Washington, D.C.: Government Printing Office.

U.S. Department of Energy. 1982. *Report of Department
of Energy Task Force on Nuclear Licensing and Regulatory Reform.* Washington, D.C.: Government Printing Office.

U.S. Department of Energy, Energy Information Adminis-
tration. 1982. *Short-Term Energy Outlook Quarterly
Projections.* August. Washington, D.C.: Government
Printing Office.

U.S. General Accounting Office. 1980. *Three Mile Island:
The Most Studied Nuclear Accident in History.*
Washington, D.C.: Government Printing Office.

U.S. General Accounting Office. 1981. *Changes in Natural
Gas Prices and Supplies Since Passage of the Natural
Gas Policy Act of 1978. June. Washington, D.C.:
Government Printing Office*

*U.S. General Accounting Office. 1981. Greater
Commitment Needed to Solve Continuing Problems at
Three Mile Island.* Washington, D.C.: Government
Printing Office

U.S. General Accounting Office. 1978. *Region at the
Crossroads: The Pacific Northwest Searches for New
Sources of Electrical Energy.* Washington, D.C.:

Government Printing Office
Washington State Energy and Utilities Committee. 1981.
*Causes of Cost Overruns and Schedule Delays on the
Five WPPSS Nuclear Power Plants.* January.

NEWSPAPERS AND MAGAZINES

Benjamin, Milton R. and Howard Kurtz. 1982. "Congress
Passes Nuclear Waste Measure." *Washington Post,*
December, 21, p. A-5.
Brand, David. 1982. "Energy Enigma: Europeans
Subsidized Soviet Pipeline Work to Save Jobs." *Wall
Street Journal,* November 2, pp. 1, 20.
Economist, The(editorial). 1982. "Life with Andropov."
October 9, p. 12.
Emshwiller, John R. 1982. "Many Nuclear-Plant Perils
Remain Three Years after Three Mile Island." *Wall
Street Journal,* February 26, p. 29.
Ibrahim, Youssef. 1981a. "Oil Discounts Seem Obstacle to
OPEC Pact." *Wall Street Journal,* October 29, p. 2.
------. 1981b. "OPEC Oil Ministers Signal Effort to End
Group's Bitter Disagreement Over Prices." *Wall Street
Journal,* October 15, p. 4.
------. 1981c. "Saudi Arabia to Store Oil Near Red Sea to
Avoid Vulnerable Persian Gulf Area." *Wall Street
Journal,* October 13, p. 2.
------. 1983a. "OPEC Meeting Fails to Agree on Oil
Prices, Output, Clearing Way for Possible Round of
Lower Quotes." *Wall Street Journal,* January 25, p. 3.
------. 1983b. "Geneva Discord: How OPEC's Oil Pact
Collapsed at 11th Hour Over Price Discounts." *Wall
Street Journal,* January 27, pp.1, 16.
Large, Arlen J. 1981a. "Atomic Snarl: Nuclear Power
Industry, and Agency Seek to Speed Procedures for
Licensing Plants." *Wall Street Journal,* July 8, p. 46.
------. 1981b. "Fallout: Battle Opens on Paying $1
Billion Cleanup Bill for Three Mile Island." *Wall Street
Journal,* October 21, p. 1.
------. 1982a. "Consensus for Nuclear-Waste Burial
Grows, but a Sharp Debate Over Methods Persists."
Wall Street Journal, June 6, p. 29.
------. 1982b. "NPC Sees Utilities Cancelling or Delaying
19 Nuclear Plants Currently Being Built." *Wall Street
Journal,* March 15, p. 20.
Lave, Lester B. 1981. "Conflicting Objectives in
Regulating the Automobile." *Science,* vol. 212, May 22,
pp. 893-99.

Mathews, Jay. 1982. "Pacific Northwest May Face a Long Rainy Day if 'Whoops' Busts." *Washington Post,* December 29, p. A2.

Mufson, Steve. 1983. "Oil Firms' Fourth-Quarter Profits to Be Down; Slump Seen Running Through Early '83." *Wall Street Journal,* January 17, p. 3.

Navarro, Peter. 1983. "Utility Bills: The Real Price of Electricity." *Wall Street Journal,* January 13.

O'Donnell, Patrick. 1981. "Energy Crisis: Fate of Nuclear Power in U.S. Could Depend on Troubled Project." *Wall Street Journal,* January 8, p. 1.

Pasztur, Andy. 1981. "Reagan Advisers Divided over Pace of Gas Decontrol, Link with Taxes." *Wall Street Journal,* December 7, p. 29.

------. 1982. "Agency Speeds Gas Control Stirring Fight." *Wall Street Journal,* February 9, p. 27.

Prewo, Wilfried. 1982. "The Pipeline: White Elephant or Trojan Horse." *Wall Street Journal,* September 18.

Schlender, Benton R. 1981. "Energy Savers: Passive-Solar Homes Are Enjoying a Boom Amid Housing Slump." *Wall Street Journal,* September 1, p. 11.

Shao, Maria. 1982. "Despite Glut of Heating Oil and Natural Gas, Prices Aren't Expected to Drop This Winter." *Wall Street Journal,* October 6, p. 31.

Tucker, William. 1981. "The Energy Crisis Is Over!" *Harper's,* November 1, pp. 33-34.

Verleger, Phillip K. 1981. "OPEC's Threat to Mr. Reagan's Balanced Budget." *Wall Street Journal,* October 15, p. 28.

WSJ Staff Reporter. 1982. "Washington Public Power May Delay Completion of a Fourth Nuclear Reactor." *Wall Street Journal,* January 12, p. 7.

Zonna, Victor F. 1982a. "Rebellion Breaks Out in the Northwest Over Skyrocketing Electricity Rates." *Wall Street Journal,* March 19, p. 27.

------. 1982b. "Oil Executives Say Industry's Deep Slump Will Continue Even if Economics Recover." *Wall Street Journal,* November 9, p. 6.

------. 1982c. "Gas Consumers Say Pipelines Are Paying More Than Necessary for Their Supplies." *Wall Street Journal,* November 11, p. 52.

------. 1982d. "Huge Gas Fields off Coast of Norway." *Seattle Times,* November 5, p. A3.

------. 1983. "Bethlehem Steel Reports Net Loss of $1.5 Billion." *Wall Street Journal,* January 27, p. 3.

INDEX

Adelman, M.A., 20

Boeing Company:
  conservation programs,
  149-50
Bonneville Power
  Administration (BPA),
  84-85, 140
Bradford, Peter, 119

Carter, Jimmy, 186

demand for energy: by
  industry in OECD area,
  147-49; by
  residential/commercial
  users, 150, 151; in
  transportation sector,
  151-54

earth sheltered
  structures, 151
energy conservation:
  barriers to, 160;
  definitions, 146,
  155-57; and
  externalities, 158-59;
  and prices, 147; and
  uncertainty, 159
energy conservation
  policies and public
  utilities' rate
  structure, 157-58
energy conservation
  programs: effectiveness
  thereof, 166-67, 168;
  energy performance
  standard in buildings
  (BEPS), 168; and federal

government's
  conservation record,
  169-70; and federal
  government's role,
  164-65; and R & D,
  161-63, 164
energy policies: of the
  Carter administration,
  187-88; and equity
  issues, 183-84, 188-89;
  and free energy markets,
  196; and income
  distribution, 182-83; of
  the Reagan
  administration, 197, 202
energy pricing policies:
  and adjustment to market
  prices, 193-94; and
  marginal costs of energy
  production, 189-90; of
  public utilities,
  198-99; and structural
  changes, 199, 200-02
enhanced oil recovery
  (EOR) methods, 14
Evans, Daniel J., 134

Federal Energy Regulatory
  Commission, 197
Federal Power Commission,
  57

Garvin, Clifton C., Jr.,
  170
Great Plains Coal
  Gasification project,
  70-71

Kalt, Joseph P., 196-97

219

WIDENER UNIVERSITY WOLFGRAM LIBRARY CHESTER, PA.

ABOUT THE AUTHOR

THOMAS C. LOWINGER is Professor of Economics at Washington State University, Pullman, Washington. He was a visiting professor at the University of Haifa, Israel and the University of Stockholm, Sweden.

Dr. Lowinger has published extensively in the fields of energy economics, international trade, commercial policy, and economic development. His articles and reviews have appeared in the *American Economic Review, Quarterly Journal of Economics,* and the *Journal of Energy and Development,* among others.

He has served twice on the economic research staff of the U.S. Department of the Treasury.

Dr. Lowinger holds a B.A. from the University of California at Los Angeles and an M.A. and Ph.D. from Michigan State University.